BERLITZ®

JAPANESE 1

STUDENT'S BOOK

日本語一

Berlitz Guides
Lausanne, Switzerland

U.S. ISBN 0-02-443100-1
Printed in Switzerland
8th printing – September 1988

Berlitz Guides
Avenue d'Ouchy, 61
1000 Lausanne 6, Switzerland

MOKUJI

DAI SAN-SHŌ (3)

DAI YON-SHŌ (4)

DAI GO-SHŌ (5)

DAI ROKU-SHŌ (6)

DAI NANA-SHŌ (7)

DAI HA-SSHŌ (8)

DAI KYŪ-SHŌ (9)

DAI JŪ-SAN-SHŌ (13)

DAI JŪ-YON-SHŌ (14)

DAI JŪ-HA-SSHŌ (18)

DAI JŪ-KYŪ-SHŌ (19)

DAI NIJU-SSHŌ (20)

PREFACE

According to M. D. Berlitz, who founded the Berlitz schools in 1878, the Berlitz Method requires "constant and exclusive use of the foreign language and direct association of concepts and thought with foreign sounds and utterances."

The means of achieving this objective are:

1. the teaching of *concrete* concepts through visual demonstration and dramatization;

2. the teaching of *abstract* concepts by association of ideas;

3. the teaching of *grammar* through examples and as a product of analogy.

"Translation is entirely excluded as a means of acquiring a foreign language. From the first lesson the student hears and speaks only the language he wishes to learn. What cannot be taught by means of demonstration is made clear by analogy; the value of the unknown quantity *X* is revealed in terms of its relation to the known quantities *A* and *B*."

In the prefaces to the first editions of his textbooks, M. D. Berlitz explained in detail his reasons for rejecting grammar-translation techniques and for insisting on the exclusive use of the target language. He felt it "unlogical" to use the student's mother tongue during the greater part of the lesson. He believed that a language was best taught "within the framework of the language itself." Only in this way could the student "get hold of its spirit and get accustomed to *thinking* in it." The difficulties of grammar, which are themselves frequently the result of translation and constant comparison with the mother tongue, are greatly reduced by the Berlitz Method.

Although a number of learned educators of the time were beginning to reshape their thinking along similar lines, M. D. Berlitz was the first to put the "direct" method to use in a systematized manner. He perceived clearly the implications the approach suggested for the design of practical language teaching programs and materials. What emerged was a constellation of practical guidelines and texts which remain unique to the Berlitz organization.

Among the practical conclusions drawn by Berlitz and subsequently implemented in all his schools were the following:

1. The teaching aim of the Berlitz Method is, primarily, comprehension and speaking. Reading and writing were considered to be secondary objectives: language is taught as *speech* rather than as *literature.*

2. Berlitz teaches languages as a practical *skill* rather than merely as theoretical knowledge. Students are taught to *use* the language rather than to merely *describe* it.

3. Berlitz courses are based on a careful selection of high frequency words and structures, which are incorporated into practical *teachable* programs.

4. The *sequence* in which vocabulary and grammatical points are introduced and practiced is determined by the need to explain each element of the language without resorting to translation.

5. Increasingly complex concepts and situations are arranged in order of difficulty, always with a view to what has preceded.

6. Simplicity of design remains a primary objective: the ability of the student to learn effectively is directly affected by the ability of the instructor to understand and implement Berlitz guides and materials in the classroom.

Since its modest beginnings a century ago, the Berlitz organization has grown into a world-wide network of language schools. The original materials have been revised and refined over and over to keep up with changing language patterns and the changing make-up of Berlitz students; cassettes have been introduced to help the student proceed faster by providing more opportunities for home review; teachers' manuals have been created to increase the effectiveness of Berlitz instructors, as have sophisticated procedures for teacher training. The spectrum of courses has expanded to include everything from private instruction both at Berlitz schools or "on location," to semi-private, group and, of course, the by now world-famous Total Immersion® courses, in which the student is literally saturated with a new language over a period of weeks.

We would like to take this opportunity to welcome you to the proud ranks of the Berlitz organization, and to wish you every success with your new language.

DAI I-SSHŌ — MATOME

Kore wa pen desu ka?

Hai, kore wa pen desu.
Iie, kore wa pen ja arimasen.

Nan / Dare desu ka?

Kore wa nan desu ka?
— Kore wa enpitsu desu.

Kore wa dare desu ka?
— Tanaka-san desu.

. . . mo . . .

Kore mo pen desu ka?
Kore mo are mo pen ja arimasen.
Kore wa enpitsu demo arimasen.

Soretomo . . .

Kore wa pen desu ka, (soretomo)
  enpitsu desu ka?
— Kore wa enpitsu desu.

Donna / Donna hon desu ka?

Sore wa akai / ōkii desu.
Sore wa akai / ōkii hon desu.

Nani-jin desu ka?

Watashi wa Nihon-jin desu.
Anata wa Amerika-jin desu ka?

. . . to . . . (to) wa

Pen to enpitsu wa kuroi desu.
Tanaka-san to Noguchi-san wa
  Nihon-jin desu.

. . . desu / -san desu

Watashi wa Tanaka desu.
Anata wa Noguchi-san desu.

Nani-iro desu ka?

Akai / shiroi / kuroi . . . desu.
Denwa wa akai desu.
Shiroi denwa wa ōkii desu.

Watashi / anata

Watashi wa sensei desu.
Anata wa seito desu.

Kaiwa-hyōgen

"Konnichiwa!"
"Sayonara."
"Hai, sō desu."
"Iie, sō ja arimasen."

NAN DESU KA?

> ... *desu*
>
> ... *ja arimasen*

Kore wa pen desu ka?

— *Hai, kore **wa** pen desu.*

Kore mo pen desu ka?

— *Hai, kore **mo** pen desu.*

Kore mo pen desu ka?

— *Iie, kore wa pen **ja arimasen**.*

Kore wa matchi desu ka, raitā desu ka?

— *Kore wa raitā desu.*

Kore wa pen desu ka?

— *Iie, kore wa pen **ja arimasen**.*

Kore wa hon desu ka?

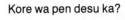

— *Iie, kore wa hon **demo arimasen**.*

Kore wa nan desu ka?

— *Kore wa tabako desu.*

Mondai 1

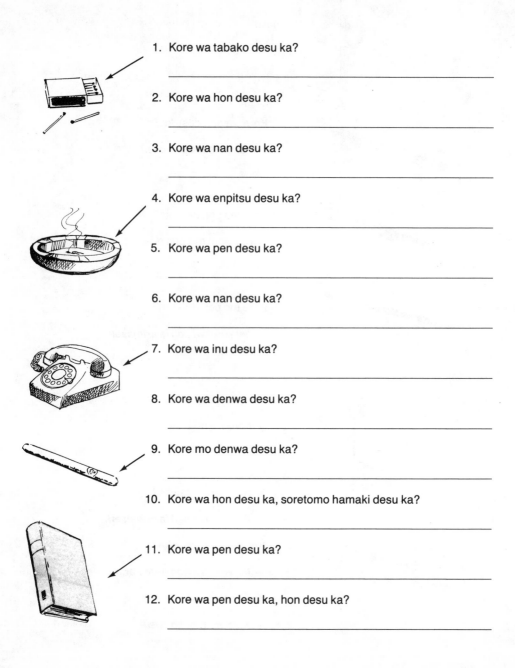

1. Kore wa tabako desu ka?

   _____

2. Kore wa hon desu ka?

   _____

3. Kore wa nan desu ka?

   _____

4. Kore wa enpitsu desu ka?

   _____

5. Kore wa pen desu ka?

   _____

6. Kore wa nan desu ka?

   _____

7. Kore wa inu desu ka?

   _____

8. Kore wa denwa desu ka?

   _____

9. Kore mo denwa desu ka?

   _____

10. Kore wa hon desu ka, soretomo hamaki desu ka?

    _____

11. Kore wa pen desu ka?

    _____

12. Kore wa pen desu ka, hon desu ka?

    _____

DARE DESU KA?

Kore wa Tanaka-san desu ka?
— *Iie, Tanaka-san ja arimasen.*
Kore wa **dare** desu ka?
— *Kore wa **Noguchi-san** desu.*

Kore wa **Tanaka-san** desu ka?
— *Hai, kore wa Tanaka-san desu.*
Tanaka-san wa **Nihon-jin** desu ka?
— *Hai, Tanaka-san wa Nihon-jin desu.*

NANI-JIN DESU KA?

Kore wa Tanaka-san desu ka?
— *Iie, Tanaka-san ja arimasen.*
Kore wa dare desu ka?
— *Kore wa Shumitto-san desu.*
Shumitto-san wa Nihon-jin desu ka?
— *Iie, Nihon-jin ja arimasen.*
Shumitto-san wa Doitsu-jin desu ka?
— *Hai, Doitsu-jin desu.*

Dubaru-san mo Doitsu-jin desu ka?
— *Iie, Doitsu-jin ja arimasen.*
Nihon-jin desu ka?
— *Iie, Nihon-jin de mo arimasen.*
Dubaru-san wa **nani-jin** desu ka?
— *Dubaru-san wa **Furansu-jin** desu.*

Kore wa dare desu ka?
— *Kore wa **Mōgan**-san desu.*
Mōgan-san wa Doitsu-jin desu ka,
Furansu-jin desu ka?
— *Mōgan-san wa Doitsu-jin de mo
Furansu-jin de mo arimasen.*
Mōgan-san wa nani-jin desu ka?
— *Mōgan-san wa **Amerika-jin** desu.*

NANI-JIN DESU KA?

Amerika-jin	Kanada-jin
Chūgoku-jin	Mekishiko-jin
Doitsu-jin	Nihon-jin
Furansu-jin	Porutogaru-jin
Igirisu-jin	Roshia-jin
Itaria-jin	Supein-jin
	Kankoku-jin

Mondai 2

1. Kore wa Tanaka-san desu ka?

   _____

2. Kore wa dare desu ka?

   _____

3. Dubaru-san wa Doitsu-jin desu ka?

   _____

4. Dubaru-san wa nani-jin desu ka?

   _____

5. Shumitto-san wa Furansu-jin desu ka,
   soretomo Doitsu-jin desu ka?

   _____

6. Berutini-san wa Itaria-jin desu ka?

   _____

7. Kore wa Berutini-san desu ka?

   _____

8. Kore wa dare desu ka?

   _____

9. Jōnzu-san wa Itaria-jin desu ka?

   _____

10. Jōnzu-san wa nani-jin desu ka?

   _____

KORE — SORE — ARE

Kore wa tabako desu.
Kore wa **shiroi** tabako desu. ➡

Sore wa raitā desu.
Sore wa **chiisai** raitā desu. ➡

Are wa haizara desu.
Are wa **ōkii** haizara desu. ➡

DONNA / NANI-IRO DESU KA?

	akai		Akai	
	kuroi		Kuroi	
	shiroi		Shiroi	
	aoi		Aoi	
Hon wa	chairo	desu.	Chairo no	hon wa . . .
	kiiro		Kiiro no	
	midoriiro		Midoriiro no	
	haiiro		Haiiro no	
Hon wa	(akaku arimasen)			
	(chairo ja arimasen)			
Hon wa	ōkii / chiisai	desu.	Ōkii / Chiisai	hon wa . . .
Hon wa	(ōkiku arimasen)			

1-25

Mondai 3

1. Denwa wa ōkii desu ka?

   _____

2. Denwa wa akai desu ka?

   _____

3. Denwa wa nani-iro desu ka?

   _____

4. Hon mo kuroi desu ka?

   _____

5. Hon wa shiroi desu ka, soretomo haiiro desu ka?

   _____

6. Kore wa enpitsu desu ka, tabako desu ka?

   _____

7. Tabako wa ōkii desu ka?

   _____

8. Tabako wa shiroi desu ka?

   _____

9. Enpitsu mo shiroi desu ka?

   _____

10. Enpitsu wa kuroi desu ka?

    _____

11. Inu mo kuroi desu ka?

    _____

12. Inu wa nani-iro desu ka?

    _____

. . . TO . . . WA . . .

Denwa wa shiroi desu ka?

— *Hai, denwa **wa** shiroi desu.*

Pen mo shiroi desu ka?

— *Hai, pen **mo** shiroi desu.*

Denwa to pen wa shiroi desu ka?

— *Hai, denwa **to** pen **wa** shiroi desu.*

Tanaka-san wa Nihon-jin desu ka?

— *Hai, **sō** desu.*

Noguchi-san mo Nihon-jin desu ka?

— *Hai, **sō** desu.*

Tanaka-san **to** Noguchi-san **wa** Nihon-jin desu.

Inu wa nani-iro desu ka?

— *Inu wa shiro **to** kuro desu.*

ŌKII / CHIISAI

Inu wa **ōkii** desu.

Inu wa **chiisai** desu.

Isu wa **ōkii** desu.

Matchi wa **chiisai** desu.

Mondai 4

1. Anata wa sensei desu ka? _____

2. Anata wa seito desu ka? _____

3. Anata wa Nihon-jin desu ka?_____

4. Tanaka-san wa Nihon-jin desu ka? _____

5. Noguchi-san mo Nihon-jin desu ka? _____

Mondai 5

Rei: Inu wa haiiro desu.

__*Inu wa haiiro ja arimasen.*_____

1. Pen wa midoriiro desu.

   _____

2. Tsukue wa chairo desu.

   _____

3. Watashi wa sensei desu.

   _____

4. Anata wa Doitsu-jin desu.

   _____

5. Kore wa enpitsu desu.

   _____

Mondai 6

Rei: Hai, watashi wa seito desu.

Anata wa seito desu ka?
_____

1. Hai, hon wa ōkii desu.

_____

2. Iie, denwa wa kiiro ja arimasen.

_____

3. Hai, isu to tsukue wa chairo desu.

_____

4. Iie, watashi wa Chūgoku-jin ja arimasen.

_____

5. Iie, haizara wa chiisaku arimasen.

_____

Mondai 7

Rei: Isu wa **chairo** desu.

Isu wa nani-iro desu ka?
_____

1. Noguchi-san wa **Nihon-jin** desu.

_____

2. Kore wa **Tanaka-san** desu.

_____

3. Are wa **inu** desu.

_____

4. Mōgan-san wa **Amerika-jin** desu.

_____

DAI NI-SHŌ — MATOME

Nani ga . . . ?

Nani ga akai desu ka?
— Enpitsu ga akai desu.

Dare ga . . . ?

Dare ga Nihon-jin desu ka?
— Tanaka-san ga Nihon-jin desu.

Dochira ga . . . ?

Dochira ga nagai desu ka?
— Kuroi kagi ga nagai desu.

Dore ga . . . ?

Dore ga mijikai desu ka?
— Enpitsu ga mijikai desu.

Watashi no / watashi no hon desu.

Kore wa dare no kuruma desu ka?
— Kore wa watashi no kuruma desu.

Tanaka-san no kuruma wa ōkii desu ka?
— Iie, Tanaka-san no kuruma wa ōkiku
arimasen.

Dare no ga ōkii desu ka?
— Mōgan-san no ga ōkii desu.

Kuni / toshi

Nihon wa kuni desu.
Tōkyō wa toshi desu.

-te imasu / -te imasen

Watashi wa pen o totte imasu ka?
— Iie, anata wa pen o totte imasen.

Nani o shite imasu ka?

Watashi wa hon o totte imasu.
Anata wa hon o oite imasu.
Tanaka-san wa e o mite imasu.

. . . to . . . to, dochira ga . . . ?

Basu to kuruma to, dochira ga ōkii
desu ka?
— Basu ga (kuruma yori) ōkii desu.

Basu wa kuruma yori ōkii desu.

Keredomo

Kore wa nagai desu.
Keredomo sore wa mijikai desu.

Kaiwa-hyōgen

"Sumimasen!"
" . . . yo!"
"Kochira wa . . . -san desu."
"Hajimemashite."
"Dōzo yoroshiku."
"O-genki desu ka?"
"Okagesamade!"
"Ē, genki desu."
" . . . o kudasai."
"Dōzo!"
"(Dōmo) arigatō (gozaimasu)."
"Dō-itashimashite."

DARE GA . . . ?

Kore wa Dubaru-san desu.

Dubaru-san wa Furansu-jin desu.

Kore wa Tanaka-san desu.

Tanaka-san wa Nihon-jin desu.

Kore wa Mōgan-san desu.

Mōgan-san wa Amerika-jin desu.

> **Dare ga** Nihon-jin desu ka?
> — *Tanaka-san **ga** Nihon-jin desu.*

DORE GA . . . ?

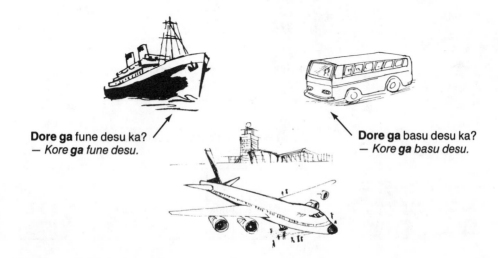

Dore ga fune desu ka?
— *Kore **ga** fune desu.*

Dore ga basu desu ka?
— *Kore **ga** basu desu.*

. . . TO . . . TO, DOCHIRA GA . . . ?

> Kuroi kuruma **to** shiroi kuruma **to, dochira ga** ōkii desu ka?
> — *Kuroi kuruma ga ōkii desu.*
>
> Kuroi kuruma wa shiroi kuruma **yori** ōkii desu.
>
> Shiroi kuruma wa kuroi kuruma **yori** chiisai desu.

Mondai 8

1. Enpitsu to kagi to, dochira ga nagai desu ka?

   _____

2. Kagi wa enpitsu yori mijikai desu ka?

   _____

3. Hikōki to kagi to, dochira ga chiisai desu ka?

   _____

4. Basu to kagi to, dochira ga ōkii desu ka?

   _____

5. Enpitsu wa tabako yori mijikai desu ka?

   _____

NIHON WA ŌKII KUNI DESU KA?

○ 6 ○

Nihon wa kuni desu ka, soretomo toshi desu ka? Nihon wa kuni desu. Tōkyō mo kuni desu ka? Iie, Tōkyō wa kuni ja arimasen. Tōkyō wa toshi desu. Tōkyō wa ōkii toshi desu. Fujisawa mo toshi desu. Keredomo, Fujisawa wa ōkii toshi ja arimasen. Fujisawa wa chiisai toshi desu.

on the other hand

Ginza-dōri mo toshi desu ka? Iie, Ginza-dōri wa toshi ja arimasen. Ginza-dōri wa michi desu. Ginza-dōri wa nagai michi desu ka? Iie, Ginza-dōri wa nagaku arimasen.

Sobieto mo michi desu ka? Iie, michi ja arimasen. Toshi desu ka? Iie, toshi de mo arimasen. Sobieto wa kuni desu. Ōkii kuni desu. Monako mo kuni desu. Monako wa ōkii desu ka? Iie, ōkiku arimasen. Sobieto to Monako to, dochira ga ōkii desu ka? Sobieto ga Monako yori ōkii desu. Dochira no kuni ga chiisai desu ka? Monako ga Sobieto yori chiisai desu.

> *Nyūyōku wa Pari yori ōkii desu.*

Pari wa ōkii toshi desu ka? Hai, ōkii toshi desu. Nyūyōku mo ōkii toshi desu ka? Hai, Nyūyōku mo ōkii desu. Pari wa Nyūyōku yori ōkii desu ka? Iie, Pari wa Nyūyōku yori ōkiku arimasen. Nyūyōku to Pari to, dochira ga ōkii desu ka? Nyūyōku wa Pari yori ōkii desu.

Mondai 9

1. Fujisawa wa kuni desu ka, soretomo toshi desu ka?

   _____

2. Fujisawa to Tōkyō to, dochira ga ōkii desu ka?

   Fujisawa ga Tokyo yori

3. Sobieto wa ōkii kuni desu ka, soretomo chiisai kuni desu ka?

   _____

4. Sobieto to Nihon to, dochira ga chiisai desu ka?

   _____

5. Pari to Nyūyōku to, dochira ga ōkii desu ka?

   _____

DONO DENWA GA . . . ?
KONO — SONO — ANO

Kore wa denwa desu.
Kono denwa wa kuroi desu. ⟶

Sore mo denwa desu.
Sono denwa wa shiroi desu. ⟶

Are mo denwa desu.
Ano denwa wa haiiro desu. ⟶

> **Dono denwa ga** shiroi desu ka?
> — *Sono denwa **ga** shiroi desu.*

DOCHIRA (NO KURUMA) GA . . . ?

Kore wa Tanaka-san no kuruma desu.
Kono kuruma wa shiroi desu.
Kono kuruma wa chiisai desu.

Kore wa Mōgan-san no kuruma desu.
Kono kuruma wa kuroi desu.
Kono kuruma wa ōkii desu.

> **Dochira ga** shiroi desu ka?
> — *Chiisai kuruma **ga** shiroi desu.*
>
> **Dochira** no kuruma **ga** kuroi desu ka?
> — *Ōkii kuruma **ga** kuroi desu.*
>
> **Dochira** no kuruma **ga** ōkii desu ka?
> — *Kuroi kuruma **ga** ōkii desu.*

Mondai 10

1. Dono denwa ga kuroi desu ka?

   _____

2. Dono denwa ga haiiro desu ka?

   _____

3. Dochira no kuruma ga Tanaka-san no desu ka?

   _____

4. Dochira no kuruma ga ōkii desu ka?

   _____

5. Dochira no kuruma ga shiroi desu ka?

   _____

Mondai 11

Rei: Iie, kono basu wa midoriiro ja arimasen.

   Kono basu wa midoriiro desu ka?
   _____

1. Iie, kono hikōki wa ōkiku arimasen.

   _____

2. Iie, Tōkyō wa Kyōto yori chiisaku arimasen.

   _____

3. Iie, kono enpitsu wa nagaku arimasen.

   _____

4. Iie, sono kagi wa mijikaku arimasen.

   _____

5. Iie, basu wa densha yori nagaku arimasen.

   _____

○ 6 ○

BERURITTSU NO SEITO

Noguchi:	Tanaka-san! Konnichiwa!
Tanaka:	Ā! Noguchi-san! O-genki desu ka?
Noguchi:	Ē okagesamade genki desu. Tanaka-san mo o-genki desu ka?
Tanaka:	Dōmo arigatō, genki desu!
Noguchi:	Tanaka-san, kochira wa Jōnzu-san desu.
Tanaka:	Sō desu ka! Jōnzu-san, hajimemashite!
Jōnzu:	Hajimemashite! Dōzo yoroshiku!
Tanaka:	Jōnzu-san wa Amerika-jin desu ka?
Jōnzu:	Iie! Watashi wa Amerika-jin ja arimasen. Igirisu-jin desu.
Tanaka:	Sō desu ka. Jōnzu-san, sore wa nan desu ka?
Jōnzu:	Kore desu ka?
Tanaka:	Hai, sore desu.
Jōnzu:	Kore wa hon desu.
Tanaka:	Hon desu ka?
Jōnzu:	Hai! Berurittsu no hon desu. Watashi wa Berurittsu no seito desu.
Tanaka:	Sō desu ka!

Mondai 12

1. Noguchi-san wa genki desu ka?

Noguchi-san okagesamade -genki desu.

2. Jōnzu-san wa Amerika-jin desu ka?

Iie Jōnzu-san wa Amerika-jin ja arimasen.

3. Jōnzu-san wa nani-jin desu ka?

Jōnzu-san wa ~~Amerika~~ Igirisu-jin desu

4. Jōnzu-san wa Berurittsu no seito desu ka?

Iie, Jōnzu-san wa Berurittsu no seito ja arimasen

Mondai 13

Rei: Konnichiwa! (**D**)

1. O-genki desu ka? (**A**)

2. Hajimemashite. (   )

3. Arigatō. (**B**)

4. Hon o totte kudasai. (   )

5. Nani o shite imasu ka? (   )

A. Okagesamade.

B. Dō-itashimashite.

C. E o mite imasu.

D. O-genki desu ka?

E. Dōzo yoroshiku.

F. Dōzo.

HAIZARA O KUDASAI

— *Sumimasen!*
— *Hai!*
— *Haizara o kudasai.*
— *Dōzo!*
— *Dōmo arigatō!*
— *Dō-itashimashite!*

Mondai 14

Rei: Anata no denwa wa kuroi desu ka?

lie, *watashi no denwa wa kuroku arimasen.*

1. Watashi no nekutai wa ao to aka desu ka?

   lie, _____

2. Watashi no tabako wa nagai desu ka?

   lie, _____

3. Watashi wa tabako o oite imasu ka?

   lie, _____

4. Anata wa haizara o totte imasu ka?

   lie, _____

5. Sensei wa watashi o mite imasu ka?

   lie, _____

6. Anata no tsukue wa ōkii desu ka?

   lie, _____

7. Watashi no pen wa chairo desu ka?

   lie, _____

Mondai 15

1. Kono hikōki wa shiroi desu ka?

_____

2. Kono hikōki wa kuroi desu ka?

_____

3. Kono hikōki mo kuroi desu ka?

_____

4. Dochira no hikōki ga chiisai desu ka?

_____

5. Chūgoku to Nihon to, dochira ga ōkii desu ka?

_____

6. Anata wa Berurittsu no seito desu ka?

_____

7. Anata no namae wa Tanaka-san desu ka?

_____

8. Anata no namae wa nan desu ka?

_____

9. Anata no sensei wa dare desu ka?

_____

10. Anata no kuni wa Nihon yori ōkii desu ka, soretomo chiisai desu ka?

_____

DAI SAN-SHŌ — MATOME

Sūji

zero			
ichi	shi	nana	jū
ni	go	hachi	jū-ichi
san	roku	ku	nijū

Kazoete kudasai

Ikutsu desu ka?
Roku tasu ni wa hachi desu.
Roku hiku ni wa yon desu.

... pēji / ... ban

Nan-pēji desu ka?
Denwa bangō wa nan-ban desu ka?

Osake wa ikaga desu ka?

Hai, itadakimasu.
Iie, kekkō desu.
Dochira demo ii desu.

Suki desu / Kirai desu

Sashimi ga (dai-)suki desu.
Tenpura ga (dai-)kirai desu.
Amari suki ja arimasen.

Tabemono: (washoku / yōshoku)

sashimi, tenpura, sukiyaki
sakana, gohan
Oishii desu.

Nomimono

kōhii, ocha, osake, kōcha
budōshu, miruku, biiru, uokka
uisukii

Dochira ga ii desu ka / ... no hō ga ii desu

Tōkyō to Pari to, dochira ga ōkii desu ka?
Tōkyō no hō ga (zutto) ōkii desu.

Dore ga ichi-ban ... ka?

Tōkyō to Pari to Nyūyōku dewa, dore ga
ichi-ban ōkii desu ka?
— Tōkyō ga ichi-ban ōkii desu.

Doko ni arimasu ka?

Isu wa doko ni arimasu ka?
— Isu wa kyōshitsu ni arimasu.
— Isu wa doko ni mo arimasen.

Ue / shita / naka

Tokei wa tsukue no ue ni arimasu.
Shashin wa tsukue no shita ni arimasu.
Okane wa poketto no naka ni arimasu.

Wakarimasu / Wakarimasen

Wakarimasu ka?
Iie, (zenzen) wakarimasen.

Nani ka ... ? / Nani mo ... sen

Nani ka arimasu ka?
— Hai, nani ka arimasu.
— Iie, nani mo arimasen.

Nihon no / gaikoku no

Nihon no kuruma wa chiisai desu.
Gaikoku no kuruma wa ōkii desu.

Kaiwa-hyōgen

"Moshimoshi ... "
"Dōmo sumimasen."
"Sumimasen."
"Nan deshō ka?"
"Dōmo arigatō gozaimashita."

KAZOETE KUDASAI!

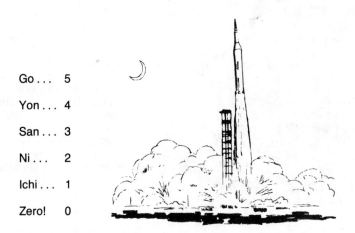

Go . . . 5

Yon . . . 4

San . . . 3

Ni . . . 2

Ichi . . . 1

Zero! 0

1	2	3	4	5
ichi	ni	san	shi (yon)	go
6	7	8	9	10
roku	shichi (nana)	hachi	ku (kyū)	jū
11	12	13	14	15
jū-ichi	jū-ni	jū-san	jū-shi (jū-yon)	jū-go
16	17	18	19	20
jū-roku	jū-shichi (jū-nana)	jū-hachi	jū-ku (jū-kyū)	nijū

DENWA-BANGŌ WA NAN-BAN DESU KA?

— Moshi moshi. Satō-san desu ka?

— Iie, chigaimasu.

— Satō-san ja arimasen ka?

— Iie, Noguchi desu.

— Ā, Noguchi-san desu ka!
Sumimasen ga, Satō-san no
denwa-bangō wa nan-ban desu ka?

— Nana roku go no ni ni san yon desu.

— Ā, dōmo arigatō gozaimashita.

— Dō-itashimashite.

Mondai 16

Rei: 321-6082

san ni ichi no roku zero/rē hachi ni

1. 789-3351

2. 600-2873

3. 779-4413

4. 350-2867

5. 223-4948

OSAKE WA IKAGA DESU KA?

Tanaka:	Noguchi-san, kōhii wa ikaga desu ka?
Noguchi:	Iie, amari suki ja arimasen.
Tanaka:	Dewa, ocha wa ikaga desu ka?
Noguchi:	Hai, arigatō! Itadakimasu.
Tanaka:	Soretomo, osake no hō ga ii desu ka?
Noguchi:	Dochira de mo ii desu.

Tanaka-san to Noguchi-san wa Nihon-jin desu. Nihon-jin wa osake ga totemo suki desu. Shumitto-san wa Nihon-jin ja arimasen. Shumitto-san wa osake yori biiru no hō ga suki desu.

Osake wa nomimono desu. Biiru ya budōshu mo nomimono desu. Sukiyaki mo nomimono desu ka? Iie, sukiyaki wa nomimono ja arimasen. Sukiyaki wa tabemono desu. Tenpura mo tabemono desu. Sukiyaki mo tenpura mo totemo oishii desu.

Mondai 17

1. Tanaka-san wa nani-jin desu ka?

_____

2. Nihon-jin wa osake ga suki desu ka?

_____

3. Shumitto-san wa osake to biiru to, dochira ga suki desu ka?

_____

4. Sukiyaki wa nomimono desu ka?

_____

5. Tenpura wa oishii desu ka?

_____

Pari to Nyūyōku to Tōkyō wa ōkii desu.

Nyūyōku wa Pari **yori** ōkii desu.
Tōkyō wa Nyūyōku **yori** ōkii desu.

Pari **to** Nyūyōku **to** Tōkyō **de wa,** dono toshi **ga** ichi-ban ōkii desu ka?
— _Tōkyō_ **ga** _ichi-ban ōkii desu._

Dono toshi **ga** ichi-ban chiisai desu ka?
— _Pari_ **ga** _ichi-ban chiisai desu._

Mondai   18

1. Furansu wa ōkii desu ka?

_____

2. Amerika mo ōkii desu ka?

_____

3. Furansu wa Amerika yori ōkii desu ka?

_____

4. Furansu to Amerika to Sobieto de wa, dono kuni ga ichi-ban ōkii desu ka?

_____

5. Dono kuni ga ichi-ban chiisai desu ka?

_____

6. Doitsu to Kanada to Nihon de wa, dono kuni ga ichi-ban chiisai desu ka?

_____

7. Ginza-dōri wa nagai desu ka?

_____

8. Ginza-dōri wa Mishishippi yori nagai desu ka?

_____

9. Dochira no hō ga nagai desu ka?

_____

10. Dochira no hō ga mijikai desu ka?

_____

11. Basu wa ōkii desu ka?

_____

12. Hikōki mo ōkii desu ka?

_____

13. Basu to hikōki to, dochira no hō ga ōkii desu ka?

_____

14. Kuruma wa basu yori ōkii desu ka?

_____

15. Basu to kuruma to hikōki de wa, dore ga ichi-ban ōkii desu ka?

_____

UE — SHITA — NAKA

> Pen wa tsukue **no ue ni** arimasu.
> Handobaggu wa tsukue **no shita ni** arimasu.
> Okane wa handobaggu **no naka ni** arimasu.

Mondai 19

1. Hon wa tsukue no ue ni arimasu ka?

   _____

2. Denwa wa tsukue no shita ni arimasu ka?

   _____

3. Denwa wa doko ni arimasu ka?

   _____

4. Handobaggu no naka ni hon ga arimasu ka?

   _____

5. Handobaggu no naka ni nani ga arimasu ka?

   _____

NANI KA / NANI MO

Koko **ni** tsukue ga arimasu ka?
— *Hai, koko **ni** tsukue ga arimasu.*

Tsukue no **ue ni** nani ka arimasu ka?
— *Hai, nani ka arimasu.*

Nani ga arimasu ka?
— *Pen to denwa **ga** arimasu.*

Pen to denwa no hoka ni, tsukue no ue
ni **nani ka** arimasu ka?
— *Iie, **nani mo** arimasen.*

Tsukue no shita ni **nani ka** arimasu ka?
— *Hai, **nani ka** arimasu.*

Tsukue no shita ni **nani ga** arimasu ka?
— *Handobaggu **ga** arimasu.*

Handobaggu no hoka ni, tsukue no shita ni
nani ka arimasu ka?
— *Iie, **nani mo** arimasen.*

Mondai 20

1. Tsukue no ue ni nani ka arimasu ka?

   _____

2. Nani ga arimasu ka?

   _____

3. Handobaggu mo tsukue no ue ni arimasu ka?

   _____

4. Handobaggu wa doko ni arimasu ka?

   _____

5. Tsukue no shita ni, enpitsu mo arimasu ka?

   _____

6. Tsukue no shita ni, handobaggu no hoka ni nani ka arimasu ka?

   _____

Kore wa kōhii desu.
Kōhii wa kappu no
naka ni arimasu.

Kore wa budōshu desu.
Budōshu wa bin no
naka ni arimasu.

DOKO NI . . . ?

Kōhii wa kappu no naka ni arimasu ka?
— *Hai, kappu no naka ni arimasu.*
Budōshu mo kappu no naka ni arimasu ka?
— *Iie, kappu no naka ni arimasen.*
Gurasu no naka ni arimasu ka?
— *Iie, gurasu no naka ni arimasen.*
Budōshu wa **doko ni** arimasu ka?
— *Bin no naka ni arimasu.*

Mondai 21

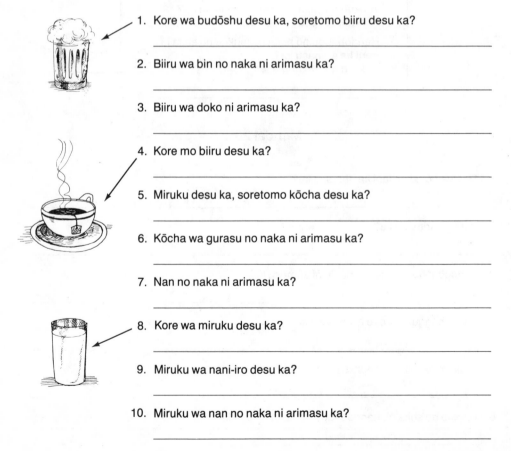

1. Kore wa budōshu desu ka, soretomo biiru desu ka?
   _____

2. Biiru wa bin no naka ni arimasu ka?
   _____

3. Biiru wa doko ni arimasu ka?
   _____

4. Kore mo biiru desu ka?
   _____

5. Miruku desu ka, soretomo kōcha desu ka?
   _____

6. Kōcha wa gurasu no naka ni arimasu ka?
   _____

7. Nan no naka ni arimasu ka?
   _____

8. Kore wa miruku desu ka?
   _____

9. Miruku wa nani-iro desu ka?
   _____

10. Miruku wa nan no naka ni arimasu ka?
    _____

FUJISAN WA NIHON DE ICHI-BAN
TAKAI YAMA DESU

Tōkyō wa ōkii toshi desu. Nihon wa kuni desu. Tōkyō wa Nihon ni arimasu. Ginza-dōri wa michi desu. Ginza-dōri wa Tōkyō ni arimasu. Berurittsu wa gakkō desu. Berurittsu-gakkō wa Tōkyō ni arimasu.

Rondon mo ōkii toshi desu. Keredomo Rondon wa Nihon ni wa arimasen. Rondon wa Igirisu ni arimasu. Igirisu wa Yōroppa ni arimasu. Igirisu wa ōkii kuni ja arimasen.

Mishishippi wa kuni desu ka, soretomo michi desu ka? Mishishippi wa kuni de mo michi de mo arimasen. Mishishippi wa kawa desu. Mishishippi-gawa wa Nihon ni arimasu ka? Iie, Amerika ni arimasu. Mishishippi-gawa wa Amerika de ichi-ban nagai kawa desu. Amazon mo kawa desu ka? Hai, kawa desu. Nihon ni arimasu ka, soretomo Furansu ni arimasu ka? Amazon wa Nihon ni mo Furansu ni mo arimasen. Amazon wa doko ni arimasu ka? Burajiru ni arimasu.

Fujisan wa yama desu. Fujisan wa Nihon ni arimasu. Fujisan wa kawa ja arimasen. Yama desu. Totemo takai yama desu. Fujisan wa Nihon de ichi-ban takai yama desu. Eberesuto mo yama desu. Eberesuto mo totemo takai yama desu. Keredomo Nihon ni wa arimasen. Eberesuto wa Fujisan yori takai desu. Sekai de ichi-ban takai yama desu.

Mondai 22

1. Rondon wa Igirisu ni arimasu ka?

_____

2. Mishishippi wa Amerika de ichi-ban nagai kawa desu ka?

_____

3. Amazon wa doko ni arimasu ka?

_____

4. Fujisan wa sekai de ichi-ban takai yama desu ka?

_____

5. Nani ga sekai de ichi-ban takai yama desu ka?

_____

DAI YON-SHŌ — MATOME

Nan-bon desu ka?

Enpitsu (pen, tabako, nekutai, ashi)
wa ni-hon arimasu ka?

Nan-mai desu ka?

Shashin (kippu, hagaki, chizu,
kami) wa go-mai arimasu ka?

Nan-bai desu ka?

Kōhii (ocha, kōcha, osake, miruku,
biiru, nomimono) o i-ppai kudasai.

Nan-satsu desu ka?

Jisho (zasshi, nōto, hon) o san-satsu
oite imasu.

Doko ni imasu ka?

Seito wa sensei no mae ni imasu.
Sensei wa seito no ushiro ni imasu.

Seito to sensei no aida ni imasu.
Dare ga seito no tonari ni imasu ka?

Tanaka-san wa uchi ni imasu.

-te imasu

sunde imasu
irete / dashite imasu

akete / shimete imasu
suwatte / tatte imasu

Dare ka . . . ka? / Dare mo . . . sen

Dare ka imasu ka?
— Hai, dare ka imasu.
— Iie, dare mo imasen.

Higashi, nishi, minami, kita

Kyōto wa Nihon no nishi
ni arimasu.
Kyōto wa Hiroshima no higashi
ni arimasu.

. . . ga, . . . wa

Amerika wa ōkii desu ga, Nihon
wa chiisai desu.

Anata wa . . . ga arimasu.

Anata wa okane ga arimasu ka?

Kaiwa-hyōgen

"Asoko desu."
"Hora!"

KONO KYŌSHITSU NI NANI GA ARIMASU KA?

○ 6 ○

> Kono kyōshitsu ni **tsukue** ga **arimasu**.
>
> Kono kyōshitsu ni **sensei** ga **imasu**.

Kore wa kyōshitsu desu. Kono kyōshitsu ni sensei to seito ga imasu. Sensei wa tatte imasu, keredomo seito wa tatte imasen. Seito wa isu ni suwatte imasu, soshite sensei no mae ni suwatte imasu. Sensei wa seito no mae ni tatte imasu. Kono kyōshitsu ni chizu ga arimasu. Chizu wa sensei no ushiro ni arimasu. Sensei wa seito to chizu no aida ni tatte imasu. Tsukue no ue ni enpitsu ga arimasu ka? Kono kyōshitsu ni enpitsu wa arimasu ga, tsukue no ue ni wa arimasen. Enpitsu wa tsukue no shita ni arimasu.

Kono e ni haizara ga arimasu ka? Hai, arimasu. Seito no yoko ni arimasu. Seito no hidari ni arimasu ka? Iie, hidari ni wa arimasen. Seito no migi ni arimasu.

DARE KA / DARE MO

Seito no yoko ni Tanaka-san ga suwatte imasu ka?
— *Iie, Tanaka-san wa suwatte imasen.*
Anata ga suwatte imasu ka?
— *Iie, watashi mo suwatte imasen.*
Dare ga suwatte imasu ka?
— ***Dare mo** suwatte **imasen**.*
Kono heya ni **dare ka** tatte imasu ka?
— *Hai, **dare ka** tatte imasu.*
Dare ga tatte imasu ka?
— *Sensei ga tatte imasu.*
Isu no ushiro ni dare ka tatte imasu ka?
— *Iie, dare mo tatte imasen.*

Mondai 23

1. Tsukue wa doko ni arimasu ka?

_____

2. Sensei wa suwatte imasu ka, soretomo tatte imasu ka?

_____

3. Sensei wa seito no yoko ni tatte imasu ka?

_____

4. Sensei wa doko ni tatte imasu ka?

_____

5. Sensei no ushiro ni dare ga tatte imasu ka?

_____

6. Seito mo tatte imasu ka?

_____

7. Seito wa doko ni suwatte imasu ka?

_____

8. Sensei to seito no aida ni dare ka imasu ka?

_____

9. Kono kyōshitsu ni enpitsu ga arimasu ka?

_____

10. Dare ga enpitsu o totte imasu ka?

_____

11. Enpitsu wa doko ni arimasu ka?

_____

12. Yōroppa no chizu wa doko ni arimasu ka?

_____

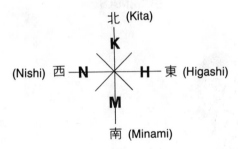

北 (Kita)

(Nishi) 西 — N ✕ H — 東 (Higashi)

南 (Minami)

HIGASHI, NISHI, MINAMI, KITA

Tōkyō wa Nihon no mannaka ni arimasu. Aomori mo Nihon no toshi desu ga, Nihon no mannaka ni arimasen. Aomori wa Tōkyō no kita ni arimasu. Sendai mo Tōkyō no kita ni arimasu. Sendai wa Tōkyō to Aomori no aida ni arimasu.

Kyōto wa doko ni arimasu ka? Nihon no kita ni arimasu ka? Iie, Kyōto wa Nihon no nishi ni arimasu. Hiroshima mo Nihon no nishi ni arimasu. Kyōto wa Hiroshima no higashi ni arimasu. Kyōto wa Hiroshima to Tōkyō no aida ni arimasu. Nara wa Kyōto no minami ni arimasu.

Mondai 24

Rei: Aomori wa Tōkyō no _____*kita*_____ni arimasu.

1. Niigata wa Tōkyō no _____ ni arimasu.

2. Nagoya wa Tōkyō no _____ ni arimasu.

3. Sapporo wa Aomori no _____ ni arimasu.

4. Ōsaka wa Hiroshima no _____ ni arimasu.

5. Okinawa wa Nagasaki no _____ ni arimasu.

SUMIMASEN!

— Sumimasen!

— Hai!

— Menyū o kudasai.

— Hai, dōzo.

— Arigatō! Sukiyaki o kudasai.

— Sukiyaki dake desu ka?

— Dewa, osake mo kudasai.

— Hai, hoka ni nani ka . . . ?

— Sore dake desu.

— Hai, wakarimashita.

Mondai 25

1. Tanaka-san wa doko ni imasu ka?

_____

2. Tanaka-san wa tatte imasu ka, suwatte imasu ka?

_____

3. Uētā wa migi no te ni enpitsu o motte imasu ka?

_____

4. Uētā wa hidari no te ni nani o motte imasu ka?

_____

5. Dare ga menyū o mite imasu ka?

_____

NANI O MITE IMASU KA?

— Heya ni nani ga arimasu ka?
 Dare ga imasu ka?

— Wakarimasen ga, otoko no hito
 ga imasu!

— Nani o shite imasu ka?

— Isu ni suwatte imasu! Sono
 hito no mae ni tsukue ga
 arimasu!

— Sō desu ka! Tsukue no ue ni
 nani ka arimasu ka?

— Hai, bin ga arimasu!

— Bin no naka ni nani ga arimasu ka?

— Wakarimasen!

— Miruku no bin desu ka?

— Iie, chigaimasu! Miruku ja
 arimasen. Osake desu! Iie!
 Uisukii desu! Ā! Ima poketto
 kara okane o dashite imasu!

— Okane desu ka?

— Hai, okane desu! Okane o
 takusan tsukue no ue
 ni oite imasu!

— Ima nani o shite imasu ka?

— Sono okane o kazoete imasu!

— Sore wa Nihon no okane desu ka?

— Wakarimasen! Zenzen wakarimasen!

Mondai 26

1. Kono heya ni dare ka imasu ka?

   _____

2. Sono hito no mae ni dare ka suwatte imasu ka?

   _____

3. Bin wa doko ni arimasu ka?

   _____

4. Bin no naka ni nani ga arimasu ka?

   _____

5. Denki wa sono hito no mae ni arimasu ka?

   _____

6. Sono hito no migi no te ni nani ka arimasu ka?

   _____

7. Hidari no te ni nani ka arimasu ka?

   _____

8. Nani ga arimasu ka?

   _____

9. Ima okane o poketto ni irete imasu ka?

   _____

10. Ima sono hito wa nani o shite imasu ka?

    _____

11. Okane o takusan kazoete imasu ka?

    _____

12. Anata no okane desu ka?

    _____

IKUTSU ARIMASU KA?

Kono e o mite kudasai! Kono heya ni nani ga arimasu ka? Tsukue to isu ga arimasu. Tsukue no ue ni nani ka arimasu ka? Hai, arimasu. Haizara ga arimasu ka? Iie, haizara wa arimasen. Tsukue no ue ni pen to hon to enpitsu to hamaki to tabako ga arimasu.

Tabako wa takusan arimasu ka? Hai, takusan arimasu. Tabako o kazoete kudasai! —I-ppon, ni-hon, san-bon, yon-hon, go-hon. Tsukue no ue ni tabako ga go-hon arimasu.

Anata wa ōkii isu o mite imasu ka? Kono isu no ue ni tabako ga go-hon arimasu ka? Iie, go-hon wa arimasen. Yon-hon arimasu ka? Iie, yon-hon mo arimasen. Nan-bon arimasu ka? San-bon arimasu.

Chiisai isu no ue ni tabako wa nan-bon arimasu ka? Yon-hon arimasu. Tsukue no ue ni mijikai enpitsu wa nan-bon arimasu ka? I-ppon arimasu. Nagai enpitsu wa ni-hon arimasu. Yuka no ue ni ōkii hon ga i-ssatsu to chiisai hon ga yon-satsu arimasu. Ōkii isu no ue ni chiisai hon wa nan-satsu arimasu ka? Ni-satsu arimasu.

Mondai 27

A) 1. Tsukue no ue ni hon ga san-satsu arimasu ka?

   _____

   2. Nan-satsu arimasu ka?

   _____

   3. Doko ni hon ga san-satsu arimasu ka?

   _____

   4. Chiisai isu no ue ni kami ga nan-mai arimasu ka?

   _____

   5. Chiisai isu no ue ni enpitsu wa nan-bon arimasu ka?

   _____

B) *Rei:* tsukue / hamaki

   Tsukue no ue ni hamaki ga yon-hon arimasu.

   1. yuka / hon

   _____

   2. chiisai isu / enpitsu

   _____

   3. tsukue / pen

   _____

   4. ōkii isu / kami

   _____

   5. ōkii isu / tabako

   _____

TŌKYŌ ICHI-MAI!

東海道本線上り
東京　上野方面

— Sumimasen! Tōkyō made
no kippu o kudasai.

— Hai, nan-mai desu ka?

— Ichi-mai kudasai.

— Hai, Tōkyō ichi-mai. Dōzo.

— Arigatō!

Nan-bon . . . ?	Nan-mai . . . ?	Nan-bai . . . ?	Nan-satsu . . . ?
bin, enpitsu, pen, hamaki, tabako, paipu, nekutai, ashi	hankachi, shashin, kami, kippu, hagaki, kabe, chizu, e	kōhii, ocha, kōcha, sake, uisukii, budōshu, miruku, biiru, nomimono	hon, nōto, jisho, zasshi
i-ppon	ichi-mai	i-ppai	i-ssatsu
ni-hon	ni-mai	ni-hai	ni-satsu
san-bon	san-mai	san-bai	san-satsu
yon-hon	yon-mai	yon-hai	yon-satsu
go-hon	go-mai	go-hai	go-satsu

DAI GO-SHŌ — MATOME

Nan-nin . . . ?

Otona ga san-nin imasu.
Watashi wa kodomo ga futari arimasu.

Ikutsu arimasu ka?

Hitotsu, futatsu . . .

. . . o kite / haite imasu

Doresu / ōbā o kite imasu.
Kutsu / zubon o haite imasu.

ii desu / yoku arimasen

Anata no kuruma wa ii desu ne.
Watashi no kuruma wa yoku arimasen.

. . . ni / o

Anata ni misete imasu.
Chizu o misete kudasai.

kanai / okusan

kanai / okusan, kazoku / go-kazoku
musume / musume-san . . .

. . . (o) . . . (ni) . . . te imasu

Kimono o kite imasu.
Kutsu o haite imasu.
Hon o watashite imasu.
Anata ni misete imasu.
Kekkon shite imasu.
Kaite imasu.
Yonde imasu.
Hanashite imasu.

. . . de

Pen de kaite imasu.
Nihon-go de kaite imasu.
Denwa de hanashite imasu.

Sūji

nijū-ichi . . . ichiman

Kaiwa-hyōgen

"Ja, (mata)."
"Ēto . . ."
"Onegai shimasu."
"Irasshaimase!"
"Konbanwa."
"Ikaga desu ka?"
"Shitsurei desu ga . . ."

NIHON-JIN TO KIMONO

Kono e o mite kudasai. Kono onna no hito wa Nihon-jin desu. Kono hito wa ima tatte imasu ka? Iie, kono hito wa suwatte imasu. Soshite kono hito wa ima Nihon no uchi ni imasu. Koko ni mado ga arimasu ka? Hai, kanojo no ushiro ni mado ga arimasu. Kanojo wa ima yōfuku o kite imasu ka? Iie, kanojo wa yōfuku o kite imasen. Dewa nani o kite imasu ka? Kanojo wa kimono o kite imasu. Anata mo ima kimono o kite imasu ka? Iie, anata wa kimono o kite imasen. Anata wa yōfuku o kite imasu ne! Burausu ya sukāto ya zubon wa yōfuku desu.

Sorekara Nihon-jin no tabemono wa Amerika-jin ya Furansu-jin no tabemono to onaji ja arimasen. Nihon-jin wa sukiyaki ya sashimi ya tenpura ga suki desu. Sashimi ya tenpura wa washoku desu. Keredomo bifuteki ya hanbāgā wa yōshoku desu. Nihon no ōkii toshi ni wa yōshoku ya washoku no resutoran ga takusan arimasu. Anata wa donna tabemono ga ichi-ban suki desu ka?

Mondai 28

1. Kono onna no hito wa Nihon-jin desu ka, Amerika-jin desu ka?

   _____

2. Kono hito wa yōfuku o kite imasu ka, kimono o kite imasu ka?

   _____

3. Anata mo ima kimono o kite imasu ka?

   _____

4. Nihon-jin no tabemono wa Amerika-jin ya Furansu-jin no tabemono to onaji desu ka?

   _____

5. Nihon-jin wa donna tabemono ga suki desu ka?

   _____

6. Sashimi ya tenpura wa yōshoku desu ka, washoku desu ka?

   _____

7. Nihon no ōkii toshi ni wa yōshoku no resutoran ga takusan arimasu ka?

   _____

8. Anata wa tenpura to sukiyaki to, dochira ga suki desu ka?

   _____

9. Anata wa donna tabemono ga ichi-ban suki desu ka?

   _____

10. Shitsurei desu ga, anata wa kekkon shite imasu ka?

   _____

どうも
ありがとう

Mondai 29

1. Kono onna no hito wa kodomo ni hanashite imasu ka?

   _____

2. Dare ni hanashite imasu ka?

   _____

3. Onna no hito wa chizu o misete imasu ka?

   _____

4. Dare ga chizu o misete imasu ka?

   _____

5. Dare ni misete imasu ka?

   _____

6. Kare wa Yōroppa no chizu o watashite imasu ka?

   _____

7. Doko no kuni no chizu o watashite imasu ka?

   _____

8. Dare ga chizu o totte imasu ka?

   _____

HITO GA NAN-NIN IMASU KA?

Kore wa Tanaka-san no kazoku desu.
Kare no kazoku wa go-nin desu. Tanaka-san
wa musuko-san ga hitori to musume-san ga
futari arimasu.

Tanaka-san wa ōkii isu ni suwatte imasu.
Okusan wa kare no mae ni tatte imasu.
Kanojo wa migi no te ni kōhii o motte imasu.
Kōhii wa shiroi kappu no naka ni arimasu.
Kanojo wa go-shujin ni kōhii o watashite
imasu. Tanaka-san wa migi no te de kōhii
o totte imasu.

Hito ga nan-nin imasu ka?

hitori
futari
san-nin
yo-nin
go-nin

| Otoko no hito | o mite kudasai.

Kare wa **go-shujin** desu.
(Kare no namae wa Tanaka desu.)

| Onna no hito | o mite kudasai.

Kanojo wa **okusan** desu.
(Kanojo no namae mo Tanaka desu.)

Mondai 30

1. Kono e ni onna no hito ga nan-nin imasu ka?

_____

2. Otoko no hito wa nan-nin imasu ka?

_____

3. Onna no hito wa suwatte imasu ka?

_____

4. Dare ga suwatte imasu ka?

_____

5. Dare ga doresu o kite imasu ka? Otoko no ko desu ka, onna no ko desu ka?

_____

6. Otoko no hito wa uwagi o kite imasu ka?

_____

7. Kare wa kōhii o motte imasu ka?

_____

8. Dare ga kōhii o motte imasu ka?

_____

9. Kōhii o isu no ue ni oite imasu ka?

_____

10. Dare ni watashite imasu ka?

_____

11. Dochira no te ni kōhii o motte imasu ka?

_____

12. Otoko no hito wa okusan kara nani o totte imasu ka?

_____

13. Kodomo wa nan-nin imasu ka?

_____

14. Otoko no ko wa nani ka kaite imasu ka?

_____

15. Nani ka yonde imasu ka?

_____

16. Hon o yonde imasu ka, soretomo shinbun desu ka?

_____

17. Ōkii onna no ko mo hon o yonde imasu ka?

_____

18. Nani o shite imasu ka?

_____

19. Kanojo wa suwatte imasu ka, soretomo tatte imasu ka?

_____

20. Hidari no te ni nani ka motte imasu ka?

_____

SŪJI

21	22	23	24	25
nijū-ichi	nijū-ni	nijū-san	nijū-shi	nijū-go

30	40	50	60	70
sanjū	yonjū	gojū	rokujū	nanajū

80	90	100	200	300
hachijū	kyūjū	hyaku	nihyaku	sanbyaku

400	500	600	700	800
yonhyaku	gohyaku	roppyaku	nanahyaku	happyaku

900	1,000	2,000	3,000	4,000
kyūhyaku	sen	nisen	sanzen	yonsen

---

31 — sanjū-ichi	29 — nijū-ku
46 — yonjū-roku	85 — hachijū-go
58 — gojū-hachi	392 — sanbyaku-kyūjū-ni
67 — rokujū-shichi	474 — yonhyaku-nanajū-shi
173 — hyaku-nanajū-san	617 — roppyaku-jū-shichi
185 — hyaku-hachijū-go	836 — happyaku-sanjū-roku
101 — hyaku-ichi	1,143 — sen-hyaku-yonjū-san
113 — hyaku-jū-san	2,581 — nisen-gohyaku-hachijū-ichi
130 — hyaku-sanjū	4,010 — yonsen-jū

Mondai 31

Tsugi no sūji o kaite kudasai.

A) *Rei:*   125   *hyaku-nijū-go* _____

    1.   38   _____

    2.   61   _____

    3.   114   _____

    4.   96   _____

    5.   179   _____

B) *Rei:*   3 + 4   *San tasu yon wa nana desu.* _____

    1.   12 − 5   _____

    2.   6 + 6   _____

    3.   8 + 10   _____

    4.   20 − 5   _____

    5.   9 + 8   _____

    6.   85 − 15   _____

    7.   20 + 20   _____

    8.   32 + 11   _____

    9.   56 − 8   _____

   10.   12 − 12   _____

   11.   19 − 9   _____

   12.   7 + 8   _____

   13.   25 + 8   _____

   14.   23 − 2   _____

   15.   18 + 2   _____

ANATA NI DENWA DESU

Yamada: Moshimoshi . . . Hai, imasu ga . . .
donata[1] desu ka? Ā, Tanaka-san no
okusan desu ka! Tanaka-san! Anata ni
denwa desu.

Tanaka: Dare kara desu ka?

Yamada: Okusan kara desu.

Tanaka: Ā, sō desu ka. Moshimoshi . . .
ā, Yuriko . . . ā, sō . . . hai . . .
ā, sō . . . sore dake? . . . ii desu yo! . . .
jā, mata!

watashi no	*anata no*

musuko	*musuko-san*
musume	*musume-san*
shujin	*go-shujin*
kanai	*okusan*
namae	*o-namae*
kazoku	*go-kazoku*

O-genki desu ka?
— Hai, genki desu.

[1] donata — dare

DARE NI TEGAMI O KAITE IMASU KA?

Kono hito wa migi no te ni nani o motte imasu ka? Pen o motte imasu ka? Hai, motte imasu. Kono hito wa nani o shite imasu ka? Hon o yonde imasu ka? Denwa de hanashite imasu ka? Iie, kono hito wa tegami o kaite imasu. Nan de kaite imasu ka? Pen de kaite imasu. Shiroi pen de kaite imasu ka? Iie, kuroi pen de kaite imasu.

Kono hito wa Yamada-san ni tegami o kaite imasu. Yamada-san ni Nihon-go de kaite imasu. Ima Yamada-san wa Kyōto ni imasu. Anata mo Yamada-san ni tegami o kakimasu ka? Anata wa watashi ni tegami o kakimasu ka? Anata wa gakkō de wa Furansu-go de hanashimasu ka? Doitsu-go de hanashimasu ka? Gakkō de wa nani-go de hanashimasu ka? Furansu-go no seito wa nani-go de hanashimasu ka?

Kore wa pen desu.
Watashi wa pen **o** motte imasu.
Watashi wa pen **de** kaite imasu.

Anata wa dochira no te **de** kakimasu ka?

Mondai 32

1. Kono hito wa hidari no te de kaite imasu ka?

_____

2. Dochira no te de kaite imasu ka?

_____

3. Kare wa anata ni kaite imasu ka?

_____

4. Dare ni kaite imasu ka?

_____

5. Yamada-san wa anata no tomodachi desu ka?

_____

6. Anata wa ima kono mondai o yonde imasu ka?

_____

7. Anata wa me de yonde imasu ka, soretomo te desu ka?

_____

8. Anata wa musuko-san to mondai o yonde imasu ka?

_____

9. Anata wa ima kimono o kite imasu ka?

_____

10. Anata wa ima waishatsu o kite imasu ka, burausu o kite imasu ka?

_____

11. Anata wa sensei ni Chūgoku-go de hanashimasu ka?

_____

12. Nani-go de hanashimasu ka?

_____

DAI ROKU-SHŌ — MATOME

Nan-ji desu ka?

Chōdo 5-ji-han desu.
Ima 6-ji-10-ppun mae desu.
12-ji-5-fun desu.

. . . ni / kara

12-ji ni / kara tabemasu.

. . . de . . .

Gakkō de hanashimasu.
Resutoran de tabemasu.

. . . de . . .

Takushii de ikimasu ka?
— Iie, aruite ikimasu.

Mō sukoshi / mō i-(ppai) / motto

Mō sukoshi yukkuri hanashite kudasai.
Kōhii o mō i-ppai onegai shimasu.
Hikōki wa motto hayai desu.

Hayai / osoi

Shinkansen wa hayai desu.
Basu wa densha yori osoi desu.

-masu / . . . te imasu

12-ji ni tabemasu.
Ima tabete imasu.
suimasu — sutte imasu
nomimasu — nonde imasu
shimasu — shite imasu
arukimasu — aruite imasu

Asa-gohan / hiru-gohan / ban-gohan

Nan-ji ni asa-gohan o tabemasu ka?
12-ji ni hiru-gohan o tabemasu.

. . . e / ni, . . . kara

Gakkō e ikimasu ka?
Hikōki wa Tōkyō kara Ōsaka made
ikimasu.

Kaiwa-hyōgen

"Dōmo . . ."
"Nani ni shimasu ka?"
"Sore ni shimasu."
"Sāte . . ."
" . . . de gozaimasu."
"Irasshaimasu."
"Gomen nasai."
"Hontō desu ka?

○ 6 ○

MŌ SUKOSHI YUKKURI HANASHITE KUDASAI!

Noguchi:	Tanaka-san, konnichiwa! Ikaga desu ka?
Tanaka:	Arigatō, genki desu. Anata wa?
Noguchi:	Ē, watashi mo genki desu. Okusan wa o-genki desu ka?
Tanaka:	Ē, genki desu.
Noguchi:	Tanaka-san, kochira wa Burēku-san desu. Amerika no tomodachi desu.
Burēku:	Hajimemashite.
Tanaka:	Burēku-san, anata wa Tōkyō ni sunde imasu ka?
Burēku:	Sumimasen ga, mō sukoshi yukkuri hanashite kudasai.
Tanaka:	Gomen nasai! Anata wa Tōkyō ni sunde imasu ka?
Burēku:	Iie, Nyūyōku ni sunde imasu. Keredomo Tōkyō ni tomodachi ga takusan imasu.
Tanaka:	Ā! Jōzu ni Nihon-go o hanashimasu nē!
Burēku:	Iie, sukoshi dake desu.
Tanaka:	Sumimasen ga, ima nan-ji desu ka?
Noguchi:	Chōdo san-ji desu.
Tanaka:	Ā, sō desu ka? Jā, watashi wa jimusho ni kaerimasu.
Noguchi:	Jā, mata ato de . . .

Mondai 33

Rei: Arigatō.   **B**

1. Anata wa Nihon-jin desu ka? _____

2. Hoka ni nani ka? _____

3. Osake wa ikaga desu ka? _____

4. Moshimoshi. _____

5. Nani o shimasu ka? _____

6. Hajimemashite. _____

7. Tabako o onegai shimasu. _____

8. Dochira no hō ga suki desu ka? _____

9. Doko e ikimasu ka? _____

10. Ikaga desu ka? _____

11. Ano hito wa jū-nin kodomo
    ga arimasu. _____

12. Sayōnara. _____

13. Ima nan-ji desu ka? _____

14. Anata wa ocha ga suki
    desu ka? _____

A. Arigatō.

B. Dō-itashimashite.

C. Jā mata . . .

D. Sore dake desu.

E. Honto desu ka?

F. Chōdo go-ji desu.

G. Hai, Tanaka desu.

H. Hai, sō desu.

I. Iie, kirai desu.

J. Doko e mo ikimasen.

K. Dochira de mo ii desu.

L. Hai, dōzo.

M. Dōzo yoroshiku.

N. Genki desu. Anata wa?

O. Terebi o mimasu.

SATŌ-SAN WA IMASU KA?

— Moshimoshi . . .
— Satō-san wa imasu ka?
— Iie, ima imasen ga . . .
— Nan-ji ni kimasu ka?
— Jū-ji-han goro ni kimasu.
— Sō desu ka! Sumimasen ga, ima
    nan-ji desu ka?
— Jū-ji-jū-go-fun mae desu ga . . .
— Dōmo arigatō. Jā, jū-ichi-ji
    ni mata denwa shimasu.
— Dōzo onegai shimasu.
— Sayonara.

Harada-san

NAN-JI DESU KA?

3:00	San-ji desu.
3:10	San-ji-ju-ppun desu.
3:15	San-ji-jū-go-fun desu.
3:25	San-ji-nijū-go-fun desu.
3:30	San-ji-han desu.
3:45	Yo-ji-jū-go-fun mae desu.
3:55	Yo-ji-go-fun mae desu.

Nan-ji desu ka?
— *San-ji desu.*

Nan-ji ni gakkō e ikimasu ka?
— *Hachi-ji ni gakkō e ikimasu.*

Bankūbā   Nyūyōku   Pari   Mosukuwa   Tōkyō

Mondai 34

A) *Nan-ji desu ka?*

1.
   _____

2.
   _____

3.
   _____

4.
   _____

5.
   _____

B)

1. Nan-ji ni jimusho e ikimasu ka? *(8:30)*

   _____

2. Nan-ji ni resutoran de tabemasu ka? *(12:15)*

   _____

3. Nan-ji ni uchi e kaerimasu ka? *(5:45)*

   _____

4. Nan-ji ni gakkō e ikimasu ka? *(6:00)*

   _____

5. Nan-ji ni shinbun o yomimasu ka? *(10:20)*

   _____

TANAKA-SAN NO ICHI-NICHI

Ima gozen ku-ji-han desu. Tanaka-san wa jimusho ni imasu. Kare wa isu ni suwatte imasu. Kare wa tabako o sutte imasu. Soshite shinbun o yonde imasu.

Harada-san mo suwatte imasu. Harada-san wa shiroi burausu to aoi sētā o kite imasu. Sorekara akai sukāto o haite imasu. Kutsu no iro mo akai desu.

Harada-san wa kanojo no isu ni suwatte imasu. Ima kanojo wa kami o taipuraitā ni irete imasu.

Ima chōdo jū-ji desu. Tanaka-san wa denwa de hanashite imasu. Harada-san wa kare no mae ni tatte imasu. Kanojo wa tsukue no ue ni kami o oite imasu. Soshite Tanaka-san ni ocha o watashite imasu.

Tanaka-san wa ima tegami o yonde imasu. Soshite ocha o nonde imasu. Harada-san wa isu ni suwatte imasu. Tegami o kaite imasu.

Ima Tanaka-san wa jimusho ni imasen. Resutoran ni imasu. Tomodachi no Noguchi-san to tabete imasu. Harada-san wa resutoran ni imasen. Kanojo wa jimusho ni imasu. Satō-san to denwa de hanashite imasu.

Mondai 35

Rei: Ima gozen **kuji-han** desu.

Ima nan-ji desu ka?
_____

1. Ku-ji-han ni Tanaka-san wa **jimusho** ni imasu.
   _____

2. Ku-ji-han ni kare wa **shinbun** o yonde imasu.
   _____

3. Harada-san wa **shiroi** burausu o kite imasu.
   _____

4. Harada-san wa **akai** kutsu o haite imasu.
   _____

5. Harada-san wa jū-ji ni Tanaka-san ni **ocha** o watashimasu.
   _____

6. Jū-ji ni Harada-san wa **Tanaka-san** no mae ni tatte imasu.
   _____

7. Jū-ji ni Harada-san wa tsukue no ue ni **kami** o oite imasu.
   _____

8. Tanaka-san wa jū-ji-jū-go-fun ni **tegami** o yomimasu.
   _____

9. Jū-ji-jū-go-fun ni Harada-san wa **tegami o kaite imasu.**
   _____

10. Jū-ni-ji-han ni Tanaka-san wa **tomodachi no Noguchi-san** to resutoran de tabete imasu.
    _____

NANI O SHIMASU KA?

Kore wa Tanaka-san desu. Tanaka-san wa ima jimusho ni imasu ka? Iie, jimusho ni wa imasen. Ima wa uchi ni imasu. Tanaka-san wa nani o shite imasu ka? Tegami o kaite imasu ka? Iie, tegami o kaite imasen. Denwa de hanashite imasu ka? Iie, denwa de hanashite imasen. Tanaka-san wa tabete imasu ka, soretomo shinbun o yonde imasu ka? Ima shinbun o yonde imasu. Soshite okusan wa kōhii o nonde imasu.

Ima chōdo gozen shichi-ji desu. Hachi-ji ni Tanaka-san wa jimusho e ikimasu. Kare wa ima tegami o kaite imasen ga, jimusho de wa tegami o takusan kakimasu. Ima Tanaka-san wa tabete imasen. Keredomo, jū-ni-ji ni wa resutoran de tomodachi to tabemasu.

Tanaka-san wa ima tabako o sutte imasen ga, jimusho de wa tabako o suimasu. Kare wa uchi de okusan to Nihon-go o hanashimasu. Keredomo, jimusho de wa Eigo to Nihon-go o hanashimasu.

> *Tanaka-san wa ima shinbun o **yonde imasu**.*
>
> *Tanaka-san wa uchi de shinbun o **yomimasu**.*

Mondai 36

1. Ima Tanaka-san wa jimusho ni imasu ka?

   _____

2. Ima doko ni imasu ka?

   _____

3. Ima nani o yonde imasu ka?

   _____

4. Jimusho de tegami o yomimasu ka?

   _____

5. Jū-ni-ji ni doko de tabemasu ka?

   _____

6. Resutoran de tomodachi to issho ni tabemasu ka, soretomo okusan
   to tabemasu ka?

   _____

7. Tanaka-san wa ima hanashite imasu ka?

   _____

8. Uchi de nani-go o hanashimasu ka?

   _____

9. Anata wa ima nani ka o yonde imasu ka?

   _____

10. Anata wa uchi de shinbun o yomimasu ka?

   _____

RESUTORAN DE

— Sumimasen!

— Hai, irasshaimase. Nan de gozaimasu ka?

— Tēburu ga arimasu ka?

— Hai, nan-nin-sama[1] desu ka?

— Futari desu.

— Hai, gozaimasu. Dōzo kochira e . . .

— Menyū o onegai shimasu.

— Hai, dōzo . . .

— Ēto . . . Sashimi wa arimasu ka?

— Iie, kyō wa sashimi wa gozaimasen.

— Jā, tenpura o onegai shimasu.

— Sumimasen. Tenpura mo gozaimasen.

— Sate . . . sukiyaki wa arimasu ka?

— Hai, gozaimasu.

— Jā, sore ni shimasu.

— Hoka ni nani ka?

— Ē, sorekara teriyaki mo kudasai.

— Hai, sorekara, nomimono wa nani ga ii desu ka?

— Biiru o kudasai.

— Hai, wakarimashita.

Nan-ji ni gohan o tabemasu ka?

(gozen)	7:00	asa-gohan
(hiru)	12:00	hiru-gohan
(gogo)	6:00	ban/yū-gohan

[1] nan-nin-sama — nan-nin

Mondai 37

1. Kono e ni onna no hito ga imasu ka?

_____

2. Kanojo wa Nagoya kara kite imasu ka?

_____

3. Doko kara kite imasu ka?

_____

4. Ōsaka e ikimasu ka?

_____

5. Doko e ikimasu ka?

_____

6. Hikōki de ikimasu ka?

_____

7. Nan de ikimasu ka?

_____

8. Anata wa Tōkyō kara Nyūyōku made kuruma de ikimasu ka?

_____

9. Nan de ikimasu ka?

_____

10. Anata wa jimusho kara resutoran made chikatetsu de ikimasu ka, soretomo aruite ikimasu ka?

_____

Mondai 38

Kono inu wa nagai desu.   *Ano inu wa mijikai desu.*

HANTAI WA NAN DESU KA?

Rei: Nagai desu.   *Mijikai desu.* _____

1. Ōkii desu. _____
2. Osoi desu. _____
3. Otoko no hito desu. _____
4. Are wa . . . _____
5. Okusan desu. _____
6. Watashi wa . . . _____
7. . . . no mae ni . . . _____
8. . . . no ue ni . . . _____
9. . . . no migi ni . . . _____
10. Suwatte imasu. _____
11. Akete imasu. _____
12. Irete imasu. _____
13. Totte kudasai! _____
14. Ikimasu. _____
15. Nani ka arimasu. _____
16. Dare ka imasu. _____
17. Gozen ni-ji desu. _____
18. Go tasu ni wa . . . _____
19. Chigaimasu. _____
20. Yukkuri hanashite kudasai. _____

DAI NANA-SHŌ — MATOME

Itsu . . . ka?

Asa kao o araimasu.
Hiru resutoran e ikimasu.
Yoru uchi de nemasu.

iu

"Ohayō" to iimasu.
Jikan o iimasu.
Berurittsu to iu gakkō e ikimasu.
Nihon-go de "Konbanwa" to iimasu.

Nan-yōbi desu ka?

Kyō wa getsu-yōbi desu.
Ashita wa ka-yōbi desu.
Kinō wa nichi-yōbi deshita.

. . . de . . . desu

Kyō wa nichi-yōbi de,
   ashita wa getsu-yōbi desu.

. . . mashō / . . . mashō ka / . . . masen ka?

Eiga e ikimashō ka?
Ē, issho ni ikimashō.
Eiga e ikimasen ka?

. . . deshita / . . . ja arimasen deshita

Kinō wa do-yōbi deshita.
Kinō wa nichi-yōbi ja arimasen deshita.

. . . no tsugi / . . . no mae

Nichi-yōbi no tsugi wa getsu-yōbi desu.
Nichi-yōbi no mae wa do-yōbi desu.

hajimaru / owaru

Konsāto wa hachi-ji ni hajimarimasu.
Soshite jū-ji ni owarimasu.

imashita / arimashita

Watashi wa kinō gakkō ni imashita.
Hon ga tsukue no ue ni arimashita.

Nani o shimashita ka?

(okimasu) okimashita
(nemasu) nemashita
(nemurimasu) nemurimashita
(araimasu) araimashita
(nugimasu) nugimashita
. . . o (shimasu) shimashita
(kotaemasu) kotaemashita
(hajimarimasu) hajimarimashita
(kakarimasu) kakarimashita
(komimasu) komimashita
(owarimasu) owarimashita
(suite imasu) suite imashita
(kikimasu) kikimashita
(arukimasu) arukimashita
(machimasu) machimashita

Kaiwa-hyōgen

"Yorokonde."
"Ja, mata ato de."
"Mochiron."
"Ā, sō deshita."

NAN-YŌBI DESU KA?

月曜日	getsu-yōbi
火曜日	ka-yōbi
水曜日	sui-yōbi
木曜日	moku-yōbi
金曜日	kin-yōbi
土曜日	do-yōbi
日曜日	nichi-yōbi

12月						
月	火	水	木	金	土	日
---	---	1	2	3	4	5
6	7	8	9	10	11	12
13	14	15	16	17	18	19
20	21	22	23	24	25	26
27	28	29	30	31	---	---

Kyō wa nichi-yōbi desu.
Ashita wa getsu-yōbi desu.
Kinō wa do-yōbi **deshita**.

Asatte wa ka-yōbi desu.
Ototoi wa kin-yōbi **deshita**.

Anata wa nan-yōbi **ni** gakkō
e ikimasu ka?
— Moku-yōbi **ni** ikimasu.

Suzuki-san wa sui-yōbi ni
gakkō e ikimasu.

Kinō wa sui-yōbi deshita.
Kinō wa gakkō e **ikimashita**.

Ototoi wa sui-yōbi ja
arimasen deshita.
Ototoi wa gakkō e ikimasen
deshita.

	ototoi	kinō	kyō	ashita	asatte	"Konnichiwa!"
asa	ototoi no asa	kinō no asa	kesa	ashita no asa	asatte no asa	"Ohayō-gozaimasu!"
yoru	ototoi no yoru	kinō no yoru (yūbe)	konban	ashita no yoru	asatte no yoru	"Konbanwa!"

Mondai 39

A) Kyō wa sui-yōbi desu.

    1. Kinō wa _____ deshita.

    2. Ashita wa _____ desu.

    3. Ototoi wa _____ deshita.

    4. Asatte wa _____ desu.

B) 1. Kin-yōbi no tsugi wa _____ desu.

    2. Getsu-yōbi no mae wa _____ desu.

    3. Sui-yōbi to kin-yōbi no aida wa _____ desu.

    4. Ka-yōbi no tsugi wa _____ desu.

    5. Nichi-yōbi to ka-yōbi no aida wa _____ desu.

    6. Do-yōbi no mae wa _____ desu.

    7. Moku-yōbi no tsugi wa _____ desu.

    8. Sui-yōbi no mae wa _____ desu.

    9. Do-yōbi no tsugi wa _____ desu.

C) Kyō wa kin-yōbi desu.

    1. _____ wa nichi-yōbi desu.

    2. _____ wa do-yōbi desu.

    3. _____ wa sui-yōbi deshita.

    4. _____ wa moku-yōbi deshita.

ISSHO NI IKIMASHŌ

Horikawa: Makita-san! Ikaga desu ka?

Makita: Ā, Horikawa-san! Konnichiwa.

Horikawa: Konban o-hima desu ka?

Makita: Ē, konban hima desu ga . . .

Horikawa: Issho ni eiga ni ikimasen ka?

Makita: Ē, yorokonde! Eiga wa nan-ji ni hajimarimasu ka?

Horikawa: Sā, yoku shirimasen ga, shichi-ji goro kara hajimarimasu. Go-ji-han goro ni ikimashō ka?

Makita: Ē, sō shimashō.

Horikawa: Jā, mata ato de.

Makita: Dōmo arigatō gozaimasu.

Horikawa-san wa Makita-san ni "Ikaga desu ka" to iimashita.
Makita-san wa "Konnichiwa" to iimashita.
Horikawa-san wa "Konban o-hima desu ka" to iimashita.
Makita-san wa "Ē, konban hima desu" to kotaemashita.

SUMISU-SAN WA SEITO DESU

Sumisu-san wa Nihon-go o benkyō shite imasu. Maishū ka-yōbi to moku-yōbi ni Berurittu-gakkō e ikimasu. Jugyō wa roku-ji kara hajimarimasu ga, shichi-ji-sanjū-go-fun ni owarimasu.

Kyō wa ka-yōbi desu. Sumisu-san wa chikatetsu de Berurittsu- gakkō e ikimasu. Kinoshita-sensei ga kare no sensei desu. Sumisu-san wa sensei ni "Konbanwa" to iimasu. Sensei mo "Konbanwa" to Nihon-go de iimasu. Kurasu de wa sensei wa Nihon- go dake de hanashimasu. Soshite Sumisu-san mo Nihon-go dake de kotaemasu. Futari tomo zenzen Eigo o hanashimasen.

Ima schichi-ji-sanjū-go-fun desu. Jugyō wa owarimashita. Sumisu-san wa rōka de tabako o suimasu. Sensei wa kōhii o nomimasu. Soshite Sumisu-san wa sensei ni "Sayonara" to iimasu. Sensei mo "Sayonara" to iimasu.

Yoru uchi de Sumisu-san wa hitori de Nihon-go o benkyō shimasu. Nihon-go no hon o san-pēji gurai yomimasu. Soshite mondai o takusan shimasu. Tēpu mo kikimasu.

NAN TO IIMASHITA KA?

"Watashi wa Tanaka desu."
Anata ni **namae o iimashita.**

"Tanaka-san, ima ni-ji desu."
Tanaka-san ni **jikan o iimashita.**

"Konnichiwa, Hiroshi-san!"
Hiroshi-san ni konnichiwa **to iimashita.**

Kono gakkō wa Berurittsu to iimasu.
Kore wa **Berurittsu to iu gakkō** desu.

Kore wa Nihon-go no kotoba desu.
Kono kotoba wa **Furansu-go de nan to iimasu ka?**

NANI O SHIMASU KA? NANI O SHIMASHITA KA?

Sumisu-san wa Nihon-go o benkyō shite imasu.

Kare wa ka-yōbi to moku-yōbi ni Berurittsu-gakkō e ikimasu.

Jugyō wa roku-ji kara hajimarimasu.

Jugyō wa shichi-ji sanjū-go-fun ni owarimasu.

Kare wa chikatetsu de gakkō e ikimasu.

Kinoshita-sensei ga Sumisu-san no sensei desu.

Sumisu-san wa sensei ni "Konbanwa" to iimasu.

Kurasu de wa sensei wa Nihon-go dake de hanashimasu.

Futari tomo zenzen Eigo o hanashimasen.

Sumisu-san wa rōka de tabako o suimasu.

Sensei wa kōhii o nomimasu.

Yoru, uchi de kare wa hitori de Nihon-go o benkyō shimasu.

Nihon-go no hon o yomimasu.

Mondai o takusan shimasu.

Soshite kare wa tēpu o kikimasu.

Sumisu-san wa Nihon-go o benkyō shite imashita.

Kare wa ka-yōbi to moku-yōbi ni Berurittsu-gakkō e ikimashita.

Jugyō wa roku-ji kara hajimarimashita.

Jugyō wa shichi-ji sanjū-go-fun ni owarimashita.

Kare wa chikatetsu de gakkō e ikimashita.

Kinoshita-sensei ga Sumisu-san no sensei deshita.

Sumisu-san wa sensei ni "Konbanwa" to iimashita.

Kurasu de wa sensei wa Nihon-go dake de hanashimashita.

Futari tomo zenzen Eigo o hanashimasen deshita.

Sumisu-san wa rōka de tabako o suimashita.

Sensei wa kōhii o nomimashita.

Yoru, uchi de kare wa hitori de Nihon-go o benkyō shimashita.

Nihon-go no hon o yomimashita.

Mondai o takusan shimashita.

Soshite kare wa tēpu o kikimashita.

Kanojo wa denwa o shimasu.

Kanojo wa denwa o shimashita.

Mondai 40

Rei: Maeda-san wa shichi-ji ni okimasu.

Maeda-san wa shichi-ji ni okimashita.

1. Shichi-ji-jū-go-fun ni kao o araimasu.

2. Asa shinbun o yomimasu ka?

3. Ofisu de "Ohayō" to iimasu.

4. Shigoto wa ku-ji-han ni hajimarimasu ka?

5. Doko de hiru-gohan o tabemasu ka?

6. Takusan taipu shimasu.

7. Jimusho ni Mōgan-san to iu hito ga kimasu.

8. Roku-ji goro uchi e kaerimasu.

Mondai 41

1. Asa hachi-ji goro chikatetsu wa taihen komimasu ka?

_____

2. Itsu konbanwa to iimasu ka?

_____

3. Kono tsugi no nichi-yōbi ongaku-kai e ikimashō ka?

_____

4. Anata wa nichi-yōbi ni wa osoku made nete imasu ka?

はい、私は 日とび に わ遅刻) まで ねて います。

5. Kinō eiga o hitori de mimashita ka?

は、日　　を一人で 見ました

6. "Book" wa Nihon-go no kotoba desu ka?

Book は 日本語 の ことば が 本です。

7. "Book" wa Nihon-go de nan to iimasu ka?

Book は 日本語で 本 です。

8. Anata wa nan to iu gakkō e ikimasu ka?

私 日本語・

9. Honda to iu kuruma wa takai desu ka?

田

10. Nihon de ichi-ban ōkii toshi wa nan to iimasu ka?

_____

JIKOKU-HYŌ

	Tōkyō	Nagoya	Kyōto	Ōsaka	Miyazaki
	10:00	10:30	—	11:05	12:45
	9:00	10:15	11:25	12:00	—

Kore wa hikōki to Kodama to iu densha no jikoku-hyō desu. Hikōki mo Kodama mo Tōkyō kara Nagoya to Ōsaka e ikimasu. Keredomo hikōki wa Kyōto e wa ikimasen. Soshite Kodama wa Miyazaki e wa ikimasen.

Tōkyō kara Ōsaka made hikōki de dono kurai kakarimasu ka? Tōkyō kara Ōsaka made hikōki de ichi-jikan-go-fun kakarimasu. Jā, densha de wa dono kurai kakarimasu ka? Chōdo san-jikan kakarimasu. Kodama to hikōki to, dochira no hō ga hayai desu ka? Hikōki no hō ga zutto hayai desu.

Ima jū-ichi-ji-ju-ppun mae desu. Hikōki wa sanju-ppun inai ni Ōsaka ni kimasu ka? Hai, hikōki wa sanju-ppun inai ni Ōsaka ni kimasu. Kodama mo sugu Ōsaka e kimasu ka? Iie, Kodama wa sugu kimasen.

Watashi wa ototoi no asa, ku-ji no Kodama de Kyōto e ikimashita. Densha wa konde imashita ka? Iie, densha wa taihen suite imashita. Soshite watashi wa densha no naka de hiru-gohan o tabemashita. Itsu Tōkyō e kaette kimashita ka? Yūbe osoku Tōkyō e kaette kimashita.

Mondai 42

1. Hikōki mo densha mo Tōkyō kara Ōsaka e ikimasu ka?

   _____

2. Hikōki mo densha mo Kyōto e ikimasu ka?

   _____

3. Dono norimono ga Miyazaki e ikimasu ka?

   _____

4. Kono densha no namae wa nan to iimasu ka?

   _____

5. Tōkyō kara Ōsaka made Hikōki de dono kurai kakarimasu ka?

   _____

6. Tōkyō kara Kyōto made densha de dono kurai kakarimasu ka?

   _____

7. Densha to hikōki to, dochira no hō ga osoi desu ka?

   でんしゃ の ほが 遅り

8. Watashi wa itsu Kyōto e ikimashita ka?

   私は

9. Watashi no densha wa konde imashita ka?

   _____

10. Watashi wa itsu Tōkyō e kaette kimashita ka?

    _____

DAI HA-SSHŌ — MATOME

Nan-do . . . ?

Mainichi nan-do denwa shimasu ka?
I-sshūkan ni nan-do gakkō e ikimasu ka?

. . . no mae ni / ato de / . . . no aida ni

Shokuji no mae ni te o araimasu.
Shigoto no ato de eiga ni ikimasu.
Asa-gohan to hiru-gohan no aida ni
nani mo tabemasen.

. . . te . . . masu / . . . te . . . mashita

Nekutai o shite kaisha ni ikimasu ka?
Isu ni suwatte hanashimashita.

. . . te kara

Uchi ni kaette kara, terebi o mimasu.

. . . mae ni . . . mashita / . . . go ni . . . masu

Densha wa 3-pun mae ni eki o demashita.
Tsugi no densha wa 2-fun go ni demasu.

. . . no tame ni

Hisho wa bosu no tame ni taipu shimasu.

. . . shika . . . masen

Kono heya ni isu wa hitotsu shika arimasen.
Watashi wa okane o sukoshi shika motte
imasen.

Mō . . . mashita / Mada . . . te imasen

Mō tabemashita ka?
— Iie, mada tabete imasen.

. . . mashita / . . . masen deshita

2-nen mae hajimete Tanaka-san
ni aimashita.
Kinō Tanaka-san wa kaisha
e ikimashita ga, hisho wa
ikimasen deshita.

. . . te imashita / . . . te imasen deshita

Kinō 10-ji goro anata wa terebi o
mite imashita ka?
— Iie, watashi wa terebi o mite
imasen deshita. Watashi wa nete
imashita.

. . . shimasu

sain / kopii / fairu shimasu

moraimasu / dashimasu

Watashi wa tomodachi kara tegami
o moraimashita.
Kyō watashi wa sono tomodachi ni
tegami o dashimashita.

demasu / tsukimasu

Kaisha o 5-ji goro demasu.
Soshite 6-ji goro uchi ni
tsukimasu.

norimasu / orimasu

Tōkyō eki kara chikatetsu ni
notte kudasai.
Tsugi no eki de chikatetsu o
orite kudasai.

Kaiwa-hyōgen

"Mata, dōzo."
"Demo . . ."
"Donata-sama."
"Chotto o-machi kudasai."
"Orimasen."

○ 6 ○

ASUTORIA DE NO YŪSHOKU

Yamada-san to Sasaki-san wa taihen ii tomodachi desu. Futari wa onaji gakkō o demashita. Tōkyō no Keiō-Daigaku[1] desu. Ima futari wa onaji kaisha de shigoto o shite imasen ga, i-sshūkan ni ichi-do futari de issho ni shokuji o shimasu. Maishū kin-yōbi ni Ginza de aimasu. Sorekara resutoran e ikimasu.

Ashita futari wa issho ni ongaku-kai e ikimasu. Soshite sono ato de shokuji o shimasu. Futari tomo Ginza no Furansu-resutoran "Asutoria" ga taihen suki desu. Do-yōbi no gogo shichi-ji goro resutoran wa taihen komimasu. Yamada-san wa "Asutoria" ni denwa o shimasu.

— Ā, moshimoshi . . .

— Moshimoshi, Asutoria de gozaimasu.

— Yamada desu ga, ashita no yoru shichi-ji goro futari no seki[2] ga arimasu ka?

— Chotto[3] o-machi kudasai.
Hai, o-futari no tēburu ga gozaimasu.

— Jā, sore o onegai shimasu.

— Hai, arigatō gozaimasu.

— Dōmo arigatō.

[1] Keiō-Daigaku — Gakkō no namae
[2] seki — tēburu
[3] Chotto — Sukoshi

Mondai 43

1. Yamada-san to Sasaki-san wa tomodachi desu ka?

   _____

2. Onaji kaisha de hataraite imasu ka?

   _____

3. Futari wa onaji gakkō o demashita ka?

   _____

4. I-sshūkan ni nan-do futari de shokuji o shimasu ka?

   _____

5. Ashita Sasaki-san wa doko e ikimasu ka?

   _____

6. Hitori de ikimasu ka?

   _____

7. Dare to ikimasu ka?

   _____

8. Ongaku-kai no ato de dono resutoran e ikimasu ka?

   _____

9. Ima Yamada-san wa denwa shite imasu ka?

   _____

10. Do-yōbi no yūgata resutoran wa taihen komimasu ka?

    _____

TAKAGI MIEKO-SAN NO ICHI-NICHI

Takagi-san wa Yamada-san no hisho desu. Kanojo wa maiasa hayaku okimasu. Kao o aratte yōfuku o kite shichi-ji ni asa-gohan o tabemasu. Asa-gohan wa mainichi tamago to tōsuto to kōhii desu. Chōshoku-chū ni shinbun o yomimasu.

Hachi-ji-niju-ppun ni Mieko-san wa uchi o demasu. Soshite chikatetsu no eki made aruite ikimasu. Chikatetsu no eki wa kanojo no uchi no mae ni arimasu. Chikatetsu ni notte kaisha e ikimasu. Kaisha e ku-ji-jū-go-fun mae ni tsukimasu. Chikatetsu wa jū-go-fun kakarimasu. Shigoto wa ku-ji ni hajimarimasu.

Takagi-san wa ōkii Nihon no kaisha no Tōkyō no jimusho de hataraite imasu. Jimusho de mainichi taipu o takusan shimasu. Jū-ni-ji ni jimusho o dete shokuji ni ikimasu. Kanojo wa tomodachi to issho ni resutoran e aruite ikimasu. Resutoran wa taihen konde imasu.

Gogo ichi-ji ni jimusho e kaette kite, mata shigoto o hajimemasu. Soshite go-ji made shigoto o shimasu. Go-ji-go-fun goro kaisha o dete chikatetsu de uchi e kaerimasu. Kanojo wa chikatetsu no eki made aruite ikimasu. Kono jikan wa chikatetsu wa ichi-ban konde imasu. Chikatetsu kara orite, kanojo wa roku-ji mae ni uchi e tsukimasu.

Shichi-ji-han ni ban-gohan o kazoku to tabete kara, terebi o mimasu. Yoru jū-ichi-ji goro nemasu. Kore ga Takagi-san no ichi-nichi desu.

Mondai 44

1. Takagi-san wa dare no hisho desu ka?

_____

2. Asa hayaku okimasu ka?

_____

3. Nan-ji ni asa-gohan o tabemasu ka?

_____

4. Chōshoku ni nani o tabemasu ka?

_____

5. Itsu shinbun o yomimasu ka?

_____

6. Takagi-san wa takushii de kaisha e ikimasu ka?

_____

7. Kaisha de donna shigoto o shimasu ka?

_____

8. Nan-ji goro kaisha o dete, chikatetsu no eki e ikimasu ka?

_____

9. Chikatetsu no eki wa kanojo no uchi no mae ni arimasu ka?

_____

10. Ban-gohan o tabete kara, nani o shimasu ka?

_____

MŌ . . . MASHITA / MADA . . . TE IMASEN

> Watashi wa asa-gohan o 7-ji ni tabemasu.
> 12-ji ni hiru-gohan o tabemasu.
>
> Ima 10-ji desu:
>
> Watashi wa **mō** asa-gohan o tabe**mashita**.
> **Mada** hiru-gohan o tabe**te imasen**.

Mondai 45

Rei: Anata wa mō Nihon e ikimashita ka?

Hai, mō ikimashita.

Iie, mada itte imasen.

1. Kyō wa mō Ishii-san ni aimashita ka?

2. Mō tenpura o tabemashita ka?

3. Mō Nihon-go de denwa shimashita ka?

4. Mō Nihon-go de tegami o kakimashita ka?

5. Ongaku-kai wa mō hajimarimashita ka?

GETSU-YŌBI NI JIMUSHO DE

○ 6 ○

Kyō wa getsu-yōbi desu. Harada-san wa ima jimusho ni imasu. Kanojo wa getsu-yōbi kara kin-yōbi made kaisha de hatarakimasu. Jimusho de wa shigoto ga takusan arimasu. Hajime ni Harada-san wa tegami o taipu shite sorekara kopii o ni-mai torimasu.

Ima gogo ni-ji-han desu. Harada-san wa tegami o taipu shite imasu. Mō resutoran e itte kaette kimashita ga, mada uchi e kaerimasen. Kanojo no shigoto wa mō owarimashita ka? Iie, mada owatte imasen. Go-ji ni owarimasu. Kanojo wa go-ji-go-fun goro jimusho o dete uchi ni kaerimasu.

Kinō wa nichi-yōbi deshita. Kinō wa shigoto ga arimasen deshita. Kanojo wa kaisha e ikimasen deshita. Zenzen taipu o shimasen deshita. Kesa hayaku okimashita ga, kinō no asa wa osoku made nete imashita. Kinō no gogo uchi de hon o yomimashita. Sorekara yoru tomodachi to eiga ni ikimashita. Yoru osoku uchi ni kaerimashita.

Mondai 46

Rei: Kyō wa **getsu-yōbi** desu.

    Kyō wa nan-yōbi desu ka?
    ―――――――――――――――――――

1. Harada-san wa ima **jimusho** ni imasu.

   ――――――――――――――――――――――――――――――――――――――

2. Jimusho de wa **shigoto** ga takusan arimasu.

   ――――――――――――――――――――――――――――――――――――――

3. Harada-san wa **tegami** o taipu shimasu.

   ――――――――――――――――――――――――――――――――――――――

4. Kanojo wa kopii o **ni-mai** torimasu.

   ――――――――――――――――――――――――――――――――――――――

5. Kanojo wa **go-ji-go-fun goro** jimusho o dete, uchi e kaerimasu.

   ――――――――――――――――――――――――――――――――――――――

6. Kinō wa **nichi-yōbi** deshita.

   ――――――――――――――――――――――――――――――――――――――

7. **Kinō no asa** osoku made nete imashita.

   ――――――――――――――――――――――――――――――――――――――

8. Kinō no gogo uchi de **hon o yomimashita.**

   ――――――――――――――――――――――――――――――――――――――

9. Kinō **tomodachi** to eiga ni ikimashita.

   ――――――――――――――――――――――――――――――――――――――

10. Kinō no **yoru osoku** uchi e kaerimashita.

   ――――――――――――――――――――――――――――――――――――――

GAKKŌ E IKIMASU

Suzuki:	Konnichiwa! Shibata-san, o-genki desu ka?
Shibata:	Konnichiwa! Okagesamade . . . Anata mo o-genki desu ka?
Suzuki:	Ē, arigatō gozaimasu.
Shibata:	Suzuki-san, doko e ikimasu ka?
Suzuki:	Gakkō e ikimasu.
Shibata:	Gakkō e?
Suzuki:	Hai! I-sshūkan ni san-do shigoto no ato de gakkō e itte imasu.
Shibata:	Nani o benkyō shite imasu ka?
Suzuki:	Eigo desu!
Shibata:	Sō desu ka . . . Eigo o kakimasu ka?
Suzuki:	Iie, kakimasen.
Shibata:	Jā, gakkō de nani o shimasu ka?
Suzuki:	Eigo dake hanashimasu.
Shibata:	Kyōshitsu wa konde imasu ka?
Suzuki:	Iie, zenzen konde imasen. Watashi hitori ga seito desu. Sensei to seito no futari dake desu.
Shibata:	Kyōshitsu de Nihon-go o hanashimasu ka?
Suzuki:	Iie, zenzen hanashimasen.
Shibata:	Hontō desu ka? Doko no gakkō desu ka?
Suzuki:	Berurittsu desu.
Shibata:	Gakkō wa nan-ji ni hajimarimasu ka?
Suzuki:	Gogo shichi-ji-jū-go-fun desu.
Shibata:	Dono gurai kakarimasu ka?
Suzuki:	Ni-jikan-han desu.
Shibata:	Sō desu ka . . . Sore wa ii desu nē!
Suzuki:	Issho ni Berurittsu e ikimasen ka?
Shibata:	Ē, yorokonde! Gakkō wa doko desu ka?
Suzuki:	Kono michi o massugu ikimasu.
Shibata:	Jā, ikimashō!

Mondai 47

1. Suzuki-san wa dare ni aimashita ka?

   _____

2. Suzuki-san wa ima doko e ikimasu ka?

   _____

3. I-sshūkan ni nan-do gakkō e ikimasu ka?

   _____

4. Itsu gakkō e ikimasu ka?

   _____

5. Gakkō de ongaku o benkyō shite imasu ka?

   _____

6. Nani o benkyō shite imasu ka?

   _____

7. Kyōshitsu de wa hon o yomimasu ka?

   _____

8. Kyōshitsu de wa nani o shimasu ka?

   _____

9. Kyōshitsu ni seito wa nan-nin imasu ka?

   _____

10. Kare no benkyō wa nan-ji ni hajimarimasu ka?

    _____

11. Jugyō wa dono gurai kakarimasu ka?

    _____

12. Konban futari wa issho ni Berurittsu-gakkō e ikimasu ka?

    _____

KONSĀTO NI IKIMASEN KA?

Koyama:	Ō-ta-sā-n . . . !
Ōta:	Ā, Koyama-san! Konnichiwa!
Koyama:	Konnichiwa, Ōta-san. Yūbe anata no uchi ni denwa o shimashita ga, anata wa imasen deshita ne?
Ōta:	Ē, yūbe wa uchi ni imasen deshita. Tomodachi to eiga ni ikimashita.
Koyama:	Hontō? Nan no eiga o mimashita ka?
Ōta:	Furansu no desu. Taihen ii eiga deshita.
Koyama:	Nan to iu eiga desu ka?
Ōta:	"Ashita Pari de" to iu eiga desu. Anata wa mō mimashita ka?
Koyama:	Iie, mada mite imasen ga, yoku shitte imasu.
Ōta:	Anata wa konban nani o shimasu ka?
Koyama:	Sā, mada nani mo . . .
Ōta:	Konsāto no kippu ga ni-mai arimasu ga, issho ni ikimasen ka?
Koyama:	Nan no konsāto desu ka?
Ōta:	Kurashikku desu. "Bētōben no yūbe" to iu konsāto desu.
Koyama:	Ā, sore wa ii desu nē! Nan-ji ni hajimarimasu ka?
Ōta:	Hachi-ji ni hajimatte, jū-ji-han goro owarimasu.
Koyama:	Doko de aimashō ka?
Ōta:	Konsāto-hōru no mae de shichi-ji-han ni aimashō.
Koyama:	Sore wa doko ni arimasu ka?
Ōta:	Kono michi o massugu ni itte hidari ni arimasu. Asoko ni basu-noriba ga arimasu. Soko kara basu ga dete imasu.
Koyama:	Sō, dōmo arigatō! Jā, mata ato de!
Ōta:	Jā, mata.

Mondai 48

1. Koyama-san wa dare ni konnichiwa to iimashita ka?

_____

2. Ōta-san wa yūbe dare to nani o shimashita ka?

_____

3. Ōta-san wa Amerika no eiga o mimashita ka, soretomo Furansu no desu ka?

_____

4. Nan to iu eiga deshita ka?

_____

5. Koyama-san wa sono eiga o mō mimashita ka?

_____

6. Dare ga konsāto no kippu o motte imasu ka?

_____

7. Sore wa nan to iu konsāto desu ka?

_____

8. Konsāto wa nan-ji ni hajimatte, nan-ji goro owarimasu ka?

_____

9. Konsāto wa doko de arimasu ka?

_____

10. Koyama-san to Ōta-san wa nan-ji ni doko de aimasu ka?

_____

11. Ōta-san to Koyama-san wa konsāto-hōru made nan de ikimasu ka?

_____

12. Basu wa doko kara dete imasu ka?

_____

DAI KYŪ-SHŌ — MATOME

Nan-gatsu desu ka?

ichi-gatsu . . . jū-ni-gatsu

Nan-nen desu ka?

Kotoshi wa 1986-nen desu.
Kyonen wa 1985-nen deshita.
Rainen wa 1987-nen desu.

Tenki wa dō desu ka?

Harete imasu.
Ame ga futte imasu.
Yuki wa futte imasen.
Kaze ga tsuyoi desu.

itsumo / yoku / tokidoki / futsū

Itsumo chikatetsu de kaisha e ikimasu.
Yoku chikatetsu no eki de Tanaka-san
ni aimasu.
Tokidoki densha de uchi e kaerimasu.
Futsū nichi-yobi wa osoku made nete
imasu.

Kesshite / mettani . . . masen

Kurasu de wa kesshite Eigo o
hanashimasen.
Tōkyō de wa mettani yuki ga
furimasen.

dandan / kyūni

Dandan samuku narimasu.
Kyūni atsuku narimasu.

-ku nai-n(o) desu / . . . ja nai-n(o) desu

Atsuku arimasen.
Atsuku nai-n desu.

Kirai ja arimasen.
Kirai ja nai-n desu.

. . . no tame (ni)

Ame no tame ni, Shinkansen ga demasen.

. . . no toki

Ame no toki, rēnkōto o kimasu.
Kodomo no toki, doko ni sunde imashita
ka?

. . . wa . . . , . . . wa . . .

Soto wa samui desu ga, naka wa
samuku wa arimasen.

-ku naru / . . . ni naru

Dandan suzushiku narimasu.
Watashi wa kyonen Berurittsu no seito
ni narimashita.

NAN-NEN DESU KA?

> 1900 — Sen-kyūhyaku-nen
>
> 1950 — Sen-kyūhyaku-gojū-nen
>
> 1976 — Sen-kyūhyaku-nanajū-roku-nen

Mondai 49

Rei: 1976   *Kotoshi wa sen-kyūhyaku-nanajū-roku-nen desu.*

               Kyonen wa sen-kyūhyaku-nanajū-go-nen deshita.

               Rainen wa sen-kyūhyaku-nanajū-nana-nen desu.

1. 1922

2. 1847

3. 1729

4. 1503

5. 1651

TENKI WA DŌ DESU KA?

Harete imasu.

Ame ga futte imasu.

Kaze ga fuite imasu.

Yuki ga futte imasu.

ITSUMO / KESSHITE / TOKIDOKI / FUTSŪ

Shiberia wa **itsumo** samui desu. **(Kesshite** atsuku ari**masen.)**

Asa ni-ji wa itsumo kurai desu. **(Kesshite** akaruku arimasen.)

Watashi wa **tokidoki** eiga o mimasu.

Watashi wa **futsū** uchi de asa-gohan o tabemasu.

Mondai 50

1. Tōkyō no natsu wa atsui desu ka?

_____

2. Natsu wa tokidoki ame ga furimasu ka?

_____

3. Fuyu wa tokidoki yuki ga furimasu ka?

_____

4. Aki ni sakura no hana o mimasu ka?

_____

5. Dono kisetsu ni sakura no hana o mimasu ka?

_____

6. Ku-gatsu ni wa yoru suzushiku narimasu ka?

_____

7. Haru ni wa yoku ame ga furimasu ka?

_____

8. Aki ni wa yuki ga furimasu ka, soretomo mettani furimasen ka?

_____ 吶 め、た/こ _____

9. Anata wa itsumo Nihon-go de tegami o kakimasu ka?

_____

10. Anata wa natsu ni ōbā o kimasu ka?

_____

ŌSAKA KARA NO DENWA

Noguchi:	Moshimoshi, Tanaka-san desu ka?
Tanaka:	Hai, Tanaka desu.
Noguchi:	Konnichiwa, Noguchi desu.
Tanaka:	Ā, Noguchi-san desu ka? O-genki desu ka?
Noguchi:	Ē, totemo genki desu. Ima Ōsaka kara denwa shite imasu.
Tanaka:	Ōsaka kara desu ka? Itsu kara Ōsaka ni imasu ka?
Noguchi:	Sengetsu kimashita.
Tanaka:	Sō desu ka? Tenki wa dō desu ka?
Noguchi:	Sengetsu wa ame ga mainichi furimashita yo! Demo kongetsu wa yoku narimashita. Kyō wa harete imasu.
Tanaka:	Yuki mo furimashita ka?
Noguchi:	Iie, Ōsaka de wa yuki wa mettani furimasen yo!
Tanaka:	Sō desu ka? Ōsaka wa Tōkyō yori atatakai-n desu ka?
Noguchi:	Ē, zutto atatakai-n desu yo.
Tanaka:	Itsu Tōkyō ni kaette kimasu ka?
Noguchi:	Raigetsu kaette kimasu.
Tanaka:	Jā, raigetsu aimashō.
Noguchi:	Ē, jā mata.

Mondai 51

1. Noguchi-san wa ima doko kara denwa shite imasu ka?

   大坂 から 電話して います

2. Ōsaka de wa sengetsu ame ga mainichi furimashita ka?

   はい 大坂

3. Yuki mo furimashita ka?

   いいえ ゆき が ふりません

4. Ōsaka no kongetsu no tenki wa sengetsu yori waruku narimashita ka?

   _____

5. Ōsaka no kongetsu no tenki wa dō desu ka?

   _____

6. Ōsaka no kyō no tenki wa dō desu ka?

   _____

7. Ōsaka de wa yoku yuki ga furimasu ka?

   _____

8. Tōkyō to Ōsaka to, dochira no hō ga samui desu ka?

   _____

9. Noguchi-san wa itsu kara Ōsaka ni imasu ka?

   _____

10. Noguchi-san wa itsu Tōkyō e kaette kimasu ka?

    _____

11. Anata no kuni de wa fuyu wa samui desu ka?

    _____

12. Anata wa dono kisetsu ga ichi-ban suki desu ka?

    _____

-KU NARU / . . . NI NARU

Tanaka-san wa ima Berurittsu
no seito desu.

Kare wa kyonen seito ja arimasen
deshita.

Kare wa kotoshi seito **ni narimashita.**

Fuyu wa samui desu.
Haru ni wa atataka**ku narimasu.**

Natsu wa atsui desu.
Aki ni wa suzushi**ku narimasu.**

Mondai 52

Rei: Kodomo wa chiisai desu.

Dandan   *ōkiku narimasu.*

1. Yoru wa kurai desu.

   Asa ni wa _____

2. Haru wa atatakai desu.

   Natsu ni wa _____

3. Fuyu wa hi ga mijikai desu.

   Natsu ni wa _____

4. Harada-san wa Tanaka-san no hisho desu.

   Ni-nen mae _____

5. Totemo ii tenki deshita.

   Keredomo kyūni _____

YOKU / METTANI . . . MASEN

> *Hokkaidō de wa yoku yuki ga furimasu.*
> *Tōkyō de wa **mettani** yuki ga furi**masen**.*
>
> *Watashi wa yoku terebi o mimasu.*
> ***Mettani** eiga e iki**masen**.*

Mondai 53

Rei: Sakura wa **shi-gatsu** ni sakimasu.

  Sakura wa nan-gatsu ni (/ itsu) sakimasu ka?

1. **Haru** ga ichi-ban suki desu.

2. **Yuki** no tame ni, hikōki ga demasen.

3. Watashi wa futsū asa-gohan ni **tōsuto to tamago** o tabemasu.

4. **Ame no toki,** rēnkōto o kimasu.

5. Kōen de **sanpo** shimasu.

6. **Nihon-go no benkyō no toki,** Nihon-go no tēpu o kikimasu.

7. Watashi-tachi wa **fuyu** ni Hokkaidō e ikimasu.

8. Tōkyō de wa **ame** ga yoku furimasu.

DAI JU-SSHŌ — MATOME

Nan-nichi desu ka?

Tsuitachi, futsuka, . . . tōka
Jū-ichi-nichi, hatsuka, sanjū-ichi-nichi

Kyūka / shutchō / shigoto de

Kyūka de Amerika e ikimashita.
Shigoto de mikka-kan Ōsaka ni ikimasu.
Shutchō de Doitsu ni ikimashita.

Donna supōtsu o shimasu ka?

Gorufu, tenisu, jūdō . . .

. . . ka . . . ni / de / e / o

Shigoto de Ōsaka ka Kyōtō e ikimasu.
Hoteru ka ryokan ni tomarimasu.
Resutoran ka uchi de tabemasu.
Kōhii ka kōcha o nomimasu.

. . . no (shi) -kata

Unten no shi-kata o shitte imasu ka?
Hashi no tsukai-kata o shirimasen.

-katta-n(o) desu / -ku arimasen deshita

Kyō no tenki wa warui desu.
Kinō no tenki mo warukatta-(n) desu.
Kinō no tenki wa yoku arimasen deshita.

. . . -n(o) desu / . . . nai-n(o) desu

Hoteru ni tomarimasu ka?
— Ē, tomaru(-n) desu.
— Iie, tomaranai(-n) desu.

. . . ka shitte imasu ka

Doko ni iru ka shitte imasu ka?

. . . no wa tanoshii desu / . . . no ga suki desu

Sukii o suru no wa tanoshii desu.
Hashi o tsukau no wa muzukashii desu.

Kaiwa-hyōgen

"O-genki de!"
"Itte irasshai!"

NIHON NO KISETSU

Tōkyō no shi-gatsu wa mainichi atatakai desu. San-gatsu kara go-gatsu made haru desu. Michi ni mo kōen ni mo niwa ni mo takusan no hana ga sakimasu. Sakura no hana wa futsū ni-shūkan shika saite imasen ga, taihen utsukushii desu.

Go-gatsu kara dandan atsuku narimasu. Sugu natsu desu. Ōsaka de wa roku-gatsu ni ame ga ichi-ban takusan furimasu. Tōkyō no natsu wa taihen atsui desu. Takusan no hito ga natsu no kyūka o totte umi ya yama e dekakemasu. Natsu no umi wa taihen komimasu. Umi e iku no wa tanoshii desu ga, kuruma de iku no wa taihen desu.

Jū-gatsu goro kara dandan suzushiku narimasu. Yama wa zenbu kiiro to aka ni narimasu. Totemo utsukushii desu. Mō aki desu. Aki no ryokō wa taihen tanoshii desu. Tōkyō de wa ku-gatsu ni ame ga ichi-ban takusan furimasu.

Jū-ni-gatsu ni wa samuku narimasu. Fuyu desu! Tōkyō de wa mettani yuki wa furimasen ga, takai yama no ue o mite kudasai! Sukoshi yuki ga arimasu. Fuyu ga kimashita. Tenki wa ii desu ga, tokidoki taihen samui desu. Jū-ni-gatsu, ichi-gatsu soshite ni-gatsu made samui fuyu desu.

Ima san-gatsu desu. Niwa ga dandan haru no iro o misemasu. Tōkyō no Hibiya-kōen ni mo Ginza no michi ni mo chiisai hana ga saite imasu. Totemo kirei desu. Haru desu! Tōkyō ni mo yama ni mo haru ga kimashita.

Mondai 54

A) *Rei:* 2/3   *Ni-gatsu mikka desu.* _____

    1. 6/4 _____

    2. 5/7 _____

    3. 3/9 _____

    4. 7/10 _____

    5. 12/1 _____

    6. 4/2 _____

    7. 8/8 _____

B) *Rei:* Anata wa itsu Tōkyō e ikimashita ka?

    1/7   *Ichi-gatsu nanoka ni ikimashita.* _____

    1. Itsu fune wa Nihon o demashita ka?

      11/8 _____

    2. Itsu hisho wa tegami o moraimashita ka?

      4/3 _____

    3. Itsu anata wa tomodachi ni aimashita ka?

      7/6 _____

    4. Itsu anata wa Igirisu kara kaerimashita ka?

      9/10 _____

    5. Itsu anata wa go-shujin ni tegami o kakimashita ka?

      2/5 _____

    6. Itsu kare wa Rondon e ikimashita ka?

      5/16 _____

SUZUKI-SAN WA HIROSHIMA E

Kono karendā o mite kudasai. Kyō wa nan-gatsu nan-nichi desu ka? Kyō wa jū-gatsu tōka, getsu-yōbi desu. Kinō wa nan-nichi deshita ka? Kinō wa jū-gatsu kokonoka deshita. Dewa, ashita wa nan-nichi desu ka? Ashita wa jū-gatsu jū-ichi-nichi desu. Suzuki-san wa asatte kara shigoto de Hiroshima e ikimasu. Asatte wa nan-nichi desu ka? Asatte wa jū-gatsu jū-ni-nichi desu. Suzuki-san no shutchō wa yōka-kan desu. Hiroshima de takusan no shigoto o shimasu ga, nichi-yōbi ni wa tomodachi to gorufu mo shimasu. Soshite Hiroshima-Hoteru ni tomarimasu.

Suzuki-san wa hikōki de ikimasu. Tōkyō kara Hiroshima made ni-jikan gurai kakarimasu. Jū-gatsu jū-ni-nichi no yoru Haneda-Kūkō o demasu. Onaji hi no yoru ni-jikan go ni hikōki wa Hiroshima-Kūkō ni tsukimasu. Soko kara hoteru made takushii de ikimasu.

Nan-gatsu desu ka?

ichi-gatsu
ni-gatsu
san-gatsu
shi-gatsu
go-gatsu
roku-gatsu
shichi-gatsu
hachi-gatsu
ku-gatsu
jū-gatsu
jū-ichi-gatsu
jū-ni-gatsu

Kongetsu wa ni-gatsu desu.
Sengetsu wa ichi-gatsu deshita.
Raigetsu wa san-gatsu desu.

Nan-nichi desu ka?

tsuitachi
futsuka
mikka
yokka
itsuka
muika
nanoka
yōka
kokonoka
tōka
jū-ichi-nichi
jū-ni-nichi . . .

Kyō wa futsuka desu.
Kinō wa tsuitachi deshita.
Ashita wa mikka desu.

Mondai 55

1. Asatte wa nan-gatsu nan-nichi desu ka?

   _____

2. Kinō wa moku-yōbi deshita ka?

   _____

3. Suzuki-san wa asatte doko e ikimasu ka?

   _____

4. Hiroshima e Shinkansen de ikimasu ka, soretomo hikōki de ikimasu ka?

   _____

5. Tōkyō kara Hiroshima made hikōki de dono gurai kakarimasu ka?

   _____

6. Hiroshima e kyūka de ikimasu ka, soretomo shigoto de ikimasu ka?

   _____

7. Suzuki-san no shutchō wa nan-nichikan desu ka?

   _____

8. Hiroshima de wa nichi-yōbi ni mo shigoto o shimasu ka?

   _____

9. Nichi-yōbi ni nani o shimasu ka?

   _____

10. Doko ni tomarimasu ka?

    _____

11. Anata wa Hiroshima ga doko ni aru ka shitte imasu ka?

    _____

12. Anata mo Hiroshima e ikitai desu ka?

    _____

○ 6 ○

YAMADA-SAN NO KYŪKA

Sengetsu Yamada-san wa kyūka o torimashita. Kuruma de Hakone e ikimashita. Hachi-gatsu jū-san-nichi ni uchi o demashita. Sono asa taihen hayaku okimashita. Asa-gohan o tabete kara, sūtsukēsu o kuruma ni iremashita. Uchi o hachi-ji mae ni demashita.

Tōkyō kara Hakone made no michi wa taihen utsukushii desu. Yamada-san wa Hakone no hoteru ni jū-ichi-ji mae ni tsukimashita. Kono hoteru wa taihen konde imashita. Hoteru ni tsuite kara hoteru no resutoran de hiru no shokuji o shimashita. Sore wa nichi-yōbi deshita.

Getsu-yōbi no asa ku-ji ni okimashita. Soshite shinbun o yonde kara, sukoshi sanpo shimashita. Hoteru e kaette kite, hiru-gohan o tabemashita. Sorekara tomodachi ni tegami o kakimashita. Kare wa Hakone de mainichi gorufu o shimashita ga, mada amari jōzu ni narimasen deshita.

Yama no tenki wa taihen yokatta desu. Ame wa zenzen furimasen deshita. Mainichi asa wa suzushikatta desu. Hiru wa sukoshi atsukatta desu ga, yoru wa taihen suzushiku narimashita. Tōkyō no tenki to yama no tenki wa taihen chigaimasu.

Hachi-gatsu nijū-roku-nichi ni Yamada-san wa kuruma de Tōkyō no uchi e kaette kimashita. Tomodachi ni o-miyage o motte kaerimashita. Gogo shichi-ji goro Tōkyō no uchi e tsukimashita. Tōkyō wa mada taihen atsukatta desu. Tōkyō wa ku-gatsu ni naru made suzushiku narimasen.

Yamada-san no Hakone no ryokō wa taihen yokatta desu.

-KATTA / -KU ARIMASEN DESHITA

> Kyō wa moku-yōbi desu.
> Kyō no tenki wa warui desu.
>
> Kinō wa sui-yōbi deshita.
> Kinō no tenki wa waru**katta desu.**
> Kinō no tenki wa yo**ku arimasen deshita.**
>
> Kinō watashi wa hon o yomimashita.
> Ano hon wa omoshiro**katta desu.**
> Ano hon wa omoshiro**ku arimasen deshita.**

Mondai 56

1. Yamada-san wa kyūka ni doko e ikimashita ka?

   _____

2. Densha de ikimashita ka, kuruma de ikimashita ka?

   _____

3. Hakone made no michi wa utsukushikatta desu ka?

   _____

4. Hakone de mainichi nani o shimashita ka?

   _____

5. Hakone de gorufu ga jōzu ni narimashita ka?

   _____

6. Yama no tenki wa dō deshita ka?

   _____

7. Hakone de wa asa to yoru wa suzushikatta desu ka?

   _____

8. Yamada-san wa itsu Tōkyō ni kaette kimashita ka?

   _____

9. Tōkyō wa mō suzushikatta desu ka, mada atsukatta desu ka?

   _____

10. Tōkyō no tomodachi ni nani o motte kaerimashita ka?

    _____

-U NO WA / -U NO GA

Yamada-san wa yoku terebi o mimasu.
Nihon no terebi wa omoshiroi desu.

Terebi o **miru no wa omoshiroi desu.**
Terebi o **miru no ga suki desu.**

Anata wa Nihon-go o kakimasu ka?
Anata ga Nihon-go o **kaku no wa
muzukashii desu ka?**

Hashi de taberu **no wa muzukashii desu**
ka, yasashii desu ka?

Mondai 57

Rei: Jitensha ni norimasu.
Muzukashii desu.

Jitensha ni noru no wa muzukashii desu.

1. Nihon-go o hanashimasu.
Yasashii desu.

2. Hitori de ryokō shimasu.
Suki desu.

3. Ongaku-kai e ikimashita.
Tanoshikatta desu.

4. Nihon-go de kazoemasu.
Muzukashii desu.

5. Kono mondai o shimashita.
Muzukashikatta desu.

UMI DE NO KYŪKA

Suzuki:	Konnichiwa, Tanaka-san! Ikaga desu ka?
Tanaka:	Ē, okagesamade! Senshū kaisha e denwa o shimashita ga, irasshaimasen deshita[1] ne . . .
Suzuki:	Ē, kyūka o totte imashita.
Tanaka:	Ryokō desu ka?
Suzuki:	Ē, kazoku to issho ni yama e ikimashita.

(Kazoku to issho ni yama e ikimashita.)

Tanaka:	Ā, sō desu ka . . . Watashi mo yama ga totemo suki desu. Tenki wa dō deshita ka?
Suzuki:	Mainichi taihen ii tenki deshita.
Tanaka:	Kaze wa arimasen deshita ka?
Suzuki:	Hai, zenzen! Yama ga taihen kirei deshita. Anata wa mada kyūka o totte imasen ka?
Tanaka:	Hai, mada desu. Raigetsu torimasu.
Suzuki:	Doko e ikimasu ka?
Tanaka:	Umi e ikimasu.
Suzuki:	Sō desu ka! . . . Go-kazoku to issho desu ka?
Tanaka:	Ē, mochiron kazoku to ikimasu.
Suzuki:	Nan-nichi ni ikimasu ka?
Tanaka:	Roku-gatsu nanoka desu.
Suzuki:	Dono gurai kyūka o toru-n desu ka?
Tanaka:	Ni-shūkan desu.
Suzuki:	Sore wa ii desu nē! O-genki de itte irasshai.
Tanaka:	Arigatō gozaimasu. Ā, mō roku-ji desu. Jā mata . . . Sayōnara!
Suzuki:	Sayōnara! Okusan ni yoroshiku.

[1] irasshaimasen deshita — imasen deshita

Mondai 58

1. Suzuki-san wa senshū kaisha ni imashita ka?

_____

2. Nani o shite imashita ka?

_____

3. Doko e ikimashita ka?

_____

4. Tanaka-san mo yama ga suki desu ka?

_____

5. Yama no tenki wa yokatta desu ka?

_____

6. Kaze ga tsuyokatta desu ka?

_____

7. Tanaka-san wa mō kyūka o torimashita ka?

_____

8. Itsu kyūka o torimasu ka?

_____

9. Kazoku to issho ni ikimasu ka?

_____

10. Tanaka-san wa doko e ikimasu ka?

_____

11. Kare no kyūka wa san-shūkan desu ka?

_____

12. Kyūka wa nan-shūkan desu ka?

_____

DAI JŪI-SSHŌ — MATOME

Ikura desu ka?

Kono hon wa sen-en desu.
Hon no nedan wa nisen-en desu.
Sanzen-en de o-tsuri ga arimasu ka?
Zenbu de ikura ni narimasu ka?
Zenbu de sanzen-gohyaku-en desu.

Chotto / chittomo . . . nai

Nichi-yōbi ni gorufu o chotto shimashita.
Kanai wa gorufu ga chittomo suki ja
  arimasen.

Sūji

    2,642 : nisen-roppyaku-yonjū-ni
  258,236 : nijū-goman-hassen-nihyaku-
              sanjū-roku
1,000,000 : hyakuman

. . . de dekite iru

Megane wa purasuchikku to garasu
  de dekite imasu.
Kono shatsu wa momen to
  poriesuteru de dekite imasu.

Mada . . . (masu) / mō . . . (masen)

Hisho wa mada taipu o shite imasu ka?
— Iie, mō taipu o shite imasen.

Nani o shi ni ikimasu ka?

Tabako o kai ni ikimasu.
Berurittsu ni Nihon-go o benkyō shi ni
  ikimasu.
Itsu kissaten ni kōhii o nomi ni
  ikimasu ka?

Kiku / oshieru

Denwa-bangō o kikimashita.
Jūsho o oshiete kudasai.

Kau / uru

Ten-in wa hon o urimasu.
Okyaku wa hon o kaimasu.

Doko de kaimasu ka?

depāto, sūpā, hon-ya, kamera-ya
kutsu-ya, sakana-ya nado

Kaiwa-hyōgen

"Sō desu ne . . . "
"Mā ii deshō."
"Sore (dake) de kekkō desu."

NEKUTAI-URIBA DE

Kinō Toshiko-san wa tomodachi no Hiroko-san to, Tōkyō no ōkii depāto ni ikimashita. Futari wa nekutai-uriba no kauntā de ten-in to hanashimashita.

Toshiko-san:	Nekutai o misete kudasai.
Ten-in:	Hai, iroiro arimasu ga, dore ga ii desu ka?
Toshiko-san:	Sō desu nē . . . Are wa ikura desu ka?
Ten-in:	Kore de gozaimasu ka?
Toshiko-san:	Sō desu.
Ten-in:	Kore wa sanzen-en de gozaimasu.
Toshiko-san:	Mō sukoshi yasui no ga arimasu ka?
Ten-in:	Ēto . . . , kore wa ikaga desu ka? Nisen-en desu ga . . .
Toshiko-san:	Nisen-en desu ka! Kirei desu nē. Demo amari suki ja arimasen. Nani ka aka to ao no ga arimasen ka?
Ten-in:	Hai, kore wa ikaga desu ka?
Toshiko-san:	Ā, sore wa kirei desu nē! Ikura desu ka?
Ten-in:	Kore wa nisen-nihyaku-en desu.
Toshiko-san:	Jā, sore o kudasai. Ichiman-en de otsuri ga arimasu ka?
Ten-in:	Hai, gozaimasu. Chotto o-machi kudasai . . . Dōzo, nanasen-happyaku-en no otsuri de gozaimasu.
Toshiko-san:	Arigatō.
Ten-in:	Dōmo arigatō gozaimashita.

Mondai 59

1. Toshiko-san wa depāto e nani o kai ni ikimashita ka?

   _____

2. Nekutai-uriba de dare ni hanashimashita ka?

   _____

3. Ten-in wa Toshiko-san ni nekutai o ju-ppon misemashita ka?

   _____

4. Nan-bon misemashita ka?

   _____

5. Kanojo wa nekutai no nedan o kikimashita ka?

   _____

6. Kanojo wa nekutai o kaimashita ka?

   _____

7. Nani-iro no nekutai o kaimashita ka?

   _____

8. Sono nekutai wa sanzen-en deshita ka?

   _____

9. Ikura deshita ka?

   _____

10. Kanojo wa ten-in ni chōdo nisen-nihyaku-en o watashimashita ka?

    _____

11. Ikura watashimashita ka?

    _____

12. Ten-in wa Toshiko-san ni otsuri o ikura watashimashita ka?

    _____

SŪJI

100	200	300	400
hyaku	*nihyaku*	*sanbyaku*	*yonhyaku*

1,000	2,000	10,000	20,000
sen	*nisen*	*ichiman*	*niman*

100,000	200,000	1,000,000	2,000,000
jūman	*nijūman*	*hyakuman*	*nihyakuman*

126	*hyaku-nijū-roku*
803	*happyaku-san*
2,642	*nisen-roppyaku-yonjū-ni*
4,924	*yonsen-kyūhyaku-nijū-yon*
10,501	*ichiman-gohyaku-ichi*
22,681	*niman-nisen-roppyaku-hachijū-ichi*
152,003	*jūgoman-nisen-san*

Mondai 60

Rei: 121   *hyaku-nijū-ichi* _____

1. 150 _____
2. 360 _____
3. 1,630 _____
4. 7,950 _____
5. 28,000 _____
6. 73,560 _____
7. 224,800 _____
8. 350,000 _____
9. 434,200 _____
10. 658,750 _____

MADA / MŌ . . . -MASEN

> *Wada-san wa 7-ji ni okimasu.*
>
> 6:30   *Mada nete imasu.*
>
> 7:30   *Mō nete imasen.*

Mondai 61

Rei: 8:00   Hisho wa uchi o demasu.

7:00   *Mada uchi ni imasu.*

8:05   *Mō uchi ni imasen.*

1. 9:30   Seito wa kyōshitsu o demasu.

9:25   _____

9:35   _____

2. 9:00   Buchō wa kagi o poketto kara dashimasu.

9:05   _____

8:55   _____

3. 12:00   Tanaka-san wa jimusho kara soto e demasu.

12:05   _____

11:55   _____

> *Watashi wa hon-ya e ikimashita.*
> *Hon-ya de hon o kaimashita.*
>
> *Watashi wa hon-ya e hon o **kai ni** ikimashita.*

Mondai 62

Rei: Tanaka-san wa kissaten e ikimashita.
Kissaten de kōhii o nomimashita.

Tanaka-san wa kissaten e kōhii o nomi ni ikimashita.

1. Watashi wa eiga-kan e ikimashita.
   Eiga-kan de eiga o mimashita.

   _____

2. Anata wa gakkō e kimasu.
   Gakkō de Nihon-go o hanashimasu.

   _____

3. Satō-san wa kaisha e kimashita.
   Tegami o kakimashita.

   _____

4. Michiko-san wa yūbin-kyoku e ikimashita.
   Tegami o dashimashita.

   _____

5. Kare wa kaisha e ikimasu.
   Kaisha de shigoto o shimasu.

   _____

SORE WA ZENBU DE IKURA DESU KA?

○ 6 ○

*Tanaka-san wa ima chikatetsu-
noriba no shinbun-uriba made
kimashita.*

— "Tōkyō Taimusu" onegai shimasu.

— Sumimasen, "Tōkyō Taimusu" wa arimasen.
"Mainichi Shinbun" wa ikaga desu ka?

— Hai, sore de kekkō desu. Sorekara tabako o kudasai.

— Dono tabako desu ka?

— Igirisu no tabako wa arimasu ka?

— Iie, arimasen. Nihon no tabako dake desu.

— Ā sō desu ka . . . Jā, "Hairaito" o kudasai.

— Dōzo.

— Sorekara, bōru-pen ga arimasu ka?

— Hai, iroiro arimasu ga . . .

— Ichi-ban yasui no wa ikura desu ka?

— Nihyaku-en desu.

— Ā sō desu ka . . . Jā, shinbun to tabako
dake de kekkō desu.

— Dōzo! Hoka ni nani ka?

— Iie, kore dake desu. Zenbu de ikura ni narimasu ka?

— Ēto . . . Shinbun to tabako de hyaku-sanjū-en
desu. Arigatō gozaimashita.

Mondai 63

1. Kono hito wa zasshi o kaimashita ka?

   _____

2. Nani o kaimashita ka?

   _____

3. Bōru-pen mo kaimashita ka?

   _____

4. Doko de shinbun o kaimashita ka?

   _____

5. Tabako mo arimashita ka?

   _____

6. Igirisu no tabako ga arimashita ka?

   _____

7. Doko no tabako ga arimashita ka?

   _____

8. Okyaku wa nedan o kikimashita ka?

   _____

9. Shinbun to tabako no hoka ni nani ka kaimashita ka?

   _____

10. Zenbu de ikura ni narimashita ka?

    _____

DAI JŪNI-SHŌ — MATOME

Hirosa / omosa / nagasa

mētoru, senchi, miri
guramu, kiro

(ni-jikan) de

Harada-san wa i-kkagetsu de taipu
ga jōzu ni narimashita.
Kyōto e ichi-jikan de iku koto ga
dekimasu.

Dare / itsu / nani / doko demo

Dare demo Nihon-go o hanashimasu.
Doko demo kau koto ga dekimasu.

. . . nashi de

Okane nashi de, kore o kau koto ga
dekimasen.
Kippu nashi de, hikōki ni noru koto
ga dekimasu ka?

(taka)-sugiru / (nomi)-sugiru

Kono heya wa atsu-sugimasu.
Kinō osake o nomi-sugimashita.

. . . to omoimasu / . . . deshō

Tanaka-san wa doko ni imasu ka?
— Kare wa kaisha ni iru to omoimasu.
— Kare wa kaisha ni iru deshō.

—u (okane / jikan)

(Toyota o kau okane ga arimasu ga,)
Kyaderakku o kau okane wa arimasen.

(Shigoto ga takusan arimasu kara,)
Kōhii o nomu jikan ga arimasen.

. . . koto ga dekimasu / dekimasen

Kono kuruma o kau koto ga dekimasu.
Nihon-go o hanasu koto ga dekimasu ga,
Furansu-go o hanasu koto wa
dekimasen.

. . . kara

Ame ga futte imasu kara, rēnkōto o
kimasu.
Okane o motte imasu kara, kau koto
ga dekimasu.

Dakara . . .

Ima ame ga futte imasu. Dakara
rēnkōto o kite imasu.

Dōshite . . . ? / . . . kara desu

Dōshite gorufu o shimasen ka?
— Ame ga futte iru kara desu.

Kaiwa-hyōgen

"Sugu o-mochi shimasu."
"Tenpura wa dekimasu ka?"
"Zannen desu ne!"
"Sō omoimasu."
"O-jōzu desu."

TŌKYŌ KARA YOKOHAMA MADE WA TŌI DESU KA?

Tōkyō

29	Yokohama								
180	151	Shizuoka							
360	331	180	Nagoya						
514	(485)	334	154	Kyōto					
553	524	373	193	39	Ōsaka				
590	561	410	230	76	37	Kōbe			
733	704	573	373	219	180	143	Okayama		
895	866	715	535	381	342	305	162	Hiroshima	
1108	1079	928	748	594	555	518	375	213	Fukuoka

Yokohama kara Kyōto made

485-kiro (-mētoru) arimasu.

Mondai 64

1. Kōbe kara Tōkyō made wa nan-kiro (-mētoru) arimasu ka?

   _____

2. Nagoya kara wa Tōkyō to Hiroshima to dochira no hō ga tōi desu ka?

   _____

3. Kōbe kara wa Shizuoka to Fukuoka to dochira no hō ga chikai desu ka?

   _____

4. Kyōto kara Hiroshima made to Yokohama kara Nagoya made to de wa
   dochira no hō ga tōi desu ka?

   _____

5. Fukuoka kara Okayama made to Ōsaka kara Shizuoka made to de wa
   dochira no hō ga chikai desu ka?

   _____

Mondai 65

A. kara

B. Chūgoku-go

C. chikaku ni

D. dare demo

E. ni-jikan de

F. kakarimasu

G. seikakuna

H. tabun

I. doko demo

J. nashi de

K. yomu

L. -sugi

M. gurai

Rei: Nihon de wa ___D___ terebi o motte imasu.

1. Anata wa _____ ga dekimasu ka?

2. _____ shinbun o kau koto ga dekimasu ka?

3. Ame ga futte imasu _____, rēnkōto o kimasu.

4. Koko kara Kyōto made nan-kiro _____ arimasu ka?

5. Eki no _____ takushii-noriba ga arimasu yo.

6. Shinbun o _____ jikan ga arimasen deshita.

7. Pasupōto _____, Igirisu ni iku koto ga dekimasu ka?

8. Ashita wa _____ ame ga furu deshō.

9. Kinō tabe _____ mashita.

10. Koko kara Tōkyō made _____ iku koto ga dekimasu ka?

11. Kyōto kara koko made san-jikan gurai _____.

12. Kono rōka no _____ nagasa o shitte imasu ka?

-U JIKAN / OKANE GA ARIMASEN

Kono kuruma wa totemo takai desu.
Watashi wa kono kuruma o kaimasen.

Watashi wa kono kuruma o kau okane ga arimasen.

Watashi wa ima sugu dekakemasu.
Denwa o shimasen.

Watashi wa denwa o suru jikan ga arimasen.

Mondai 66

Rei: Watashi wa totemo isogashikatta desu. Yasumimasen deshita.

Watashi wa yasumu jikan ga arimasen deshita.

1. Uchi wa totemo takai desu. Watashi wa kaimasen.

_____

2. Buchō wa shigoto ga takusan arimasu. Hiru-gohan o tabemasen.

_____

3. Hirai-san wa totemo isogashii desu. Eiga o mimasen.

_____

4. Ōkii terebi wa takai desu. Watashi wa kaimasen.

_____

. . . DESHŌ

Noguchi-san wa ima doko ni imasu ka?
— Kare wa ima Hiroshima ni iru deshō.

Sakura ga itsu saku ka shitte imasu ka?
— Shi-gatsu goro saku deshō.

Ashita wa donna tenki desu ka?
— Tabun ame ga furu deshō.

Mondai 67

Rei: Amerika no kuruma wa ikura gurai desu ka? *(Kyūsen-doru)*

    Tabun kyūsen-doru gurai deshō.

1. Anata wa ashita nan-ji ni hiru-gohan o tabemasu ka? *(12-ji)*

2. Anata wa konban nani o shimasu ka? *(terebi o miru)*

3. Anata wa raishū dare ni aimasu ka? *(Yoshikawa-san)*

4. Anata wa ashita doko de kaimono o shimasu ka? *(depāto)*

-SUGIRU

> Kono hon wa ōkii desu.
> Watashi no poketto ni ireru koto ga dekimasen.
> Hon wa **ōki-sugimasu.**
> Poketto wa **chiisa-sugimasu.**

Mondai 68

Rei: Tōkyō kara Ōsaka made wa tōi desu. Aruku koto ga dekimasen.

    Tōkyō kara Ōsaka made wa tō-sugimasu.

1. Kono tsukue wa omoi desu. Ugokasu koto ga dekimasen.

2. Atarashii kuruma wa takai desu. Kau koto ga dekimasen.

3. Kono mondai wa totemo muzukashii desu. Watashi wa kono mondai o hitori de suru koto ga dekimasen.

4. Kyō wa totemo samui desu. Sanpo suru koto ga dekimasen.

HIRAGANA TO KATAKANA

a ア あ	i イ い	u ウ う	e エ え	o オ お
ka カ か	ki キ き	ku ク く	ke ケ け	ko コ こ
sa サ さ	shi シ し	su ス す	se セ せ	so ソ そ
ta タ た	chi チ ち	tsu ツ つ	te テ て	to ト と
na ナ な	ni ニ に	nu ヌ ぬ	ne ネ ね	no ノ の
ha ハ は	hi ヒ ひ	fu フ ふ	he ヘ へ	ho ホ ほ

ma マ ま	mi ミ み	mu ム む	me メ め	mo モ も
ya ヤ や		yu ユ ゆ		yo ヨ よ
ra ラ ら	ri リ り	ru ル る	re レ れ	ro ロ ろ
wa ワ わ				o ヲ を
n ン ん				

Anata wa Nihon-go no shinbun o yomu koto ga dekimasu ka? Gaikoku-jin ga Nihon no shinbun o yomu no wa, taihen muzukashii desu. Futsū Nihon-jin wa Kanji to Hiragana o tsukaimasu. Keredomo tokidoki, Katakana mo tsukaimasu. Eigo ya Furansu-go ya Supein-go nado no kotoba wa Katakana de kakimasu. Tatoeba, HOTERU, IGIRISU, PAN nado desu. Anata wa hoka ni donna Katakana no kotoba o shitte imasu ka?

Hiragana to Katakana wa Nihon-jin dake no ji desu. Keredomo, Kanji wa ima kara 1500-nen gurai mae, Chūgoku kara Nihon e kimashita. Soshite, sorekara dandan Kanji wa Nihon-jin no ji ni narimashita. Sore wa yaku 1200-nen gurai mae desu.

Kanji wa taihen takusan arimasu. Zenbu de 50,000 gurai arimasu. Keredomo ima wa, Nihon-jin wa yaku 2000 gurai dake o tsukatte imasu. Hiragana to Katakana wa amari takusan arimasen. Hiragana wa zenbu de 46 arimasu. Katakana mo zenbu de 46 desu.

Chūgoku-jin wa Kanji dake o tsukaimasu ga, Nihon-jin wa Kanji to Hiragana to Katakana o tsukaimasu. Keredomo kono hon wa zenbu Rōmaji o tsukatte imasu. Dakara anata wa yomu koto ga dekimasu.

DŌSHITE DESU KA? / . . . KARA DESU

Ame ga futte imasu **kara,** *rēnkōto o kite imasu.*
Dōshite *rēnkōto o kite imasu ka?*
-Ame ga futte iru **kara desu.**

Watashi wa rēnkōto o kite imasu.
Dōshite *desu ka?*
-Ame ga futte iru **kara desu.**

Mondai 69

1. Depāto wa yoru jū-ni-ji ni aite imasu ka, soretomo shimatte imasu ka?

_____

2. Ima wa yoru no jū-ni-ji desu. Depāto ni hairu koto ga dekimasu ka?

_____

3. Dōshite desu ka?

_____

4. Anata wa gakkō kara resutoran made aruku koto ga dekimasu ka?

_____

5. Tōkyō kara Hiroshima made aruku koto ga dekimasu ka?

_____

6. Tō-sugimasu ka?

_____

7. Dōshite Tōkyō kara Hiroshima made aruku koto ga dekimasen ka?

_____

ANO SŪTSUKĒSU WA IKURA DESU KA?

6

Iwasaki-san wa depāto e sūtsukēsu o kai ni ikimashita. Yoru no hachi-ji-sanju-ppun ni ikimashita ga, depāto wa mada aite imashita. Depāto ni haitte Iwasaki-san wa kaban-uriba e massugu ni ikimashita. Sui-yōbi no yoru deshita kara, depāto wa amari konde imasen deshita. Ten-in wa Iwasaki-san o mite, hanashimashita.

— Irasshaimase!
— Chiisai sūtsukēsu wa arimasu ka?
— Hai, iroiro arimasu. Dōzo kochira e irashite kudasai.¹
    Kore wa ikaga desu ka?
— Sore wa chotto ōki-sugimasu. Mō sukoshi chiisai no o
    misete kudasai.
— Hai, kore wa ikaga desu ka?
— Ā, sono hō ga zutto ii desu nē. Sore wa ikura desu ka?
— Kyūsen-en desu.
— Kyūsen-en? Taka-sugimasu nē. Motto yasui no wa arimasen ka?
— Hai, hoka ni mo takusan arimasu.
— Are wa ikura desu ka?
— Are desu ka?
— Ē, ano chairo no desu. Ikura desu ka?
— Are wa nisen-en desu.
— Nisen-en desu ka? Jā, are ni shimasu. Are o kudasai.
— O-mochikaeri ni narimasu ka?²
— Ē, motte kaerimasu.
— Jā, nisen-en onegai shimasu.
— Dōzo.
— Arigatō gozaimashita.

¹ irashite kudasai — kite kudasai
² O-mochikaeri ni narimasu ka? — Motte kaerimasu ka?

Mondai 70

1. Kono hito wa depāto e uwagi o kai ni ikimashita ka?

_____

2. Nani o kai ni ikimashita ka?

_____

3. Dare ni hanashimashita ka?

_____

4. Yōfuku-uriba e ikimashita ka?

_____

5. Dono uriba e ikimashita ka?

_____

6. Kyūsen-en no sūtsukēsu o kaimashita ka?

_____

7. Dōshite desu ka?

_____

8. Hoka no ga arimashita ka?

_____

9. Mō sukoshi yasui no o kaimashita ka?

_____

10. Ikura deshita ka?

_____

NANI O SURU KOTO GA DEKIMASU KA?

Shinbun wa yasui desu.
Mainichi shinbun o kaimasu.

Hikōki wa takai desu.
Watashi wa hikōki o kaimasen.

Shinbun o ka**u koto ga dekimasu.**
Hikōki o ka**u koto ga dekimasen.**

Watashi wa Tōkyō e ikimasu.
Tōkyō made hikōki ga arimasu.
Watashi wa Tōkyō e hikōki de
   ik**u koto ga dekimasu.**

Kyōto made hikōki wa arimasen.
Kyōto made hikōki de ik**u koto**
   ga dekimasen.

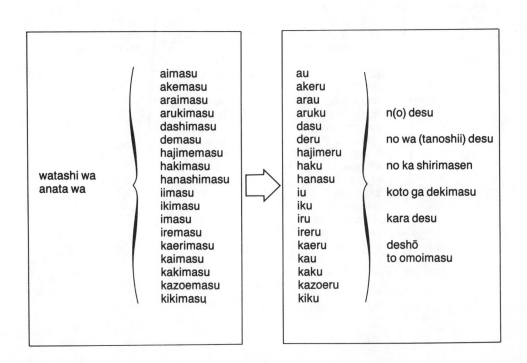

watashi wa anata wa	aimasu	au	n(o) desu
	akemasu	akeru	
	araimasu	arau	
	arukimasu	aruku	no wa (tanoshii) desu
	dashimasu	dasu	
	demasu	deru	no ka shirimasen
	hajimemasu	hajimeru	
	hakimasu	haku	koto ga dekimasu
	hanashimasu	hanasu	
	iimasu	iu	kara desu
	ikimasu	iku	
	imasu	iru	
	iremasu	ireru	deshō
	kaerimasu	kaeru	to omoimasu
	kaimasu	kau	
	kakimasu	kaku	
	kazoemasu	kazoeru	
	kikimasu	kiku	

watashi wa anata wa	kimasu	kiru	
	kimasu	kuru	
	kotaemasu	kotaeru	
	magarimasu	magaru	
	mimasu	miru	
	misemasu	miseru	
	mochiagemasu	mochiageru	
	mochimasu	motsu	
	narimasu	naru	
	nemasu	neru	
	nemurimasu	nemuru	
	nomimasu	nomu	
	norimasu	noru	
	nugimasu	nugu	
	okimasu	okiru	
	okimasu	oku	
	omoimasu	omou	no desu
	orimasu	oriru	no wa tanoshii desu
	oshiemasu	oshieru	no ka shirimasen
	owarimasu	owaru	koto ga dekimasu
	shimasu	suru	kara desu
	shimemasu	shimeru	deshō
	shirimasu	shiru	to omoimasu
	suimasu	suu	
	sumimasu	sumu	
	tabemasu	taberu	
	tachimasu	tatsu	
	tanomimasu	tanomu	
	tomarimasu	tomaru	
	torimasu	toru	
	tsukimasu	tsuku	
	tsuzukemasu	tsuzukeru	
	ugokashimasu	ugokasu	
	ukemasu	ukeru	
	urimasu	uru	
	watashimasu	watasu	
	yasumimasu	yasumu	
	yomimasu	yomu	

Mondai 71

Rei: Watashi wa pen o motte imasu. Watashi wa kakimasu.

Pen nashi de kaku koto ga dekimasen.

Watashi wa pen o motte imasu kara, kaku koto ga dekimasu.

1. Tanaka-san wa okane o motte imasu. Shinbun o kaimasu.

   _____

2. Suzuki-san wa kagi o motte imasu. Doā o akemasu.

   _____

3. Hisho wa taipuraitā o motte imasu. Tegami o taipu shimasu.

   _____

4. Sensei wa megane o motte imasu. Hon o yomimasu.

   _____

5. Satō-san wa kippu o motte imasu. Eiga-kan ni hairimasu.

   _____

6. Watashi wa kuruma o motte imasu. Yokohama e ikimasu.

   _____

7. Satō-san wa pasupōto o motte imasu. Nihon kara demasu.

   _____

DAI JŪ-SAN-SHŌ — MATOME

Donna koto . . . ?

Hashi de taberu koto wa
muzukashii desu ka?

Harada-san to donna koto o
hanashimasu ka?
— Iroiro na koto o hanashimasu.
— Kaisha no koto o hanashimasu.

-te mo ii desu ka / . . . -te wa ikemasen

Tabako o sutte mo ii desu ka?
— Iie, sutte wa ikemasen.
— Iie, sutte wa dame desu yo.
— Iie, suwanai de kudasai!

-tai (-no/n) desu / -taku arimasen

Kōhii o nomitai desu ka?
— Hai, nomitai-n desu.
— Iie, nomitaku arimasen.

. . . ga hoshii desu / . . . wa hoshiku arimasen

Ōkii kuruma ga hoshii desu ka?
— Iie, ōkii kuruma wa hoshiku
arimasen.
Chiisai kuruma ga hoshii desu.

. . . toki, . . .

Sashimi o taberu toki, o-hashi o
tsukai masu.
Kōhii ga nomitai toki, kissaten
e ikimasu.
Atsui toki, ōbā o nugimasu.

Kaisha kara nani o moraimasu ka?

kyūryō, gekkyū, shūkyū, bōnasu, nado

Yomemasu / akeraremasu

Watashi wa Nihon-go ga yomemasu.
Kagi o motte imasu kara, doa ga
akeraremasu.

(Moshi) . . . nara / . . . ja nakereba

Ii tenki nara, sanpo shimasu.
Ii tenki ja nakereba, uchi ni imasu.

(Moshi) -kereba / -ku nakereba

(Moshi) samukereba, mado o shimete
kudasai.
(Moshi) samuku nakereba, mado o
akete kudasai.

(Moshi) -(e)ba / -(a)nakereba

(Moshi) hikōki de ikeba, Ōsaka ni
ichi-ji goro tsukimasu.
(Moshi) densha de ikeba, Ōsaka ni
san-ji goro tsukimasu.
Kippu o kawanakereba, densha
ni noru koto ga dekimasen.

Kaiwa-hyōgen

"Zannen nagara/desu ga . . . "
"Oyasumi nasai."
"Tada desu."

TABAKO O SUTTE MO II DESU KA?

— Koko de tabako o sutte mo ii desu ka?

— Sumimasen ga, koko de tabako o suwanai de kudasai.
Rōka de wa sutte mo ii desu yo.

— Eigo de hanashite mo ii desu ka?

— Iie, Eigo de hanashite wa ikemasen.

— Ja, Furansu-go de hanashite mo ii desu ka?

— Iie, Furansu-go mo dame desu.

Osake o nonde mo ii desu ka?

— *Iie, nonde wa ikemasen.*

— *Iie, nomanai de kudasai.*

— *Iie, nonde wa dame desu yo!*

Kore o mite mo ii desu ka?

— *Iie, mite wa ikemasen.*

— *Iie, dame desu.*

— *Iie, minai de kudasai.*

Mondai 72

Rei: Ima hon o yonde mo ii desu ka?

     Iie, ima hon o yonde wa ikemasen.

     Iie, ima hon o yomanai de kudasai.

1. Kyō hayaku uchi e kaette mo ii desu ka?

___

2. Shigoto-chū ni eiga ni itte mo ii desu ka?

___

3. Atsui desu kara, uwagi o nuide mo ii desu ka?

___

4. Nihon no uchi no naka de, kutsu o haite mo ii desu ka?

___

5. Fōku de sashimi o tabete mo ii desu ka?

___

6. Enpitsu de sain o shite mo ii desu ka?

___

7. Samui desu kara, mado o shimete mo ii desu ka?

___

8. Ima jisho o tsukatte mo ii desu ka?

___

9. Raishū kyūka o totte mo ii desu ka?

___

10. Ashita denwa shite mo ii desu ka?

___

-TAI DESU

Onaka ga suite imasu.	⟶	Tabetai desu.
Eiga ga suki desu.	⟶	Eiga o mitai desu.
Kōhii ga hoshii desu.	⟶	Kōhii ga nomitai desu.
Ryokō ga suki desu.	⟶	Ryokō o shitai desu.

Mondai 73

Rei: Kono heya wa atsui desu.

(*akeru*) Mado o _____ *aketai desu.* _____

1. Ongaku ga dai-suki desu.

   (*kiku*) Ongaku o _____

2. Nihon-go o jōzu ni hanasu koto ga dekimasen.

   (*hanasu*) Nihon-go o jōzu ni _____

3. Ōkii uchi ga hoshii desu.

   (*sumu*) Ōkii uchi ni _____

4. Shigoto ga isogashi-sugimasu.

   (*yasumu*) Watashi wa _____

5. Totemo samui desu.

   (*kiru*) Watashi wa ōbā o _____

6. Shinkansen no kippu o kaimashita.

   (*noru*) Hayaku Shinkansen ni _____

HISHO NO HARADA-SAN

Nihon no toshi ni wa takusan no ōkii kaisha ga arimasu. Soshite takusan no jūgyō-in ga hataraite imasu. Harada-san no kaisha wa Tōkyō ni arimasu. Kanojo wa maitsuki, kaisha kara gekkyū o moraimasu. Hotondo no Nihon no kaisha wa, jūgyō-in ni kyūryō o gekkyū de haraimasu. Sorekara, Harada-san no kaisha de wa, jūgyō-in wa gekkyū no hoka ni bōnasu mo moraimasu. Futsū bōnasu wa jūni-gatsu to shichi-gatsu ni demasu.

Harada-san wa kyonen no shi-gatsu ni kono kaisha ni hairimashita. Soshite Tanaka-san no hisho ni narimashita. Kanojo no kyonen no gekkyū wa jū-niman-en deshita ga, kotoshi wa jū-niman-gosen-en ni narimashita. Hotondo no Nihon no kaisha de wa, jūgyō-in no kyūryō wa mainen ōku narimasu.

Ikeda-san mo Harada-san to onaji kaisha de hataraite imasu. Keredomo kanojo wa kono kaisha ni nagai aida tsutomete imasu kara, Ikeda-san no gekkyū wa Harada-san no yori ōi desu. Kanojo no gekkyū wa ima yaku jū-yonman-en desu ga, rainen wa motto ōku naru deshō.

Ikeda-san mo Harada-san mo kaimono ga dai-suki desu kara, futari wa yoku gekkyū-bi ni issho ni kaimono ni ikimasu.

Mondai 74

1. Harada-san no kaisha wa doko ni arimasu ka?

   _____

2. Kanojo wa maitsuki kaisha kara nani o moraimasu ka?

   _____

3. Kanojo wa gekkyū no hoka ni nani o moraimasu ka?

   _____

4. Futsū ichi-nen ni nan-do bōnasu ga demasu ka?

   _____

5. Harada-san wa itsu kono kaisha ni hairimashita ka?

   _____

6. Kanojo no kyonen no gekkyū wa ikura deshita ka?

   _____

7. Ikeda-san wa Harada-san to onaji kaisha de hataraite imasu ka?

   _____

8. Dōshite Ikeda-san no gekkyū wa Harada-san no yori ōi- (no) desu ka?

   _____

9. Ikeda-san mo Harada-san mo kaimono ga suki desu ka?

   _____

10. Futari wa itsu issho ni kaimono ni ikimasu ka?

    _____

11. Anata mo kaimono ga suki desu ka?

    _____

12. Anata mo kaisha kara bōnasu o moraimasu ka?

    _____

. . . TOKI / -TAI TOKI

Sukiyaki o tabemasu

\+

Hashi o tsukaimasu ⟹ Sukiyaki o taberu **toki,** hashi o tsukaimasu.

Nihon-go o benkyō shimasu

\+

Tēpu o kikimasu ⟹ Nihon-go o benkyō suru **toki,** tēpu o kikimasu.

Kōhii ga nomitai desu

\+

Kissaten e ikimasu ⟹ Kōhii ga nomi**tai toki,** kissaten e ikimasu.

Samui desu

\+

Sētā o kimasu ⟹ Samui **toki,** sētā o kimasu.

Mondai 75

Rei: Nani ka o moraimasu.
Arigatō to iimasu.

Nani ka o morau toki, arigatō to iimasu.

1. Isogashii desu.
Eiga o miru koto ga dekimasen.

2. Kaisha e ikimasu.
Nekutai o shimasu.

3. Kyōto e ikimasu.
   Shinkansen ni norimasu.

   _____

4. Tabako o suimasu.
   Rōka e demasu.

   _____

5. Nihon-go o benkyō shimasu.
   Eigo o hanasanaide kudasai.

   _____

6. Heya ga akaruku arimasen.
   Denki o tsukemasu.

   _____

7. Bifuteki ga tabetai desu.
   Doko e ikimasu ka?

   _____

8. Hikōki ni norimasu.
   Hikōjō e ikimasu.

   _____

9. Ame ga futte imasu.
   Rēnkōto o kimasu.

   _____

10. Hitori de mochiageru koto ga dekimasen.
    Dare ka ni tanomimasu.

    _____

HASHI DE TABERAREMASU KA?

Kono e o mite kudasai. Tanaka-san wa ima kazoku no minna to shokuji o shite imasu. Kare wa naifu to fōku de tabete imasu ka? Iie, kare wa ima hashi de tabete imasu.

Nihon-jin wa shokuji o suru toki, futsū hashi o tsukaimasu. Keredomo tokidoki, yōshoku o taberu toki wa, naifu to fōku o tsukaimasu. Chūgoku-jin ya Kankoku-jin mo shokuji o suru toki, futsū hashi o tsukaimasu. Anata mo hashi de taberaremasu ka? Tabun anata ni wa hashi o jōzu ni tsukau koto wa totemo muzukashii deshō.

Tōkyō ni wa iroiro na resutoran ga takusan arimasu. Moshi tenpura ya sashimi o tabetakereba, anata wa Nihon no resutoran e iku koto ga dekimasu. Moshi anata ga hashi de taberu koto ga dekinakereba, uētā ya uētoresu ni naifu to fōku o tanomemasu.

Itaria-jin ni wa sukiyaki o hashi de taberu koto wa muzukashii desu ga, Nihon-jin ni mo supagetti o fōku ya supūn de taberu koto wa muzukashii to omoimasu. Watashi wa supagetti o fōku de taberu no ka, supūn de taberu no ka yoku shirimasen.

miru	mimasu	miemasu
yomu	yomimasu	yomemasu
hanasu	hanashimasu	hanasemasu
kaku	kakimasu	kakemasu
toru	torimasu	toremasu
iku	ikimasu	ikemasu
morau	moraimasu	moraemasu
kiku	kikimasu	kikemasu
arau	araimasu	araemasu
kau	kaimasu	kaemasu
uru	urimasu	uremasu

Mondai 76

Rei: Watashi wa Nihon-go o yomimasen.

Watashi wa Nihon-go o yomu koto ga dekimasen.

Watashi wa Nihon-go ga yomemasen.

1. Hisho wa kuruma o kaimasen.

2. Tanaka-san wa kyō Hiroshima e ikimasen.

3. Satō-san wa Chūgoku-go o hanashimasen.

4. Kanji o kakimasen.

5. Anata wa kongetsu kyūka o torimasen.

Dubaru-san wa Nihon-go no sensei desu ka?
— Shirimasen.

Kyōshitsu de wa Nihon-go de hanashimasu ka?
— Shirimasen.

Moshi kare ga Nihon-go no sensei nara, kyōshitsu
de wa Nihon-go de hanashimasu.

Noguchi-san no kuruma wa ōkii desu ka?
Watashi no garēji ni ireru koto ga dekimasu ka?

Moshi kuruma ga ōkikereba, ireru koto ga dekimasen.
Moshi ōkiku nakereba, ireru koto ga dekimasu.

Anata wa pasupōto o motte imasu ka?
Nihon ni hairu koto ga dekimasu ka?

Moshi pasupōto o motte ireba, hairu koto ga dekimasu.
Moshi pasupōto o motte inakereba, hairu koto ga dekimasen.

		Hai	Iie
(Moshi)	sensei sake getsu-yōbi kirei suki	nara, . . .	ja nakereba, . . .
	ōki(i) taka(i) ikita(i)	-kereba, . . .	-ku nakereba, . . .
	motte i(ru) ake(ru) kae(ru)	-reba, . . .	-nakereba, . . .
	yom(u) kak(u) ik(u)	-eba, . . .	-anakereba, . . .

Mondai 77

1. Moshi anata ga o-kanemochi nara, Kyaderakku o kaitai desu ka?

   _____

2. Sashimi ga tabetai nara, Nihon no resutoran e ikimasu ka?

   _____

3. Moshi watashi ga tenisu ga jōzu nara, issho ni tenisu o shitai desu ka?

   _____

4. Shigoto ga isogashikereba, eiga ni iku koto ga dekimasen ka?

   _____

5. Atsukereba, ōbā o kimasu ka, soretomo ōbā o nugimasu ka?

   _____

6. Tanaka-san ni aeba, itsumo kaisha no koto o hanashimasu ka?

   _____

7. Sono sūtsukēsu ga takakunakereba, kaimasu ka?

   _____

8. Ashita ame ga furanakereba, gorufu o shimasu ka?

   _____

9. Nihon-go o benkyō shitakereba, Berurittsu e ikimasu ka?

   _____

10. Kōhii o takusan nomeba, yoru nemuru koto ga dekimasu ka?

    _____

DAI JŪ-YON-SHŌ — MATOME

. . . ga iru / . . . (iru) hitsuyō ga aru

Pasupōto ga irimasu.
Biza ga hitsuyō desu.
Biza o morau hitsuyō ga arimasu.

. . . tame ni

Ryokō suru tame ni, bíza o moraimasu.
Okane o kaeru tame ni, ginkō e ikimasu.

Naze . . . ? / Naze desu ka?

Naze taishikan e iku-n(o) desu ka?
Naze o-isha ni ikanai-n(o) desu ka?

. . . tokoro desu / -ta tokoro desu

Kusuri o nomu tokoro desu.
Kusuri o nonda tokoro desu.

-ta toki . . .

Taishikan e itta toki, biza o
moraimashita.
Byōki ni natta toki, byōin e ikimashita.

Kaze o hiku / Byōki ni naru

Kibun ga warui desu.
Tsukaremasu.
Atama ga itai desu.
Netsu ga demasu.
Kusuri o nomimasu.

-yasui / -nikui

Kaze o hiki-yasui desu.
Kono pen wa kaki-nikui desu.

-tara

Kuruma ga taka kattara kaemasen.
Demo yasu kattara, kaemasu.
Ame ga futtara, sanpo o shimasen.

-ta bakari desu

Ikimashita ka?
— Hai, itta bakari desu.

Kaiwa-hyōgen

"Dō shimashita ka?"
"Daijōbu desu."
"Māmā desu."
"O-daiji ni."

MOSHI NIHON E IKITAKEREBA . . .

Moshi anata ga Nihon e ikitakereba, nani ga hitsuyō desu ka? Hikōki no kippu o motte itara, anata wa Nihon e ikemasu ka? Iie, hikōki no kippu shika motte inakereba, anata wa Nihon e iku koto wa dekimasen. Hikōki no kippu no hoka ni, biza to pasupōto ga irimasu. Biza to pasupōto o ryokō suru mae ni morau tame ni, anata wa Nihon taishikan ka, Nihon ryōjikan e iku hitsuyō ga arimasu. Moshi anata ga Nihon de kankō ryokō o shitai nara, kankō-biza ga irimasu. Shikashi moshi anata ga Nihon de shigoto o suru nara, shōyō-biza o morau hitsuyō ga arimasu. Shōyō-biza o morau koto wa, kankō-biza o morau koto yori zutto muzukashii desu.

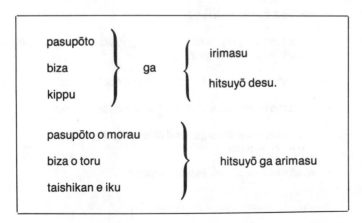

ATARASHII HANDOBAGGU GA IRIMASU

○ 6 ○

— Konnichiwa Michiko-san! Dochira e irasshaimasu ka?[1]

— Ā, Keiko-san, konnichiwa! Depāto desu.

— Nani o kai ni ikimasu ka?

— Handobaggu desu. Kono handobaggu wa mō furuku narimashita kara, atarashii no ga irimasu.

— Watashi mo atarashii handobaggu ga hoshii desu.

— Jā, issho ni irasshaimasen ka? Ima o-hima desu ka?

— Ē, ima wa hima desu ga, go-ji ni tomodachi to eiga o mi ni ikimasu.

— Ā, sō desu ka . . . Jā, isoide ikimashō!

[1] Dochira e irrasshaimasu ka? — Doko e ikimasu ka?

Mondai 78

1. Michiko-san wa gakkō e iku tokoro desu ka?

   _____

2. Doko e iku tokoro desu ka?

   _____

3. Depāto ni sukāto o kai ni iku tokoro desu ka?

   _____

4. Nani o kai ni ikimasu ka?

   _____

5. Dōshite handobaggu o kai ni ikimasu ka?

   _____

6. Michiko-san wa dare to hanashite imasu ka?

   _____

7. Keiko-san mo atarashii handobaggo o kaitai desu ka?

   _____

8. Depāto de handobaggu ga kaemasu ka?

   _____

9. Keiko-san wa ima isogashii desu ka?

   _____

10. Keiko-san wa go-ji ni doko ni ikimasu ka?

    _____

11. Kanojo wa Michiko-san to issho ni depāto ni ikimasu ka?

    _____

12. Anata mo kanojo-tachi to issho ni depāto ni ikimasu ka?

    _____

-U TAME NI

Watashi wa hon o │ *kaimasu.* │ Hon-ya e ikimasu.

Wạtashi wa hon o **kau tame ni** hon-ya e ikimasu.

Mondai 79

Rei: Nihon-go o benkyō shimasu. Gakkō e ikimasu.

Nihon-go o benkyō suru tame ni, gakkō e ikimasu.

1. Okane o kaemasu. Ginkō e ikimasu.

   _____

2. Shinkansen ni norikaemasu. Tōkyō eki de orimasu.

   _____

3. Kusuri o kaimasu. Kusuri-ya e ikimasu.

   _____

4. Te o fukimasu. Taoru o tsukaimasu.

   _____

5. Nihon e ikimasu. Pasupōto ga irimasu.

   _____

6. Kurejitto-kādo de haraimasu. Sain o shimasu.

   _____

7. Maemotte yakusoku shimasu. Denwa o shimasu.

   _____

8. Yoku nemurimasu. Osake o nomimasu.

   _____

OKANE O KAETAI DESU KA?

— Amerika no doru ga kaeraremasu ka?

— Hai, koko de kaeraremasu.
Ikura kaetai-no desu ka?

— Hyaku-doru o en ni kaetai-no desu
ga . . .

— Wakarimashita. Ichi-doru wa
nihyaku-en desu kara, niman-en
ni narimasu. Dōzo.

— Dōmo arigatō.

Nihon no okane wa en desu. Nihon de wa gaikoku no okane ga
tsukaemasen. Takushii ni noru toki mo, kaimono o suru toki mo,
resutoran de shokuji o suru toki mo, Nihon no okane ga irimasu.
Keredomo moshi anata ga Nihon no okane o motte inakereba,
ginkō de gaikoku no okane o en ni kaeru koto ga dekimasu. Kūkō
ni wa okane o kaeru tame no ginkō ga arimasu kara, Nihon ni
tsukeba hajime ni okane o kaeru koto ga dekimasu.

-RU TOKORO / -TA TOKORO

11:50	12:15	12:45
taberu tokoro desu	tabete imasu	tabeta tokoro desu
yomu tokoro desu	yonde imasu	yonda tokoro desu
hanasu tokoro desu	hanashite imasu	hanashita tokoro desu
kaku tokoro desu	kaite imasu	kaita tokoro desu
nomu tokoro desu	nonde imasu	nonda tokoro desu
kuru tokoro desu	kite imasu	kita tokoro desu
suru tokoro desu	shite imasu	shita tokoro desu

TABERU TOKI HASHI O TSUKAIMASU

Watashi wa | *tabemasu.* | Watashi wa hashi o tsukaimasu.

Watashi wa **taberu toki,** hashi o tsukaimasu.

Watashi wa kinō hachi-ji ni | *tabemashita.* | Watashi wa hashi o tsukaimashita.

Watashi wa kinō hachi-ji ni **tabeta toki,** hashi o tsukaimashita.

-u toki		*-ta toki*	
aimasu	au	aimashita	atta
akemasu	akeru	akemashita	aketa
araimasu	arau	araimashita	aratta
arimasu	aru	arimashita	atta
arukimasu	aruku	arukimashita	aruita
dashimasu	dasu	dashimashita	dashita
dekakemasu	dekakeru	dekakemashita	dekaketa
dekimasu	dekiru	dekimashita	dekita
demasu	deru	demashita	deta
fukimasu	fuku	fukimashita	fuita
furimasu	furu	furimashita	futta
hairimasu	hairu	hairimashita	haitta
hajimarimasu	hajimaru	hajimarimashita	hajimatta
hajimemasu	hajimeru	hajimemashita	hajimeta
hakimasu	haku	hakimashita	haita
hanashimasu	hanasu	hanashimashita	hanashita
haraimasu	harau	haraimashita	haratta
hatarakimasu	hataraku	hatarakimashita	hataraita
hikimasu	hiku	hikimashita	hiita
iimasu	iu	iimashita	itta
ikimasu	iku	ikimashita	itta
imasu	iru	imashita	ita
iremasu	ireru	iremashita	ireta
isogimasu	isogu	isogimashita	isoida

	-u toki		*-ta toki*
kaemasu	kaeru (okane o)	kaemashita	kaeta
kaerimasu	kaeru (uchi e)	kaerimashita	kaetta
kaimasu	kau	kaimashita	katta
kakarimasu	kakaru	kakarimashita	kakatta
kakemasu	kakeru	kakemashita	kaketa
kakimasu	kaku	kakimashita	kaita
kazoemasu	kazoeru	kazoemashita	kazoeta
keshimasu	kesu	keshimashita	keshita
kikimasu	kiku	kikimashita	kiita
kimasu (yōfuku o)	kiru	kimashita	kita
kimasu (uchi e)	kuru	kimashita	kita
kirimasu	kiru	kirimashita	kitta
komimasu	komu	komimashita	konda
kotaemasu	kotaeru	kotaemashita	kotaeta
machimasu	matsu	machimashita	matta
magarimasu	magaru	magarimashita	magatta
maniaimasu	maniau	maniaimashita	maniatta
miemasu	mieru	miemashita	mieta
mimasu	miru	mimashita	mita
misemasu	miseru	misemashita	miseta
mochiagemasu	mochiageru	mochiagemashita	mochiageta
mochimasu	motsu	mochimashita	motta
moraimasu	morau	moraimashita	moratta
naorimasu	naoru	naorimashita	naotta
narimasu	naru	narimashita	natta
nemasu	neru	nemashita	neta
nemurimasu	nemuru	nemurimashita	nemutta
nomimasu	nomu	nomimashita	nonda
norimasu	noru	norimashita	notta
nugimasu	nugu	nugimashita	nuida
okimasu (6-ji ni)	okiru	okimashita	okita
okimasu (pen o)	oku	okimashita	oita
okuremasu	okureru	okuremashita	okureta
omoimasu	omou	omoimashita	omotta

-u toki	**-ta toki**

orimasu	oriru	orimashita	orita
oshiemasu	oshieru	oshiemashita	oshieta
owarimasu	owaru	owarimashita	owatta
shimarimasu	shimaru	shimarimashita	shimatta
shimasu	suru	shimashita	shita
shimemasu	shimeru	shimemashita	shimeta
shirimasu	shiru	shirimashita	shitta
suimasu	suu	suimashita	sutta
sukimasu	suku	sukimashita	suita
sumimasu	sumu	sumimashita	sunda
suwarimasu	suwaru	suwarimashita	suwatta
tabemasu	taberu	tabemashita	tabeta
tachimasu	tatsu	tachimashita	tatta
tanomimasu	tanomu	tanomimashita	tanonda
tomarimasu	tomaru	tomarimashita	tomatta
torimasu	toru	torimashita	totta
tsukaimasu	tsukau	tsukaimashita	tsukatta
tsukaremasu	tsukareru	tsukaremashita	tsukareta
tsukemasu	tsukeru	tsukemashita	tsuketa
tsukimasu	tsuku	tsukimashita	tsuita
tsutomemasu	tsutomeru	tsutomemashita	tsutometa
tsuzukemasu	tsuzukeru	tsuzukemashita	tsuzuketa
ugokashimasu	ugokasu	ugokashimashita	ugokashita
ukemasu	ukeru	ukemashita	uketa
urimasu	uru	urimashita	utta
wakarimasu	wakaru	wakarimashita	wakatta
watashimasu	watasu	watashimashita	watashita
yasumimasu	yasumu	yasumimashita	yasunda
yomimasu	yomu	yomimashita	yonda

Mondai 80

Rei: Senshū depāto e ikimashita.
Atarashii kutsu o kaimashita.

Senshū depāto e itta toki, atarashii kutsu o kaimashita.

1. Watashi wa kesa Tanaka-san ni aimashita.
Kare to hanashimashita.

   _____

2. Nihon-go o takusan benkyō shimashita.
Tsukaremashita.

   _____

3. Kinō waishatsu o kaimashita.
Ten-in ni okane o watashimashita.

   _____

4. Yamada-san wa yūbe Tōkyō ni tsukimashita.
Watashi ni denwa shimashita.

   _____

5. Byōki ni narimashita.
Byōin ni ikimashita.

   _____

6. Yamashita-san wa senshū kaze o hikimashita.
Yamashita-san wa kusuri o nomimashita.

   _____

7. Nihon taishikan e ikimashita.
Watashi wa biza o moraimashita.

   _____

8. Kyonen watashi wa Yōroppa ni ikimashita.
Hikōki ni norimashita.

   _____

KAZE O HIITE IMASU

Kobayashi:	Konnichiwa. Dō shimashita ka?
Maeda:	Chotto kaze o hikimashita.
Kobayashi:	Sō desu ka?
Maeda:	Kinō, ame no naka o kasa nashide aruita kara desu. Anata wa ikaga desu ka?
Kobayashi:	Watashi wa genki desu. Demo watashi mo yoku kaze o hikimasu. Anata wa mō o-isha ni ikimashita ka?
Maeda:	Ē, hiru-yasumi ni itta bakari desu.
Kobayashi:	Kusuri o moraimashita ka?
Maeda:	Ē, kusuri o takusan moraimashita ga totemo nomi-nikui kusuri desu.
Kobayashi:	Jā, o-daiji ni.
Maeda:	Arigatō.

. . . -YASUI / . . . -NIKUI

Fuyu wa yoku kaze o hikimasu.
⟶ *Fuyu wa kaze o **hiki-yasui** desu.*

Hashi de taberu no wa muzukashii desu.
⟶ *Hashi de wa **tabe-nikui** desu.*

Kono kusuri wa totemo mazui desu.
⟶ *Kono kusuri wa **nomi-nikui** desu.*

Mondai 81

1. Maeda-san wa dōshite kaze o hikimashita ka?

   前田さん　　冬は風を引きやすい

2. Maeda-san wa itsu o-isha ni ikimashita ka?

3. Kaze o hiite iru toki, atama ga itai desu ka?

   時時 かぜをひっている時 あたまか痛いです

4. Kibun wa ii desu ka, warui desu ka?

   気凩は悪いです

5. Tsukarete iru toki, byōki ni nari-yasui desu ka?

   はい渡れている時、 びょうきになり-やすいです

6. Warui kaze o hiite ireba, kaisha e ikemasu ka?

   いいえ 悪 かぜを ひっていれば、会え 行けませんね

7. Isha wa doko de hatarakimasu ka?

8. Futsū wa fuyu ni kaze o hikimasu ka, soretomo natsu desu ka?

9. Kusuri wa aji ga ii desu ka?

   飲み たくい

10. Kaze o hiitara, anata wa kusuri o nomimasu ka?

DAI JŪ-GO-SHŌ — MATOME

Chichi / otōsan

Watashi no chichi wa genki desu.
Anata no otōsan wa o-genki desu ka?

Arimasu / gozaimasu

Koko ni denwa ga arimasu ka?
— Hai, gozaimasu.

Gozaimasu / irasshaimasu

Koko ni hon ga gozaimasu.
Koko ni Tanaka-san ga irasshaimasu.

Yomimasu / o-yomi ni narimasu

Watashi wa shinbun o yomimasu.
Anata wa shinbun o o-yomi ni
narimasu ka?

Suru / nasaru

Watashi wa gorufu o shimasu.
Anata wa gorufu o nasaimasu ka?

Iimasu / osshaimasu

Watashi wa ohayō to iimashita.
Anata wa ohayō to osshaimashita.

. . . to iu / . . . da to iu / ja nai to iu

Kyō wa atsui to iimashita.
Kore wa hon da to iimashita.
Kore wa hon ja nai to iimashita.

Tabako o motte iru hito

Tabako o motte iru hito wa Tanaka-san
desu.

Watashi wa sono hon-ya e ikimasu.
Sono hon-ya wa sugu soko desu.
Watashi ga iku hon-ya wa sugu
soko desu.

. . . node / . . . nanode

Ame ga furu node rēnkōto ga irimasu.
Watashi wa sashimi ga dai-suki nanode,
yoku tabemasu.

Ikimasu, kimasu, imasu / irasshaimasu

Watashi wa kaisha e ikimasu.
Anata wa kaisha e irasshaimasu ka?

Watashi wa ashita kimasu.
Anata wa ashita irasshaimasu ka?

Watashi wa koko ni imasu.
Anata wa koko ni irasshaimasu.

Kaiwa-hyōgen

"Shitsurei shimashita."
"Kashikomarimashita."
"Itashimasu."
"Chotto o-tazune shitai-n desu ga . . ."
"Komarimashita ne!"
"Shōshō o-machi kudasai."

WATASHI NO KANAI TO ANATA NO OKUSAN

Tanaka:	Konban no ongaku-kai no kippu ga ni-mai arimasu ga, issho ni irasshaimasen ka?
Satō:	Arigatō gozaimasu. Zannen desu ga, kanai ga sukoshi kibun ga warui node ikemasen.
Tanaka:	Sō desu ka? Kaze desu ka?
Satō:	Ē, sukoshi kaze o hikimashita ga, sugu yoku naru deshō . . . Otaku no okusan wa o-genki desu ka?
Tanaka:	Arigatō gozaimasu. Okagesamade kanai wa itsumo genki de, mettani byōki o shimasen. Dōzo okusan o o-daiji ni . . .
Satō:	Ē, arigatō!

watashi no	**anata no / kare no**
shujin	*go-shujin*
kazoku	*go-kazoku*
musuko	*musuko-san*
musume	*musume-san*
shigoto	*o-shigoto*
namae	*o-namae*
kanai	*okusan*
haha	*okāsan*
chichi	*otōsan*

KYŌTO E IRASSHAIMASU KA?

*Watashi wa tomodachi ni
 hanashimasu:*

Anata ni denwa desu.
Namae o oshiete kudasai.
Konban kaimono o shimasu ka?
Ashita gakkō e kimasu ka?
Asatte Kyōto e ikimasu ka?

*Watashi wa tomodachi no otōsan
 ni hanashimasu:*

Anata ni denwa de gozaimasu.
O-namae o oshiete kudasaimasen ka?
Konban kaimono o nasaimasu ka?
Ashita gakkō e irasshaimasu ka?
Asatte Kyōto e irasshaimasu ka?

Buchō wa hisho ni hanashimasu:

Dare desu ka?
Nihon-go o benkyō
 shite imasu ka?
Denwa-bangō o shitte imasu ka?
Kotoshi no natsu ni ryokō
 shimasu ka?
Kinō konsāto ni ikimashita ka?

Hisho wa buchō ni hanashimasu:

Donata desu ka?
Nihon-go o benkyō
 shite irasshaimasu ka?
Denwa-bangō o gozonji desu ka?
Kotoshi no natsu ni ryokō
 nasaimasu ka?
Kinō konsāto ni irasshaimashita ka?

Sensei wa seito ni hanashimasu:

Ototoi gakkō e kimashita ka?
Doko ni sunde imasu ka?
Tabako o suimasu ka?
Nihon no shinbun o
 yomimasu ka?
Chotto matte kudasai.

Seito wa sensei ni hanashimasu:

Ototoi gakkō e irasshaimashita ka?
Doko ni sunde irasshaimasu ka?
Tabako o o-sui ni narimasu ka?
Nihon no shinbun o
 o-yomi ni narimasu ka?
Chotto o-machi kudasai.

---

*Watashi wa anata ni watashi
 no chichi ni tsuite hanashimasu:*

Watashi no chichi wa kyō kaisha
 o yasumimasu.
Watashi no chichi wa Amerika
 e ikimashita.

*Watashi wa anata ni anata no
 otōsan ni tsuite hanashimasu:*

Anata no otōsan wa kyō kaisha o
 o-yasumi ni narimasu.
Anata no otōsan wa Amerika e
 irasshaimashita.

Mondai 82

Rei: Anata wa raishū Amerika e ikimasu ka?

   Anata wa raishū Amerika e irasshaimasu ka?

1. Anata wa nan-yōbi ni gakkō e kimashita ka?

_____

2. Anata wa ima Nihon-go o benkyō shite imasu ka?

_____

3. Berurittsu no jūsho o shitte imasu ka?

_____

4. Tanaka-san wa nan to iimashita ka?

_____

5. Konsāto e itsu ikimasu ka?

_____

6. Mō shokuji o shimashita ka?

_____

7. Kore wa Tanaka-san no kuruma desu ka?

_____

8. Ashita Tanaka-san ni aimasu ka?

_____

9. Tegami o yomimashita ka?

_____

10. Itsu sukii ni ikimasu ka?

_____

SŪPĀ DE

Suzuki Noriko-san wa sūpā de Yamada-san
no okusan ni aimashita:

Suzuki: Anō, shitsurei desu ga, Yamada-
san no okusan ja arimasen ka?

Yamada: Ē, Yamada desu ga . . .
Donata deshō ka?

Suzuki: Suzuki de gozaimasu. Tonari no
apāto ni sunde imasu.

Yamada: Ā, Suzuki-san no okusan!
Dōmo shitsurei shimashita.

Suzuki: Itsumo koko de kaimono o
nasaimasu ka?

Yamada: Iie, hoka no mise de mo kau-n
desu yo! Anata wa mō iroiro na
mise o gozonji desu ka?

Suzuki: Watashi wa mada kono mise shika shiranai-n desu.

Yamada: Ā, anata wa senshū kochira e irasshatta bakari desu ne?

Suzuki: Sō desu. San-shūkan mae ni kekkon shite, kono apāto ni kita-n desu.
Sono mae wa chichi to haha to issho ni Yokohama ni sunde imashita.

Yamada: A, sō desu ka? Anata no go-shujin wa doko ni o-tsutome desu ka?

Suzuki: Amerika no ginkō ni tsutomete imasu.

Yamada: Sō desu ka? Jā, Eigo o o-tsukai ni narimasu ka?

Suzuki: Ē, mainichi ofisu de Eigo o hanashimasu. Yamada-san wa
kodomo-san ga irasshaimasu nē!

Yamada: Hai, futari imasu. Musuko wa "Kenji", musume wa "Akiko" to iimasu.

Suzuki: Ii o-namae desu nē!

Yamada: Arigatō gozaimasu. Mō kaimono wa owarimashita ka?

Suzuki: Ē, owarimashita.

Yamada: Jā, uchi de issho ni ocha o ikaga desu ka?

Suzuki: Dōmo arigatō gozaimasu. Jā, kaerimashō!

Mondai 83

1. Suzuki-san wa "Shitsurei desu ga . . . " to iimashita ka?

_____

2. Yamada-san wa "Dōmo shitsurei shimashita" to iimashita ka?

_____

3. Yamada-san wa itsumo kono sūpā de kaimasu ka, soretomo hoka no mise demo kaimasu ka?

_____

4. Suzuki-san wa itsu kekkon shita to iimashita ka?

_____

5. Suzuki-san no go-shujin wa doko ni tsutomete imasu ka?

_____

6. Yamada-san wa kodomo ga nan-nin aru to iimashita ka?

_____

7. Yamada-san wa musume-san no namae ga Haruko da to iimashita ka?

_____

8. Yamada-san no musume-san no namae wa nan to iimasu ka?

_____

9. Yamada-san to Suzuki-san wa Suzuki-san no go-shujin ni tsuite hanashimashita ka?

_____

10. Futari wa kaimono no ato de, ocha o nomimasu ka?

_____

MICHI O KIKU

Saitō-san wa kinō Tōkyō kara Kyōto e kimashita. I-sshūkan gurai Kyōto de shigoto o shimasu. Kyō wa hima nanode o-tera o mi ni ikimasu. Michi o aruite iru toki, Honda-san to iu tomodachi ni aimashita.

Honda:	Saitō-san!
Saitō:	Ā, Honda-san konnichiwa! Anata mo Kyōto e shigoto de irasshatta-n desu ka?
Honda:	Iie, o-tera o mi ni kimashita. Kyōto ni wa subarashii o-tera ya Nihon-teien ga takusan arimasu kara . . .
Saitō:	Sō desu nē . . . Mō o-tera o takusan mimashita ka?
Honda:	Iie, mada desu. Ima kara "Kokedera" to iu o-tera o mi ni iku tokoro desu ga, michi ni mayoimashita. Koko kara Kokedera e iku michi o gozonji desu ka?
Saitō:	Zannen desu ga, watashi mo shirimasen. A, ano o-miyage-ya e ikimashō. Kitto Kyōto no chizu o utte imasu kara.

(Futari wa o-miyage-ya e hairimashita.)

Ten-in:	Irasshaimase!
Saitō:	Kyōto no chizu wa arimasu ka?
Ten-in:	Kochira ni takusan gozaimasu.
Saitō:	Honda-san, kono chizu o mite kudasai! Hora, kore ga Kokedera desu. Watashi-tachi wa ima koko ni imasu. Ēto . . . Hajime ni kono michi o massugu itte, san-banme no kado o migi e magatte, sorekara . . . A, wakarimashita! Watashi mo issho ni ikimashō!

(Futari wa mise o dete michi o aruki-hajimemashita.)

Honda:	Mō jū-go-fun arukimashita ga, mada Kokedera ga miemasen ne? Watashi-tachi wa mata mayoimashita yo! Dō shimashō?
Saitō:	Komarimashita nē! Ā, asoko ni omawarisan ga imasu kara kikimashō. Omawarisan, sumimasen! Chotto otazune shitai-n desu ga . . .
Omawarisan:	Dō shimashita ka?
Saitō:	Kokedera e ikitai-n desu ga, dō ikeba ii desu ka?
Omawarisan:	Kono michi o nihyaku-mētoru gurai ikeba hidari ni ōkii kusuri-ya ga arimasu. Soko o hidari ni magareba, sugu takusan no kankō-basu ga miemasu. Soko ga Kokedera desu. Wakarimashita ka?
Saitō:	Hai, yoku wakarimashita. Dōmo arigatō.
Omawarisan:	Dō-itashimashite. Jā . . . sayonara.
Saitō:	Sayonara!

Mondai 84

1. Saitō-san wa ima Tōkyō ni imasu ka, Kyōto ni imasu ka?

_____

2. Kyō Saitō-san wa isogashii desu ka, soretomo hima desu ka?

_____

3. Honda-san wa Saitō-san no tomodachi desu ka?

_____

4. Honda-san wa ima Kyōto de shigoto o shite imasu ka?

_____

5. Kyōto ni wa takusan no o-tera ga arimasu ka?

_____

6. Honda-san wa Kyōto e nani o shi ni kimashita ka?

_____

7. Honda-san wa Kokedera e iku michi o shitte imasu ka?

_____

8. Futari wa doko de Kyōto no chizu o mimashita ka?

_____

9. Futari wa michi ni mayotta toki, dare ni kikimashita ka?

_____

10. Moshi anata ga michi ni mayottara, omawarisan ni kikimasu ka?

_____

11. Omawarisan wa takusan no kankō-basu ga mieru tokoro ga Kokedera da to iimashita ka?

_____

12. Anata mo Kokedera ni ikitai desu ka?

_____

"YUKI-GUNI" TO IU HON

Kono e o mite kudasai. Ima hon o mite iru hito wa Shumitto-san desu. Kare wa Nihon-go o benkyō shite imasu. Soshite Hiragana o yomu koto ga dekimasu. Shumitto-san wa senshū shigoto no ato de hon-ya e ikimashita. Shumitto-san ga itsumo iku hon-ya wa Ginza ni arimasu. Soko de, "Yukiguni" to iu hon o kaimashita. Kawabata Yasunari to iu hito ga sono hon o kakimashita. Shumitto-san wa Kawabata Yasunari ga kaita hon ga dai-suki desu. Kare no kaita hon o mō go-satsu yomimashita. Mochiron zenbu Eigo de yomimashita.

Hon-ya no ten-in wa, sono hon ni wa takusan no Kanji ga aru node, totemo muzukashii to iimashita. Keredomo Shumitto-san wa Nihon-go no jisho o motte iru node, kitto yomu koto ga dekiru to iimashita.

Kare wa "Yukiguni" o yomi-hajimemashita. Sono hon ni wa takusan no muzukashii kotoba ga arimasu. Jisho de kotoba no imi o benkyō shimasu. Yoku wakaranai toki wa, tomodachi no Tanaka-san ni kikimasu. Tanaka-san wa Nihon-go de wakaranai kotoba ga aru toki wa, itsu demo kiite kudasai to iimashita. Dakara Shumitto-san wa shitsumon o nōto ni kaite, Tanaka-san ni kikimasu. Tanaka-san wa Shumitto-san no ichi-ban ii sensei desu.

Mondai 85

1. Ima hon o mite iru hito wa dare desu ka?

   _____

2. Kare wa Hiragana o yomu koto ga dekimasu ka?

   _____

3. Shumitto-san ga itsumo iku hon-ya wa doko ni arimasu ka?

   _____

4. "Yukiguni" wa dare ga kaita hon desu ka?

   _____

5. Shumitto-san wa Kawabata Yasunari no hon ga suki desu ka?

   _____

6. Hon-ya no ten-in wa "Yukiguni" wa muzukashii to iimashita ka, soretomo yasashii
   to iimashita ka?

   _____

7. Shumitto-san wa Nihon-go no jisho o motte iru node, yomu koto ga dekiru to
   iimashita ka?

   _____

8. Muzukashii kotoba ga aru toki, Shumitto-san wa nan de kotoba no imi o benkyō
   shimasu ka?

   _____

9. Wakaranai toki, dare ni kikimasu ka?

   _____

10. Tanaka-san wa nan to iimashita ka?

    _____

WATASHI GA SHOKUJI O SURU RESUTORAN

Are wa *resutoran* desu.

Resutoran wa ōkii desu.

⇨ Are wa **ōkii** *resutoran* desu.

Are wa *resutoran* desu.

Ano *resutoran* de **watashi wa shokuji o shimasu.**

⇨ Are wa **watashi ga shokuji o suru** *resutoran* desu.

Kore wa *handobaggu* desu.

Watashi wa **kinō** kono *handobaggu* o **kaimashita.**

⇨ Kore wa **watashi ga kinō katta** *handobaggu* desu.

Kōban de kikimashō.

Kōban wa **eki no mae ni arimasu.**

⇨ **Eki no mae ni aru** *kōban* de kikimashō.

Kore wa *pen* desu.

Watashi wa kono *pen* o **Tanaka-san kara moraimashita.**

⇨ Kore wa **Tanaka-san kara moratta** *pen* desu.

Mondai 86

Rei: Moshimoshi Yoshida-san o
onegai shimasu to iu toki, hisho
wa _____ *F* _____ to iimasu.

1. Murata-san ga dochira e to
   iu toki, anata wa _____ to
   iimasu.

2. Hisho ni taipu o tanomu toki,
   hisho wa _____ to iimasu.

3. Hasegawa-san ga kare no okusan ga
   byōki da to iu toki, anata wa
   _____ to iimasu.

4. Anata ga asu Nagoya e iku to iu
   toki, watashi wa _____
   to iimasu.

5. Tanaka-san ga Noguchi-san ni ikaga
   desu ka to iu toki, Noguchi-san wa
   _____ to iimasu.

6. Uētā ga sukiyaki wa dekimasen to
   itta toki, anata wa _____
   to iimashita.

7. Watashi ga o-yasumi nasai to itta
   toki, anata wa _____ to iimashita.

8. Watashi ga koko de tabako o sutte
   mo ii desu ka to iu toki, anata wa
   _____ to iimasu.

9. Okyaku ga tenpura o kudasai to iu
   toki, uētā wa _____ to iimasu.

A. Dōzo o-genki de
   itte irasshai.

B. Kashikomarimashita.

C. Mada hayai desu yo.

D. Sugu itashimasu.

E. Iie, dame desu yo.

F. Shōshō o-machi kudasai.

G. Sore wa taihen desu ne.

H. Māmā desu.

I. Sore wa zannen desu ne.

J. Chotto soko made.

DAI JŪ-ROKU-SHŌ — MATOME

. . . ka to kiku / tazuneru

"Doko ni sunde imasu ka?"
Doko ni sunde iru ka to kikimashita.

. . . (da) to kotaeru

"Tōkyō ni sunde imasu."
Tōkyō ni sunde iru to kotaemashita.

"Kore wa hon desu."
Kore wa hon da to kotaemashita.

. . . ka dōka

"Ashita ikimasu ka?"
Ashita iku ka dōka tazunemasu.
Ashita iku ka dōka shitte imasu ka?
Ashita iku ka dōka wakarimasen.

. . . (da) sō desu

Tanaka-san wa kyō kuru koto ga
  dekinai to iimashita.

Tanaka-san wa kyō kuru koto ga
  dekinai sō desu.

. . . to omou

Tanaka-san wa byōki da to omoimasu.
Hisho wa mō kaetta to omoimasu.

oshieru / narau / naosu

Sensei wa seito ni Nihon-go o
  oshiemasu.
Seito wa Nihon-go o naraimasu.
Sensei wa seito no machigai o
  naoshimasu.

. . . o wasureru / oboete iru

Yakusoku o oboete imasu.
Yakusoku o wasuremashita.

. . . koto / no o wasureru

Denki o kesu no o wasuremashita.
Yakusoku ga aru koto o wasuremashita.

. . . kamo shirenai

Ashita ame ga furu kamo shiremasen.
Kore wa Tanaka-san no hon kamo
  shiremasen.

Kaiwa-hyōgen

"Nantomo . . ."

TAKUSHII DE KŪKŌ E

Untenshu:	Dochira made desu ka?
Tanaka:	Kūkō made itte kudasai.
	Hikōki ga yo-ji ni deru node san-ji-han
	made ni tsukitai-n desu ga . . .
Untenshu:	Atarashii kōsoku-dōro o ikeba, daijōbu deshō.
Tanaka:	Koko kara ikura deshō ka?
Untenshu:	Sō desu nē . . . sanzen-gohyaku-en gurai desu.
Tanaka:	Kekkō desu. O-negai shimasu.
Untenshu:	Hai, dōzo.

Tanaka-san wa kyō Ōsaka e shutchō shimasu. Ima kara kūkō e iku tokoro desu. Soto e dete takushii o mitsukemashita. Soshite untenshu ni hikōjō made itte kudasai to iimashita. Tanaka-san no hikōki wa yo-ji ni demasu. Dakara san-ji-han made ni kūkō ni tsuku koto ga dekiru ka dōka untenshu ni kikimashita. Untenshu wa atarashii kōsoku-dōro o ikeba, jūbun maniau to kotaemashita. Sorekara Tanaka-san wa kūkō made ikura kakaru ka to kikimashita. Untenshu wa sanzen-gohyaku-en gurai da to kotaemashita.

Kōsoku-dōro wa totemo konde imashita node, kūkō ni tsuita toki wa mō yo-ji-ju-ppun mae deshita. Tanaka-san wa untenshu ni okane o haratte, kuruma o orimashita. Soshite kōkū-gaisha no kauntā e isogimashita. Kippu o motte imashita kara, kaban o watasu dake deshita. Tanaka-san wa yo-ji no hikōki ni noru koto ga dekimashita.

Mondai 87

1. Tanaka-san wa doko made ikitai to untenshu ni iimashita ka?

   _____

2. Nan-ji no hikōki ni noru to iimashita ka?

   _____

3. Untenshu wa san-ji han made ni tsuku koto ga dekiru to kotaemashita ka?

   _____

4. Tanaka-san wa kūkō made ikura kakaru ka to kikimashita ka?

   _____

5. 'Untenshu wa sanzen-gohyaku-en gurai da to kotaemashita ka?

   _____

6. Kōsoku-dōro wa suite imashita ka, soretomo konde imashita ka?

   _____

7. Nan-ji ni kūkō ni tsukimashita ka?

   _____

8. Tanaka-san wa kūkō no kauntā de kippu o kaimashita ka?

   _____

9. Kauntā de nani o shimashita ka?

   _____

10. Tanaka-san wa hikōki ni maniaimashita ka?

    _____

DENGON GA ARIMASU

Mainichi takusan no hito ga Tanaka-san ni denwa o shimasu. Shikashi Tanaka-san ga ofisu ni inai toki ya isogashii toki wa, dengon o nokoshimasu. Harada-san wa dengon o kami ni kaite, Tanaka-san no tsukue no ue ni okimasu. Kanojo wa kesshite dengon o suru koto o wasuremasen.

Kaigi ga owatte ima Tanaka-san wa jimusho e kaette kimashita. Soshite hisho no Harada-san ni denwa ga atta ka dōka kiite imasu.

Harada: Furuya-san kara san-ji ni denwa ga arimashita. Uchi e kaeru kara, mata ashita denwa suru sō desu.

Tanaka: Ā, sō desu ka . . . Sorekara?

Harada: Sorekara, Yoshida-san kara mo denwa ga arimashita.

Tanaka: Nani ka dengon ga arimasu ka?

Harada: Ashita issho ni shokuji o shitai to osshaimashita.

Tanaka: Nan-ji ni shitai to itte imashita ka?

Harada: Ichi-ji-han desu.

Tanaka: Ā, chotto komarimashita nē. Ashita no ichi-ji ni wa shachō to yakusoku ga aru-n desu yo . . . Ēto, Yoshida-san ni denwa shite asatte no ni-ji wa ii ka dōka kiite kudasai!

Harada: Hai, wakarimashita.

(Harada-san wa Yoshida-san ni denwa o shimashita.)

Yoshida-san wa asatte no ni-ji ni kono biru no resutoran de shokuji o shitai to osshaimashita.

Tanaka: Ā, ii deshō. Arigatō.

NAN TO KIKIMASHITA KA?

	kyō/ashita		**kinō**
ikimasu	iku	ikimashita	itta
ikimasen	ikanai	ikimasen deshita	ikanakatta
sen-en desu	sen-en da	sen-en deshita	sen-en datta
sen-en ja arimasen	sen-en ja nai	sen-en ja arimasen deshita	sen-en ja nakatta

Tanaka: "Resutoran e ikimasu ka?"
Noguchi: "Iie, resutoran e ikimasen."

Tanaka-san wa Noguchi-san ga resutoran e iku ka to/(dōka) kikimashita.
Noguchi-san wa resutoran e ikanai to kotaemashita.

Tanaka: "Doko e ikimasu ka?"
Noguchi: "Gakkō e ikimasu."

Tanaka-san wa doko e iku ka to kikimashita.
Noguchi-san wa gakkō e iku to kotaemashita.

Tanaka: "Kinō gakkō e ikimashita ka?"
Noguchi: "Hai, ikimashita."

Tanaka-san wa kinō gakkō e itta ka to/(dōka) kikimashita.
Noguchi-san wa itta to kotaemashita.

Tanaka: "Kinō resutoran e ikimashita ka?"
Noguchi: "Iie, ikimasen deshita."

Tanaka-san wa kinō gakkō e itta ka to/(dōka) kikimashita.
Noguchi-san wa ikanakatta to kotaemashita.

Mondai 88

Rei: Tanaka-san wa doko ni imasu ka?

Tanaka-san ga doko ni iru ka to kikimashita.

1. Densha wa nan-ji ni demasu ka?

2. Ginza-dōri wa doko ni arimasu ka?

3. Ikura desu ka?

4. Ikura deshita ka?

5. Doko ni sunde imasu ka?

6. Doko de kaimashita ka?

7. Itsu kaerimashita ka?

8. Dare to hanashimashita ka?

9. Nan-jikan gurai kakarimasu ka?

10. Kazoku wa nan-nin desu ka?

JIMUSHO DE

Hisho: Satō-san, ohayō-gozaimasu!

Satō: Ohayō-gozaimasu! Dare ka okyaku ga
arimashita ka?

Hisho: Iie, dare mo irasshaimasen deshita ga,
Tanaka-san kara o-denwa ga arimashita.
Sore dake desu.

Satō: Sō desu ka. Nani ka dengon ga arimasu ka?

Hisho: Hai, kyō ni-ji ni kuru koto ga dekinai
sō desu. Mata denwa suru to osshaimashita.

Satō: Arigatō. Watashi kara ato de denwa
shimashō.

Hisho: Sukoshi yūbin ga kite imasu ga, ima
o-yomi ni narimasu ka?

Satō: Iie, ima kara Noguchi-san to shokuji ni
ikimasu. Kaette kite kara yomimashō.

Hisho: Nan-ji ni kaette irasshaimasu ka?

Satō: Ni-ji goro kaette kimasu. Kanai kara denwa
ga aru to omoimasu ga, gekijō e hachi-ji
ni iku to itte kudasai.

Hisho: Hai, wakarimashita.

Asa Satō-san ga jimusho ni kita toki, hisho wa ohayō-gozaimasu to
iimashita. Satō-san wa dare ka okyaku ga kita ka to kikimashita.
Hisho wa dare mo okyaku wa nakatta ga, Tanaka-san kara denwa ga
atta to kotaemashita. Satō-san wa dengon ga aru ka dōka
kikimashita. Hisho wa Tanaka-san ga ni-ji ni kuru koto ga dekinai
to iimashita. Satō-san wa ato de denwa suru to iimashita. Hisho wa
yūbin ga kite iru to iimashita ga, Satō-san wa yomu jikan ga nai to
iimashita. Soshite Noguchi-san to shokuji o suru tame ni resutoran e
iku ga, ni-ji ni kaette kuru to iimashita. Satō-san wa konban okusan
to gekijō e ikimasu. Moshi okusan kara denwa ga attara, hachi-ji
ni iku to itte kudasai to hisho ni iimashita. Hisho wa wakarimashita
to kotaemashita.

Mondai 89

1. Satō-san ga jimusho e kita toki, okyaku ga kite imashita ka?

   _____

2. Dare kara denwa ga arimashita ka?

   _____

3. Tanaka-san wa nani ka dengon o shimashita ka?

   _____

4. Tanaka-san wa ni-ji ni kuru to iimashita ka?

   _____

5. Hisho wa yūbin ga kite iru to iimashita ka?

   _____

6. Hisho wa sore o ima yomu ka dōka Satō-san ni tazunemashita ka?

   _____

7. Satō-san wa dare to shokuji ni iku to iimashita ka?

   _____

8. Hisho wa nan-ji ni jimusho e kaette kuru ka to kikimashita ka?

   _____

9. Satō-san wa nan-ji goro kaette kuru to iimashita ka?

   _____

10. Konban gekijō de Tanaka-san to au to iimashita ka?

   _____

YOKU MACHIGAERU HISHO

Senshū Satō-san no kaisha ni Fujita-san to iu atarashii hisho ga kimashita. Hoka no hisho ga kanojo ni iroiro shigoto o oshiete imasu ga, Fujita-san wa mada mainichi machigai o shimasu. Tatoeba, kinō wa Tanaka-san ni dengon o suru no o wasuremashita. Sorekara jūyō na shorui no kopii o nakushimashita. Kyō wa asa kara sono kopii o sagashite imasu ga, mada mitsukete imasen. Hontō ni komarimashita nē!

Kanojo wa taipu mo mada jōzu ja arimasen. Kyō wa onaji tegami o san-do mo taipu shimashita. Itsu Fujita-san wa ii hisho ni nareru deshō ka?

KAIGI

○ 6 ○

Keiko-san to Toshiko-san wa onaji kaisha de hataraite iru hisho desu.

Keiko: Toshiko-san, Satō-san wa mō kimashita ka?

Toshiko: Dono hito ga Satō-san ka wakarimasen ga . . .

Keiko: Hora, itsumo Kyūba no hamaki o sutte iru hito desu.

Toshiko: Ā, ano hito! Ano hito wa mada desu.

Keiko: Sō. Satō-san wa shachō to san-ji ni au yakusoku ga aru-n desu yo!

Toshiko: Jūyō na kaigi desu ka?

Keiko: Ē, kitto Kyōto no atarashii jimusho ni tsuite da to omoimasu.

Toshiko: Kyōto ni atarashii jimusho o dasu-n desu ka?

Keiko: Mada atarashii jimusho o dasu ka dōka kimete imasen. Kyō wa sore o sōdan suru tokoro desu yo! Atarashii jimusho wa nioku-en gurai kakaru sō desu yo.

Toshiko: Nioku-en? Hontō desu ka?

Keiko: Ē, tashika desu.

Toshiko: Satō-san osoi desu nē . . . Mō san-ji-jū-go-fun desu. Yakusoku o wasureta-no deshō ka?

Keiko: Iie, kesa denwa de hanashita toki wa, tashika ni san-ji no yakusoku o oboete irasshaimashita yo! Mō sugu irassharu to omoimasu.

  (Dare ka ga doā o akete imasu.)

Toshiko: Ā dare ka irasshaimashita yo! Kitto Satō-san deshō!

Keiko: Ā, sō desu nē! Satō-san desu.

Satō: Konnichiwa! Dōmo, osoku natte sumimasen!

Keiko: Iie, dōzo kochira e. Shachō ga o-machi shite imasu.[1]

[1] o-machi shite imasu — matte imasu

DAI JŪ-NANA-SHŌ — MATOME

Umareru / nakunaru

Watashi wa 1950-nen ni
umaremashita.
Kenedii wa 1963-nen ni nakunarimashita.

. . . -sai desu

Watashi wa 21-sai desu.
Watashi wa wakai desu.
Watashi wa toshiyori ja arimasen.

Kureru / ageru

Anata wa watashi ni hon o
kuremashita.
Watashi wa anata ni pen o
agemashita.

-te ageru / -te kureru / -te morau

Watashi wa anata ni Nihon-go o
yonde agemasu.

Anata wa watashi ni Eigo o
yonde kuremasu.

Watashi wa anata ni Eigo o
yonde moraimasu.

. . . yōni tanomu

"Doā o akete kudasai."
Watashi wa anata ni doā o
akeru yōni tanomimashita.

-nakereba ikenai / -nakute mo ii

Kyō kaisha e ikanakereba ikemasen.

Ashita kaisha e ikanakute mo
ii desu.

-nakereba ikenai / -te wa ikenai

Nihon-go no kurasu de wa, Nihon-go
o hanasanakereba ikemasen.

Nihon-go no kurasu de wa, Eigo o
hanashite wa ikemasen.

-nakute mo ii / -te mo ii

Kurasu no ato de wa Nihon-go
o hanasanakute mo ii desu.

Kurasu no ato de wa Eigo o hanashite
mo ii desu.

-te mo, . . .

Ame ga futte mo sanpo shimasu.
Takakute mo kaimasu.

Kaiwa-hyōgen

"O-tanoshimi desu ne!"
"Kawarimashita."
"Sore jā."

TANJŌBI NO PĀTII

Mieko:	Akemi-san, Satō Shirō-san o oboete imasu ka?
Akemi:	Ē, mochiron!
Mieko:	Raishū ano hito no pātii ga aru-n desu ga, issho ni ikimasen ka?
Akemi:	Nan no pātii desu ka?
Mieko:	Tanjōbi no pātii desu.
Akemi:	Watashi ga itte mo ii-n desu ka?
Mieko:	Mochiron desu yo! Satō-san wa anata mo shōtai shite iru-n desu yo.
Akemi:	Hontō! Ureshii wa!
Mieko:	Sore jā, ashita kare ni denwa shite, futari tomo pātii ni iku to iimashō.
Akemi:	Ē onegai shimasu. Mieko-san wa kare ni donna okurimono o ageru-n desu ka?
Mieko:	Sā, donna mono ga ii to omoimasu ka?
Akemi:	Otoko no hito e no okurimono wa totemo muzukashii desu nē!
Mieko:	Sō desu nē! Kyonen no Kurisumasu ni, watashi wa Satō-san kara subarashii kōsui o moraimashita kara, watashi mo nani ka ii mono o agetai to omotte imasu.
Akemi:	Mā hontō? Ano hito wa watashi ni wa nani mo kuremasen deshita yo!

Mondai 90

1. Akemi-san to Mieko-san wa ima nani ni tsuite hanashite imasu ka?

_____

2. Satō Shirō-san no pātii wa itsu desu ka?

_____

3. Satō-san wa Akemi-san o tanjōbi no pātii ni shōtai shimashita ka?

_____

4. Kyonen no Kurisumasu ni Satō-san wa Mieko-san ni nani o agemashita ka?

_____

5. Kyonen no Kurisumasu ni Akemi-san wa Satō-san kara nani o moraimashita ka?

_____

ageru / kureru / morau

Watashi wa anata ni agemasu.
Anata wa watashi ni kuremasu.
Watashi wa anata kara (/ni) moraimasu.

watashi anata Satō-san	wa	anata Satō-san	ni	agemasu
anata Satō-san	wa	watashi	ni	kuremasu
watashi anata Satō-san	wa	anata Satō-san watashi	kara / ni	moraimasu

-TE AGERU / MORAU

Tanaka: Ni-mai kopii o totte moraemasen ka?
Hisho: Hai, kashikomarimashita.

Tanaka-san wa itsumo tegami o kaku toki, hisho ni kopii o totte moraimasu. Hisho wa
Tanaka-san no tame ni kopii o totte agemasu. Kare wa tegami ni sain shite, hisho ni sono
tegami o yūbin-kyoku ni motte itte moraimasu.

Hisho wa tegami o taipu shimasu.

Hisho wa Tanaka-san ni taipu o shite **agemasu.**
Tanaka-san wa hisho ni taipu o shite **moraimasu.**

Hisho wa watashi ni taipu o shite **kuremasu.**
Watashi wa hisho ni taipu o shite **moraimasu.**

Mondai 91

Rei: Uētā wa okyaku ni menyū o motte kimashita.

Okyaku wa *uētā ni menyū o motte kite moraimashita.*

1. Omawarisan wa Kondō-san ni michi o oshiemasu.

   Kondō-san wa _____

2. Kaisha wa jūgyō-in ni kyūryō o haraimasu.

   Jūgyō-in wa _____

3. Kanai wa watashi ni osake o motte kimashita.

   Watashi wa _____

4. Otōsan wa kodomo ni omocha o kaimashita.

   Kodomo wa _____

5. Okusan wa go-shujin ni ban-gohan o tsukurimasu.

   Go-shujin wa _____

6. Yoshida-san wa watashi no tame ni, doā o shimemashita.

   Watashi wa _____

7. Shimizu-san wa okusan ni atarashii ōbā o kaimasu.

   Okusan wa _____

8. Seito wa sensei ni enpitsu o watashimasu.

   Sensei wa _____

9. Hisho wa buchō no tame ni, taipu shimasu.

   Buchō wa _____

10. Musuko wa otōsan no tame ni, kuruma o araimasu.

    Otōsan wa _____

JIBUN DE SURU

Imai-san: Kondō-san, o-isogashii desu ka?

Kondō-san: Ē, taihen isogashii desu.
Tsukaremashita yo!

Imai-san: Anata no hisho wa inai-n desu ka?

Kondō-san: Kanojo wa kyō yasumi desu.

Imai-san: Jā, dare ga sono tegami o taipu shimashita ka?

Kondō-san: Watashi ga jibun de taipu shimashita.

Imai-san: Hontō desu ka? Taipu ga jōzu desu ne! Anata wa hisho ni naremasu
yo! Ha, ha, ha . . .

Kondō-san: Ha, ha, ha, . . . Iie, dō mo . . .

Imai-san: Kondō-san, ato de issho ni bā e nomi ni ikimasen ka?

Kondō-san: Zannen nagara kyō wa hayaku uchi e kaeranakereba ikenai-n desu. Kanai
ga byōki desu kara . . .

Imai-san: Okusan ga byōki desu ka? Sore wa komarimashita ne! Dō shimashita ka?

Kondō-san: Kaze o hiita dake desu ga, nete inakereba ikemasen.

Imai-san: Jā, dare ga yūshoku o tsukuru-n desu ka?

Kondō-san: Watashi ga jibun de tsukuranakereba ikemasen. Kesa mo watashi ga
kanai to kodomo no tame ni asa-gohan o tsukurimashita.

Imai-san: Anata wa ryōri ga dekimasu ka?

Kondō-san: Ē, kekkon suru mae ni hitori de apāto ni sunde ita toki, yoku ryōri o
tsukurimashita. Anata wa?

Imai-san: Watashi wa zenzen dekimasen. Mada ichi-do mo ryōri o shita koto ga
arimasen. Itsumo haha ga shokuji o tsukutte kuremashita. Kondō-san,
anata wa mō uchi e kaeranakute mo ii-n desu ka?

Kondō-san: Kaeritai-n desu ga . . . Shikashi kono shorui no kopii o toranakereba
ikemasen.

Imai-san: Daijōbu, watashi ga kopii o totte agemasu yo.

Kondō-san: Sō desu ka? Ja, sumimasen ga onegai shimasu.

Imai-san: Okusan hayaku yoku natte kudasai. Dōzo, o-daiji ni!

Mondai 92

1. Dōshite Kondō-san wa tsukaremashita ka?

   _____

2. Hisho ga Kondō-san ni tegami o taipu shite agemashita ka, soretomo Kondō-san ga jibun de taipu shimashita ka?

   _____

3. Kondō-san wa Imai-san to issho ni bā ni iku koto ga dekimasu ka?

   _____

4. Shigoto no ato de Kondō-san wa doko ni ikimasu ka?

   _____

5. Kondō-san no okusan wa genki desu ka?

   _____

6. Kanojo wa dō shimashita ka?

   _____

7. Dōshite kanojo wa uchi ni inakereba ikemasen ka?

   _____

8. Kondō-san no uchi de wa dare ga ryōri o tsukuranakereba ikemasen ka?

   _____

9. Imai-san wa ryōri o tsukuru koto ga dekimasu ka?

   _____

10. Anata mo jibun de ryōri o tsukuru koto ga dekimasu ka?

   _____

-NAKEREBA IKENAI / -NAKUTE MO II

> Kono hon wa sen-en desu.
> Hon o kau tame ni wa,
>   okane o motte inakereba
>   ikemasen.
>
> Kono eiga wa tada desu.
> Eiga o miru tame ni wa,
>   okane o motte inakute mo
>   ii desu.

Mondai 93

Rei: Nihon-go o hanashimasu. / Nihon-go o hanashimasen.

    Nihon-go o hanasanakereba ikemasen. / Nihon-go o hanasanakute mo ii desu.

1. Tegami o taipu shimasu. / Tegami o taipu shimasen.

   _____

2. Shinbun o yomimasu. / Shinbun o yomimasen.

   _____

3. Atarashii kuruma o kaimasu. / Atarashii kuruma o kaimasen.

   _____

4. Genkin de haraimasu. / Genkin de haraimasen.

   _____

5. Kanji de namae o kakimasu. / Kanji de namae o kakimasen.

   _____

6. Ashita gakkō e ikimasu. / Ashita gakkō e ikimasen.

   _____

7. Ima heya o demasu. / Ima heya o demasen.

   _____

DAI JŪ-HA-SSHŌ — MATOME

-ta ato de . . .

Shokuji o shita ato de, nani o
shimasu ka?
—Shokuji o shita ato de, terebi o
mimasu.

. . . to, . . .

Denki o keseba, kuraku narimasu.
Denki o kesu to, kuraku narimasu.
Byōki ni naru to, kusuri o nomimasu.

tōru

Kaisha ni hairu toki, uketsuke o
tōrimasu.
Tōkyō kara Ōsaka e iku toki, Nagoya o
tōrimasu.

-ta koto ga aru / -ta koto ga nai

Anata wa Tōkyō e itta koto ga
arimasu ka?
— Hai, Tōkyō e itta koto ga arimasu.
— Iie, ichi-do mo Tōkyō e itta koto
ga arimasen.

. . . made ni

Eiga wa 10-ji made ni owarimasu.
Kyō 6-ji-han made ni uchi e kaeru
tsumori desu.

-ku suru

Kore wa ōki-sugimasu.
Mō sukoshi chiisaku shinakereba
ikemasen.

. . . tsumori desu

Ashita kaisha e kitto ikimasu.
Ashita kaisha e iku tsumori desu.

Kaiwa-hyōgen

"Shibaraku desu ne!"

KURUMA NO SHŪRI

— Konbanwa! Ogawa desu ga, watashi no kuruma o tori ni
  kimashita.
— Ā, Ogawa-san, sumimasen. Ano kuruma wa mada naotte inai-n
  desu.
— Mada? Dōshite desu ka? Kinō denwa shita toki, anata wa
  kyō no 6-ji made ni naoshite kureru to yakusoku shimashita
  yo!
— Hai, hontō ni sumimasen. Kesa hayaku kara ano kuruma o shūri
  shite iru-n desu ga, mada owaranai-n desu. Mō ichi-nichi
  kakaru-n desu ga . . . Ashita no gogo made ni kitto naoshimasu.
— Komarimashita nē! Konban shichi-ji ni daiji na yakusoku ga
  atte torikesu no wa mō oso-sugimasu. Dō shimashō? Soko
  e kuruma nashi de wa ikemasen.
— Jā, watashi no kuruma o kashite agemasu!
— Sō desu ka! Jā, ashita kuruma o kaeshimasu. Sono toki
  made ni watashi no kuruma o kitto naoshite kuremasu
  ne?
— Hai, kashikomarimashita!
— Dōmo arigatō! Anata no kuruma o daiji ni tsukaimasu.
— Dōzo, ki o tsukete unten shite kudasai!
— Jā, mata ashita.
— Sayōnara.

Mondai 94

1. Ogawa-san wa nani o tori ni kimashita ka?

   _____

2. Ogawa-san no kuruma no shūri wa owarimashita ka?

   _____

3. Kuruma o shūri suru hito wa kinō no yakusoku o mamorimashita ka?

   _____

4. Ogawa-san wa konban nan-ji ni daiji na yakusoku ga arimasu ka?

   _____

5. Soko e kuruma nashi de iku koto ga dekimasu ka?

   _____

6. Kuruma o shūri suru hito wa Ogawa-san ni kuruma o kashite agemasu ka?

   _____

7. Ogawa-san wa kuruma o kariru no ni okane o harawanakereba ikemasen ka?

   _____

8. Anata wa Ogawa-san no kuruma ga Toyota ka dōka shitte imasu ka?

   _____

9. Anata wa Ogawa-san no kuruma ga ashita no gogo made ni naoru to omoimasu ka?

   _____

10. (Moshi anata ga kuruma o motte ireba,) anata wa jibun de kuruma o shūri
    shimasu ka, soretomo dare ka ni shūri shite moraimasu ka?

    _____

UKETSUKE

— Tanaka-san wa irasshaimasu ka?

— Kaigi-chū de gozaimasu ga . . .
Donata-sama de irasshaimasu ka?

— Ogawa desu. Kojima-Ginkō no Ogawa
desu.

— Shitsurei desu ga, o-yakusoku ga
gozaimasu ka?

— Ē, kinō denwa de 9-ji-han ni o-ai suru
yakusoku o shimashita.

— Sō de gozaimasu ka? Jā, shibaraku
o-machi kudasai. Sochira no isu ni
suwatte o-machi kudasai. Kaigi wa mō
sugu owaru to omoimasu.

Takeda-san wa kaisha no uketsuke ni imasu. Kono kaisha ni kuru hito
wa, dare demo uketsuke o tōranakereba ikemasen. Takeda-san wa
okyaku no namae to, aitai hito no namae o tazunemasu. Sorekara
yakusoku ga aru ka dōka mo kikimasu.

Takeda-san wa sono hito ni denwa o shimasu. Soshite sono hito ga
okyaku ni au koto ga dekiru ka dōka tazunemasu. Sono hito ga kaigi-chū
no toki ya, isogashii toki ni wa, okyaku wa uketsuke de matanakereba
ikemasen. Moshi okyaku ga maemotte denwa o sureba, amari nagaku
matanakute mo ii desu.

Mondai 95

1. Tanaka-san ni aitakereba, maemotte denwa shinakereba ikemasen ka?

___

2. Tanaka-san no kaisha e hairu toki, hajime ni uketsuke o tōranakereba ikemasen ka?

___

3. Tanaka-san ni au toki, nekutai o shite inakereba ikemasen ka?

___

4. Uketsuke no Takeda-san wa, okyaku ni osake o agenakereba ikemasen ka?

___

5. Tanaka-san no uchi ni hairu toki, kutsu o nuganakereba ikemasen ka?

___

6. Shinkansen ni noru toki, kippu o motte inakereba ikemasen ka?

___

7. Shinkansen ni noru toki, pasupōto o motte inakereba ikemasen ka?

___

8. Akushu shita ato de, ojigi o shinakereba ikemasen ka?

___

9. Okane o tomodachi kara karitara, narubeku hayaku kaesanakereba ikemasen ka?

___

10. Terebi o mita ato de, terebi o kesanakereba ikemasen ka?

___

11. Kissaten e iku toki, maemotte yoyaku shinakereba ikemasen ka?

___

12. Moshi jikan dōri ni ikanakereba, yakusoku o torikesanakereba ikemasen ka?

___

Mondai 96

Rei: a) Heya kara deru toki, denki o keshite kudasai.

    Heya kara deru toki, denki o kesanakereba ikemasen.

  b) Heya kara deru toki, denki o kesanai de kudasai.

    Heya kara deru toki, denki o keshite wa ikemasen.

  c) Dochira de mo ii desu.

    Heya kara deru toki, denki o kesanakute mo ii desu.

1. a) Konban no shokuji o tsukutte kudasai.

  b) Konban no shokuji o tsukuranai de kudasai.

  c) Dochira de mo ii desu.

2. a) Inoue-san o pātii ni shōtai shite kudasai.

  b) Inoue-san o pātii ni shōtai shinai de kudasai.

  c) Dochira de mo ii desu.

3. a) Tonari no neko o sagashite kudasai.

  b) Tonari no neko o sagasanai de kudasai.

  c) Dochira de mo ii desu.

TANOSHII RYOKŌ

Watashi-tachi wa ichi-do mo Kyūshū e itta koto ga arimasen. Dakara issho ni ryokō shitai to omoimashita. Iroiro sōdan shite, Kagoshima e iku koto o kimemashita. I-kkagetsu gurai mae, watashi-tachi wa ryokō-dairiten e ikimashita. Hikōki de iku yori, densha de iku hō ga, zutto omoshiroi to omoimashita kara, Shinkansen to futsū no densha de iku koto o kimemashita. Soshite ryokō-dairiten ni densha no kippu to ryokan no yoyaku o tanomimashita.

Tōkyō kara Kagoshima made yaku sen-gohyaku-kiro arimasu. Hikōki de iku to, ni-jikan gurai de ikemasu ga, densha de iku to, jū-roku-jikan gurai kakarimasu. Keredomo densha de ikeba, mado kara iroiro na mono o miru koto ga dekimasu. Sorekara iroiro na eki de oishii o-bentō[1] o kau koto ga dekimasu.

Watashi-tachi no Shinkansen wa gogo san-ji ni Tōkyō eki o dete, ima Hiroshima o tōtte imasu. Shinkansen de Hakata made ikimasu ga, soko kara futsū no densha ni norikaenakereba ikemasen. Ima soto wa totemo kurai desu. Mado no soto ni kuroi yama ga miemasu. Tōku ni umi mo miemasu. Korekara kono densha wa Shimonoseki ni tsukimasu. Soshite umi no shita o tōtte Kyūshū ni ikimasu. Kyūshū no ichi-ban minami ni aru Kagoshima ni ashita no asa tsukimasu. Maemotte ryokan o yoyaku shimashita kara, eki kara ryokan made massugu takushii de iku tsumori desu. Ryokan ni tsuitara, narubeku hayaku Tōkyō no uchi e denwa o suru tsumori desu.

---

[1] o-bentō = hiru-gohan

Mondai 97

1. Watashi-tachi wa doko e iku tokoro desu ka?

   _____

2. Watashi-tachi wa Kyūshū e itta koto ga arimasu ka?

   _____

3. Watashi-tachi wa Kagoshima e hikōki de ikimasu ka, densha de ikimasu ka?

   _____

4. Doko de densha no kippu o yoyaku shimashita ka?

   _____

5. Ima Shinkansen wa doko o tōtte imasu ka?

   _____

6. Doko de densha o norikaenakereba ikemasen ka?

   _____

7. Densha de iku to, Tōkyō kara Kagoshima made nan-jikan kakarimasu ka?

   _____

8. Anata wa Shinkansen ni notta koto ga arimasu ka?

   _____

9. Anata wa Kyūshū e itta koto ga arimasu ka?

   _____

10. Anata wa yoku ryokō shimasu ka?

    _____

11. Anata wa ryokō suru toki, ryokō-dairiten de kippu o yoyaku shite moraimasu ka?

    _____

12. Anata ga ryokō suru toki, donna norimono o tsukaimasu ka?

    _____

-TA KOTO GA ARU

Watashi wa (kyonen) Pari e | ikimashita. |

Watashi wa Pari e | **itta koto ga arimasu.** |

Watashi wa Amerika e | ikimasen deshita. |

Watashi wa Amerika e | **itta koto ga arimasen.** |

iku	ikimashita	itta koto ga arimasu
	ikimasen deshita	itta koto ga arimasen
taberu	tabemashita	tabeta koto ga arimasu
	tabemasen deshita	tabeta koto ga arimasen
sumu	sumimashita	sunda koto ga arimasu
	sumimasen deshita	sunda koto ga arimasen
kiku	kikimashita	kiita koto ga arimasu
	kikimasen deshita	kiita koto ga arimasen
miru	mimashita	mita koto ga arimasu
	mimasen deshita	mita koto ga arimasen

. . . TSUMORI DESU

> *Ashita anata wa kimasu ka?*
>
> — *Hai, watashi wa kitto kimasu.*
> — *Hai, watashi wa kuru* **tsumori** *desu.*
>
> *Itsu benkyō suru* **tsumori** *desu ka?*
> — *Konban benkyō suru* **tsumori** *desu.*

-KU SURU

> *Kono biru wa furui desu.*
> *Rainen atarashiku* **shimasu.**
>
> *Sore wa taka-sugimasu.*
> *Yasuku* **shite kudasai.**

Mondai 98

Rei: Anata wa Nihon e ikimasu ka? *(hai)*

Hai, watashi wa iku tsumori desu.

1. Anata wa dare to Nihon e ikimasu ka? *(bosu)*

2. Fune de iku-no desu ka, soretomo hikōki de iku-no desu ka? *(hikōki)*

3. Dono kurai Nihon ni imasu ka? *(ni-shūkan)*

4. Dono hoteru ni tomarimasu ka? *(Tōkyō Hoteru)*

5. Dare ni aimasu ka? *(Tanaka-san)*

6. Anata no kodomo-san ni o-miyage o kaimasu ka? *(hai)*

DAI JŪ-KYŪ-SHŌ — MATOME

Tsukurareru / hanasareru / urareru

Kamera o tsukurimasu.
Kamera ga tsukuraremasu.

Nihon-go o hanashimasu.
Nihon-go ga hanasaremasu.

Seihin o urimasu.
Seihin ga uraremasu.

Kaite imasu / kakarete imasu

Watashi wa kono tegami
o kaite imasu.

Kono tegami wa Nihon-go
de kakarete imasu.

Yushutsu / yunyū

Nihon wa seihin o gaikoku e
yushutsu shimasu.

Nihon wa zairyō o gaikoku kara
yunyū shimasu.

Keiyaku / torihiki

Anata no kaisha to watashi no
kaisha wa keiyaku o musubimashita.

Anata no kaisha wa watashi no
kaisha to torihiki ga arimasu.

Kamotsusen / torakku / tankā

Kamotsusen wa nimotsu o hakobu
fune desu.

Torakku wa nimotsu o hakobu
kuruma desu.

Tankā wa sekiyu o hakobu fune
desu.

. . . no hitotsu / hitori desu.

Kamera wa Nihon no bōeki-shōhin
no hitotsu desu.

Tanaka-san wa Nihon-jin no hitori
desu.

Kōgyō / nōgyō

Kōgyō-koku wa iroiro na seihin
o seizō shimasu.

Nōgyō-koku wa okome ya yasai
nado o tsukurimasu.

Kaiwa-hyōgen

"Yatto, . . . "

SHIMAGUNI NO NIHON

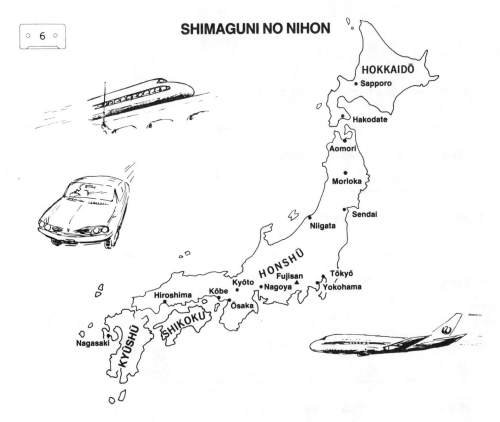

Nihon wa yottsu no ōkii shima to, hijōni takusan no chiisai shima de dekite imasu. Yottsu no ōkii shima wa Hokkaidō, Honshū, Shikoku, Kyūshū desu.

Ichi-ban kita ni aru no wa Hokkaidō desu. Koko de wa yuki ga yoku furimasu. Hokkaidō no ichi-ban ōkii toshi wa Sapporo desu.

Ichi-ban jinkō ga ōi shima wa Honshū desu. Honshū ni wa takusan no ōkii toshi ga arimasu. Tatoeba Tōkyō, Yokohama, Nagoya, Ōsaka, Hiroshima nado desu. Anata wa hoka ni donna toshi o shitte imasu ka? Kyōto wa Ōsaka no chikaku ni arimasu. Kyōto wa totemo furui toshi desu. Ima kara sen-gohyaku-nen gurai mae, koko wa Nihon de ichi-ban jūyō na tokoro deshita. Iroiro na furui tatemono ya utsukushii Nihon no niwa o miru koto ga dekimasu. Dakara hoka no toshi ya gaikoku kara takusan no kankō-kyaku ga o-tera ya jinja o mi ni kimasu.

Kyūshū wa minami ni arimasu kara, atatakai tokoro desu. Dakara yasai o fuyu ni tsukuru koto ga dekimasu. Nōjō de tsukurareru yasai wa torakku nado de Nihon-jū ni hakobaremasu. Ima de wa Shinkansen de Tōkyō kara Hakata made iku koto ga dekimasu.

Shikoku wa yottsu no shima no naka de ichi-ban chiisai shima desu. Zutto mae wa, fune de shika iku koto ga dekimasen deshita ga, ima wa hikōki de hayaku iku koto ga dekimasu. Mō sugu Shinkansen de mo iku koto ga dekiru deshō.

Mondai 99

1. Nihon ni wa ikutsu no ōkii shima ga arimasu ka?

   _____

2. Ichi-ban chiisai shima wa nan desu ka?

   _____

3. Ichi-ban ōkii shima wa nan desu ka?

   _____

4. Ichi-ban minami ni aru shima wa nan desu ka?

   _____

5. Dono shima ga ichi-ban samui desu ka?

   _____

6. Nihon no ōkii toshi no namae o mittsu kaite kudasai .

   _____

7. Doko ni takusan no furui o-tera ya jinja ga arimasu ka?

   _____

8. Sapporo wa Kyūshū ni arimasu ka, soretomo Hokkaidō ni arimasu ka?

   _____

9. Honshū kara densha de Kyūshū e iku koto ga dekimasu ka?

   _____

10. Hiroshima wa doko ni arimasu ka?

   _____

NIHON NO KŌGYŌ

Nihon no kōgyō wa iroiro arimasu. Kuruma ya kamera ya bideo wa mochiron, sono hoka iroiro na seihin ga Nihon-jū no kōjō de seizō sarete imasu. Soshite sono seihin wa sekai-jū ni urarete imasu. Toyota ya Nissan wa kuruma no ōte no mēkā desu. Sonii ya Tōshiba wa terebi ya bideo nado o seizō shite imasu. Soshite tekkō-gaisha wa kōtetsu o tsukutte, sore o gaikoku ni yushutsu shite imasu. Seikō ya Shichizun wa tokei, Kyanon wa kamera o tsukutte imasu. Nihon de tsukurareru Nihon-sei no seihin wa sekai no iroiro na kuni ni hakobarete, sekai-jū no hito ni tsukawarete imasu.

Shikashi Nihon wa iroiro na mono o gaikoku kara yunyū shinakereba ikemasen. Sono naka de sekiyu wa hijōni daiji na mono no hitotsu desu. Takusan no sekiyu ga Chūkintō no kuni kara yunyū saremasu. Sekiyu o hakobu fune wa tankā desu. Nimotsu o hakobu fune wa kamotsusen desu. Nihon wa gaikoku ni shōhin o yushutsu shite, soshite seihin o tsukuru tame no zairyō o gaikoku kara yunyū shite imasu. Nihon wa takusan no kuni to torihiki ga arimasu. Nihon wa ōkii bōeki-koku desu.

Mondai 100

1. Nihon ni wa ōkii kaisha ga takusan arimasu ka?

   _____

2. Toyota ya Nissan wa jidōsha no mēkā desu ka?

   _____

3. Anata wa hoka no jidōsha no mēkā no namae o shitte imasu ka?

   _____

4. Sonii ya Tōshiba wa nani o tsukutte imasu ka?

   _____

5. Sono hoka no Nihon no terebi no mēkā wa nan desu ka?

   _____

6. Nihon no kuruma no mēkā wa sono seihin o gaikoku ni urimasu ka?

   _____

7. Nihon-sei no kamera no namae wa nan desu ka?

   _____

8. Nihon no bōeki-shōhin wa nan de gaikoku e hakobaremasu ka?

   _____

9. Nihon wa sekiyu o yunyū shite imasu ka, soretomo yushutsu shite imasu ka?

   _____

10. Nihon wa doko kara sekiyu o yunyū shite imasu ka?

    _____

11. Sekiyu wa nan de Nihon ni hakobaremasu ka?

    _____

12. Anata no kaisha wa Nihon no kaisha to torihiki ga arimasu ka?

    _____

1982-NEN NI TSUKURARETA
KURUMA TO SONO YUSHUTSU

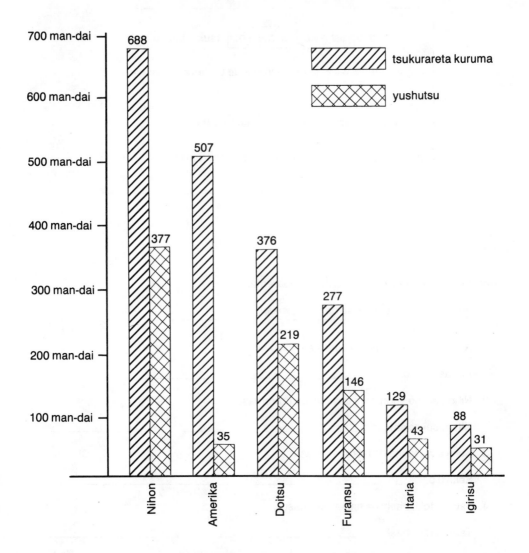

Nihon de tsukurareru jidōsha no kazu wa hijōni fuete imasu. 1960-nen
ni wa sekai de nana-banme ni takusan no jidōsha o tsukurimashita. Shikashi
1970-nen ni wa Amerika ga ichi-ban de, Nihon wa ni-banme ni narimashita.
Soshite ima dewa sekai de ichi-ban takusan no kuruma o tsukutte imasu.
1983-nen ni wa yaku 715 man-dai no jidōsha, 390 man-dai no torakku, soshite
gosen-roppyaku-dai no basu ga Nihon de tsukuraremashita.

TSUKURU / TSUKURARERU

Jidōsha-gaisha wa | *kuruma* **o** | **tsukurimasu.**

| *Kuruma* **wa** | jidōsha-gaisha de **tsukuraremasu.**

Nihon-jin wa | *Nihon-go* **o** | **hanashimasu.**

| *Nihon-go* **wa / ga** | Nihon de **hanasaremasu.**

Mondai 101

Rei: Iroiro na shōhin wa torakku de hakobaremasu.

Iroiro na shōhin o *torakku de hakobimasu.*

1. Atarashii kōjō wa rainen tateraremasu.

   Atarashii kōjō o _____

2. Nihon-sei no shōhin wa gaikoku de uraremasu.

   Nihon-sei no shōhin o _____

3. Sekiyu wa tankā de hakobaremasu.

   Sekiyu o _____

4. Taberu toki, hashi ga tsukawaremasu.

   Taberu toki, hashi o _____

5. Kono tegami wa Hiragana de kakarete imasu.

   Kono tegami o _____

6. Takusan no jidōsha wa Amerika e yushutsu saremasu.

   Takusan no jidōsha o _____

Mondai 102

A. hanasaremasu	F. gasorin	K. tekkō-gaisha
B. keiyaku	G. chokusetsu	L. kamotsusen
C. torihiki	H. mēkā	M. Kanji
D. yatto	I. hitotsu	N. yushutsu
E. yunyū	J. sekai-jū	O. nōjō

Rei: Toyota ya Nissan wa jidōsha no ____**H**____ desu.

1. Kōtetu wa _____ de tsukuraremasu.

2. Furansu de wa Furansu-go ga _____.

3. Nihon kara takusan no jidōsha ga _____ saremasu.

4. Eigo wa _____ de hanasarete imasu.

5. Amerika wa Nihon kara rajio ya terebi o _____ shite imasu.

6. Nihon no _____ de wa okome ya yasai o tsukurimasu.

7. Nihon-sei no shōhin wa _____ de gaikoku e hakobaremasu.

8. Nihon de wa _____ to Hiragana to Katakana ga tsukawarete imasu.

9. Kamera wa Nihon no jūyō na bōeki-shōhin no _____ desu.

10. Watashi no shigoto wa _____ owarimashita.

11. Watashi no kaisha to anata no kaisha to _____ o musubimashita.

12. Nihon wa Sauji Arabia kara sekiyu o _____ yunyū shite imasu.

13. _____ wa sekiyu kara tsukuraremasu.

14. Watashi no kaisha wa Nihon no kaisha to _____ ga arimasu.

DAI NIJU-SSHŌ — MATOME

Nan-pāsento desu ka?

Tōkyō no jinkō wa Nihon no jinkō no 10-pāsento ijō desu.

Bukka wa 5-pāsento agarimashita.

omo na / omo ni

Nihon no omo na yushutsu-hin wa jidōsha ya terebi desu.

Nihon wa sekiyu o omo ni Chūkintō kara yunyū shimasu.

Bukka ga agaru / sagaru

Nedan ga takaku narimasu.
Bukka ga agarimasu.

Nedan ga yasuku narimasu.
Bukka ga sagarimasu.

-bai ni / han-bun ni

Shinbun no nedan wa 50-en deshita.
Shinbun no nedan wa 100-en desu.
Shinbun no nedan wa ni-bai ni narimashita.

Jūgyō-in no kazu wa nisen-nin deshita.
Ima jūgyō-in no kazu wa sen-nin desu.
Jūgyō-in no kazu wa han-bun ni narimashita.

Seizō-gaisha / hanbai-gaisha

Seizō-gaisha wa seihin o tsukurimasu.

Hanbai-gaisha wa shōhin o urimasu.

Kōgai / inaka / toshi

Tōkyō ya Ōsaka wa toshi desu.
Toshi no chikaku wa kōgai desu.
Inaka wa toshi kara tōi desu.

. . . ni tsuide

Tōkyō wa ichi-ban ōkii desu.
Ōsaka wa ni-banme ni ōkii desu.
Ōsaka wa Tōkyō ni tsuide ōkii desu.

. . . ga sakan desu.

Nihon wa jidōsha-kōgyō ga sakan desu.
Nihon de wa yakyū ga totemo sakan desu.

Kaiwa-hyōgen

"Okashii desu ne."

TŌKYŌ

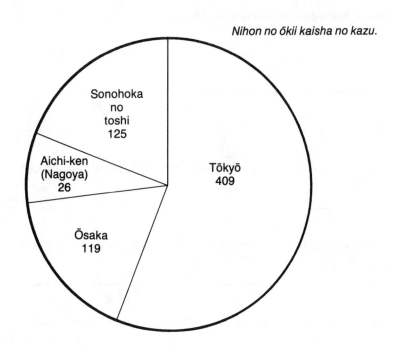

Nihon no ōkii kaisha no kazu.

Tōkyō wa Nihon de ichi-ban ōkii toshi desu ga, sekai de mo ichi-ban ōkii toshi desu. Anata wa Tōkyō ga Nihon no doko ni aru ka shitte imasu ka? Chizu o mite kudasai. Tōkyō wa Honshū no chōdo man-naka ni arimasu ne!

Tōkyō ni wa takusan no hito ga sunde imasu. Yaku sen-hyaku-rokujūman no hito ga sunde imasu. Sore wa Nihon no zenbu no jinkō no ju-ppāsento ijō desu. Soshite asa ni naru to, Tōkyō no chikaku no Chiba-ken, Saitama-ken, Kanagawa-ken nado kara takusan no hito ga hataraki ni kimasu. Dakara Tōkyō de wa asa to yūgata, densha ya chikatetsu nado no norimono wa totemo komimasu.

Tōkyō ni wa takusan no ōkii kaisha ya ginkō ga arimasu. Nihon no omo na kaisha no honsha ya gaikoku no kaisha no shisha mo koko ni arimasu. Gaikoku no taishikan ya ryōjikan mo koko ni arimasu. Mochiron Berurittsu-gakkō mo arimasu. Tōkyō wa Nihon de ichi-ban jūyō na toshi desu.

Mondai 103

1. Nihon de ichi-ban ōkii toshi wa doko desu ka?

_____

2. Tōkyō wa Kyūshū ni arimasu ka, Honshū ni arimasu ka?

_____

3. Tōkyō ni wa Nihon no jinkō no nan-pāsento no hito ga sunde imasu ka?

_____

4. Asa to yūgata, Tōkyō no densha ya chikatetsu wa taihen komimasu ka?

_____

5. Tōkyō de hataraite iru hito wa zenbu Tōkyō ni sunde iru hito desu ka?

_____

6. Chiba-ken ya Kanagawa-ken nado kara takusan no hito ga Tōkyō ni hataraki ni kimasu ka?

_____

7. Anata wa Tōkyō e itta koto ga arimasu ka?

_____

8. Anata wa Tōkyō ni sumitai desu ka?

_____

KAIGI NO ATO DE

Arakawa-san to Yamamoto-san wa ima kaisha o deru tokoro desu.

Arakawa:	Yamamoto-san, kyō wa taihen deshita ne!
Yamamoto:	Ā, Arakawa-san, kaigi wa yatto owarimashita yo!
Arakawa:	Kyō no kaigi wa nagakatta desu ne. Yaku san-jikan desu yo!
Yamamoto:	Sengetsu no kaigi wa motto nagakatta-n desu yo! Demo kyō no kaigi wa hotondo watashi hitori de hōkoku shinakereba ikemasen deshita kara, tsukaremashita yo.
Arakawa:	Kyō wa hanbai-bu no hito wa takusan no shitsumon o shimashita nē.
Yamamoto:	Ē, hanbai-buchō wa senshū Amerika kara kaetta bakari desu kara, kikitai koto ga takusan atta-n deshō.
Arakawa:	Atarashii kōkoku ni tsuite no anata no iken wa totemo yokatta desu yo.
Yamamoto:	Anata mo sō omoimasu ka? Hontō ni saikin wa shinbun-kōkoku yori terebi no kōkoku no hō ga zutto ii-n desu yo.
Arakawa:	Sō desu ka? Demo terebi no kōkoku wa takai deshō?
Yamamoto:	Ē, mochiron desu yo! Demo Arakawa-san, mō kaigi wa owarimashita yo!
Arakawa:	Ā, sō deshita ne! Gomen nasai! Watashi mo kyō wa mō shigoto ni tsuite hanashitaku arimasen yo.
Yamamoto:	Ima kara massugu uchi e kaerimasu ka?
Arakawa:	Ē, kaeru tsumori desu ga . . .
Yamamoto:	Chotto chikaku no bā e issho ni ikimasen ka?
Arakawa:	Sō desu ne. Mada hayai desu kara, i-ppai nomimashō.

Mondai 104

Rei: Arakawa-san to Yamamoto-san wa jimusho kara deru tokoro desu.

H
___

1. Kyō no kaigi wa nagakatta desu ne.

   ___

2. Honto ni tsukaremashita!

   ___

3. Hotondo watashi hitori de hōkoku shimashita.

   ___

4. Takusan no shitsumon o shimashita.

   ___

5. Totemo ii iken desu ne!

   ___

6. Bā e ikimashō!

   ___

7. Mō shigoto ni tsuite hanashitaku arimasen.

   ___

8. Ima kara massugu uchi ni kaerimasu.

   ___

9. Sengetsu no kaigi wa motto nagakatta desu.

   ___

10. Taihen deshita.

    ___

A. Kiku koto ga takusan arimashita.

B. Hoka no koto o hanashimashō.

C. I-ppai nomimashō!

D. Muzukashikatta desu.

E. Watashi mo sō omoimasu.

F. Sugu owarimasen deshita.

G. Doko e mo ikimasen.

H. Uchi ni kaerimasu.

I. Genki ga arimasen.

J. Sengetsu no kaigi ni kurabete mijikakatta desu.

K. Hoka no hito wa kiite imashita.

KŌKOKU-BUCHŌ NO HASHIMOTO-SAN

Hashimoto-san wa kamera-gaisha no Tōkyō honsha ni tsutomete imasu. Nijū-go-nen mae, kono kaisha no Ōsaka shisha ni hairimashita. Kono kaisha wa Nihon-jū ni takusan no shisha ga arimasu. Ōsaka shisha wa sono hitotsu desu. Kono kaisha wa iroiro no bu ni wakarete imasu. Tatoeba hanbai-bu, seizō-bu, kōkoku-bu nado desu.

Hashimoto-san ga kono kaisha ni haitta toki, kono kaisha wa shin-seihin o shōkai suru tame ni, shinbun to zasshi shika tsukaimasen deshita. Keredomo go-nen mae ni Hashimoto-san ga kōkoku-bu no buchō ni natte kara, terebi ni mo kōkoku shi- hajimemashita. Sono kōkoku wa hijōni yokatta node, kamera no namae wa yūmei ni narimashita. Soshite kaisha wa okane o takusan mōkeru koto ga dekimashita.

Keredomo kyōnen kara infure no tame ni, iroiro na bukka ga agarimashita. Kamera o tsukuru tame no zairyō no nedan mo agarimashita. Kaisha no jūgyō-in no kyūryō mo agarimashita. Kamera no nedan mo zutto agarimashita. Sono tame ni kamera wa amari uremasen deshita.

Kotoshi wa motto takusan uru koto ga dekiru yōni, kare wa hanbai-buchō ya shachō to iroiro sōdan shimashita. Soshite kamera no nedan o go-pāsento yasuku suru koto o kimemashita.

Mondai 105

1. Hashimoto-san wa hanbai-bu de hataraite imasu ka?

   _____

2. Nani-bu de hataraite imasu ka?

   _____

3. Kare wa buchō ni naru mae ni nan-nenkan hataraite imashita ka?

   _____

4. Terebi no kōkoku o hajimeta no wa kare ga buchō ni naru mae desu ka, natta ato desu ka?

   _____

5. Terebi no kōkoku wa yokatta desu ka?

   _____

6. Kamera no namae wa yūmei ni narimashita ka?

   _____

7. Sono toki kaisha wa okane o mōkeru koto ga dekimashita ka?

   _____

8. Kyonen kamera no nedan wa agarimashita ka, sagarimashita ka?

   _____

9. Kyonen mo kamera wa takusan uremashita ka?

   _____

10. Hashimoto-san wa dare to sōdan shimashita ka?

    _____

11. Kotoshi wa motto takusan uru tame ni, dō suru koto o kimemashita ka?

    _____

12. Ima kamera wa jūman-en desu. Atarashii nedan wa ikura ni narimasu ka?

    _____

Mondai 106

HANTAI WA NAN DESU KA?

Rei: Kuruma wa ōkii desu.   *Kuruma wa chiisai desu.*

1. Tokei ga kowaremasu.
2. Dōbutsu
3. Taihen tōi desu.
4. Sore wa yasui desu ne.
5. Kusuri wa nomi-nikui desu.
6. Kare wa o-kanemochi desu.
7. Katamichi-kippu o kudasai.
8. Kaette mo ii desu.
9. Yunyū shimasu.
10. Infure
11. Honsha ni tsutomete imasu.
12. Denki o keshite kudasai.
13. Okane o kashimasu.
14. Bukka ga agarimasu.
15. Ni-bai ni narimashita.
16. Umaremashita.
17. Sore o oboete imasu.
18. Chotto ō-sugimasu.
19. Kore wa benri desu ne!
20. Watashi wa wakai desu.
21. Michi o tazunemasu.
22. Yōfuku o kimasu.
23. Densha ni norimasu.
24. Toshi ni sunde imasu.
25. Kōgyō ga sakan desu.

OSAKE YA BIIRU MO AGARIMASHITA

— Ara! Okamoto-san no okusan! Shibaraku deshita nē!

— Mā, shibaraku! Nakayama-san no okusan! O-genki desu ka?

— Ē, okagesamade! Kyō wa anata mo o-kaimono desu ka?

— Ē, kesa kono depāto no shinbun-kōkoku o mimashita. Yōfuku-
uriba de nani ka yasui no o mitsukeru tsumori desu. Mainichi
bukka ga agatte taihen desu kara.

— Sō desu nē! Tabemono ga agatte, yōfuku mo agatta deshō.
Hon ya zasshi mo takaku narimashita nē! Densha mo takushii mo.
Sorekara osake ya biiru made. Uchi no shujin wa yoku nomu-n
desu yo.

— Uchi no mo desu. Hontō ni taihen desu ne! Kyonen wa bukka
ga sanjū-yon-pāsento mo agatta sō desu yo. Agaranai no wa
shujin no gekkyū dake desu! Watashi mo mō sugu dokoka e
hataraki ni ikimasu.

— Sore wa ii desu nē! Watashi mo hatarakitai-no desu ga, mada
dekimasen. Kodomo ga chiisai desu kara.

— Jā, kore de shitsurei shimasu. Go-shujin ni yoroshiku.

— Dōmo arigatō! Sayonara.

Mondai 107

A. yoyaku	F. keiki	K. saikin
B. bukka	G. tokuni	L. keizai
C. neko	H. hatten	M. dōbutsu
D. Nihon-sei	I. zōsen-gyō	N. tanjōbi
E. omo ni	J. tsuide	O. sekai-jū

Rei: Watashi wa Nihon no tabemono no naka de, _____**G**_____ sukiyaki ga suki desu.

1. _____ kono kaisha no _____ wa yoku arimasen.

2. _____ no shōhin wa _____ de urarete imasu.

3. Infure no toki wa _____ ga agarimasu.

4. Nihon no _____ wa _____ shimashita.

5. Maemotte seki o _____ shite kudasai.

6. Anata no _____ wa itsu desu ka?

7. Inu ya _____ wa _____ desu.

8. Nihon wa _____ Chūkintō kara sekiyu o yunyū shimasu.

9. Nihon de wa _____ ga sakan desu.

10. Hokkaidō wa Honshū ni _____ ōkii shima desu.

DŌSHI NO HENKA

Dictionary form + :
ka (dōka) shirimasen
kara desu
mae ni
jikan ga arimasen
koto ga dekimasu
deshō
toki
tokoro desu
tame ni
no desu
sō desu
to omoimasu
node

Te-form + :
wa dame desu yo
imasu
kudasai.
wa ikemasen
mo ii desu
agemasu
moraimasu
kuremasu
hoshii desu

Masu-stem + :
masu
mashita
mashō
tai desu
kata o
shitte imasu
tara

Nai-stem + :
nakereba ikemasen
naide kudasai
nakutemo ii desu

Ta-form + :
toki
tokoro desu
deshō
bakari desu
koto ga arimasu
kamo shiremasen
ato de

		masu		
agaru	agatte	agari	agara	agatta
ageru	agete	age	age	ageta
akeru	akete	ake	ake	aketa
arau	aratte	arai	arawa	aratta
aru	—	ari	—	atta
aruku	aruite	aruki	aruka	aruita
iu	itte	ii	iwa	itta
iku	itte	iki	ika	itta
isogu	isoide	isogi	isoga	isoida
iru (okane ga)	—	iri	—	itta
iru (inu ga)	ite	i	i	ita
ireru	irete	ire	ire	ireta
ukeru	ukete	uke	uke	uketa
ugokasu	ugokashite	ugokashi	ugokasa	ugokashita
ugoku	ugoite	ugoki	ugoka	ugoita
umareru	umarete	umare	umare	umareta
urikireru	urikirete	urikire	urikire	urikireta
uru	utte	uri	ura	utta

okiru	okite	oki	oki	okita
oku	oite	oki	oka	oita
okureru	okurete	okure	okure	okureta
oshieru	oshiete	oshie	oshie	oshieta
oboeru	oboete	oboe	oboe	oboeta
omou	omotte	omoi	omowa	omotta
oriru	orite	ori	ori	orita
owaru	owatte	owari	owara	owatta
kau	katte	kai	kawa	katta
kaesu	kaeshite	kaeshi	kaesa	kaeshita
kaeru (uchi e)	kaette	kaeri	kaera	kaetta
kaeru (okane o)	kaete	kae	kae	kaeta
kakaru	kakatte	kakari	kakara	kakatta
kakeru	kakete	kake	kake	kaketa
kaku	kaite	kaki	kaka	kaita
kasu	kashite	kashi	kasa	kashita
kazoeru	kazoete	kazoe	kazoe	kazoeta
kariru	karite	kari	kari	karita
kieru	kiete	kie	kie	kieta
kiku	kiite	kiki	kika	kiita
kimeru	kimete	kime	kime	kimeta
kiru (kami o)	kitte	kiri	kira	kitta
kiru (fuku o)	kite	ki	ki	kita
kuru	kite	ki	ko	kita
kureru	—	kure	kure	kureta
kesu	keshite	keshi	kesa	keshita
kotaeru	kotaete	kotae	kotae	kotaeta
komu	konda	komi	—	konda
kowareru	kowarete	koware	koware	kowareta
sagasu	sagashite	sagashi	sagasa	sagashita
sagaru	sagatte	sagari	sagara	sagatta
saku	saite	saki	saka	saita
shimaru	shimatte	shimari	shimara	shimatta
shimeru	shimete	shime	shime	shimeta
shiru	shitte	shiri	shira	shitta
suu	sutte	sui	suwa	sutta
sugiru	sugite	sugi	sugi	sugita
suku	suite	suki	suka	suita

ka (dōka) shirimasen	wa dame desu yo	masu	nakereba ikemasen	toki
kara desu	imasu	mashita	naide kudasai	tokoro desu
mae ni	kudasai	mashō	nakutemo ii desu	deshō
jikan ga arimasen	wa ikemasen	tai desu		bakari desu
koto ga dekimasu	mo ii desu	kata o		koto ga arimasu
deshō	agemasu	shitte imasu		kamo shiremasen
toki	moraimasu	tara		ato de
tokoro desu	kuremasu			
tame ni	hoshii desu			
no desu				
sō desu				
to omoimasu				
node				

sumu	sunde	sumi	suma	sunda
suru	shite	shi	shi	shita
suwaru	suwatte	suwari	suwara	suwatta
tasu	tashite	tashi	tasa	tashita
dasu	dashite	dashi	dasa	dashita
tazuneru	tazunete	tazune	tazune	tazuneta
tatsu	tatte	tachi	tata	tatta
tateru	tatete	tate	tate	tateta
tanomu	tanonde	tanomi	tanoma	tanonda
taberu	tabete	tabe	tabe	tabeta
chigau	chigatte	chigai	chigawa	chigatta
tsukau	tsukatte	tsukai	tsukawa	tsukatta
tsukareru	tsukarete	tsukare	tsukare	tsukareta
tsukuru	tsukutte	tsukuri	tsukura	tsukutta
tsuku	tsuite	tsuki	tsuka	tsuita
tsukeru	tsukete	tsuke	tsuke	tsuketa
tsuzukeru	tsuzukete	tsuzuke	tsuzuke	tsuzuketa
tsutomeru	tsutomete	tsutome	tsutome	tsutometa
dekakeru	dekakete	dekake	dekake	dekaketa
dekiru	dekite	deki	deki	dekita

deru	dete	de	de	deta
tōru	tōtte	tōri	tōra	tōtta
tomaru	tomatte	tomari	tomara	tomatta
torikesu	torikeshite	torikeshi	torikesa	torikeshita
toru	totte	tori	tora	totta
naosu	naoshite	naoshi	naosa	naoshita
naoru	naotte	naori	naora	naotta
nakusu	nakushite	nakushi	nakusa	nakushita
narau	naratte	narai	narawa	naratta
naru	natte	nari	nara	natta
nugu	nuide	nugi	nuga	nuida
nemuru	nemutte	nemuri	nemura	nemutta
neru	nete	ne	ne	neta
nokosu	nokoshite	nokoshi	nokosa	nokoshita
nomu	nonde	nomi	noma	nonda
norikaeru	norikaete	norikae	norikae	norikaeta
noru	notte	nori	nora	notta
hairu	haitte	hairi	haira	haitta
haku	haite	haki	haka	haita
hakobu	hakonde	hakobi	hakoba	hakonda
hajimaru	hajimatte	hajimari	hajimara	hajimatta
hajimeru	hajimete	hajime	hajime	hajimeta
hataraku	hataraite	hataraki	hataraka	hataraita
hanasu	hanashite	hanashi	hanasa	hanashita
harau	haratte	harai	harawa	haratta
hareru	harete	hare	hare	hareta
hiku	hiite	hiki	hika	hiita
fueru	fuete	fue	fue	fueta
fuku	fuite	fuki	fuka	fuita
furu	futte	furi	fura	futta
magaru	magatte	magari	magara	magatta
machigaeru	machigaete	machigae	machigae	machigaeta
matsu	matte	machi	mata	matta
maniau	maniatte	maniai	maniawa	maniatta
mamoru	mamotte	mamori	mamora	mamotta
mayou	mayotte	mayoi	mayowa	mayotta
mieru	miete	mie	mie	mieta

ka (dōka) shirimasen	wa dame desu yo	masu	nakereba ikemasen	toki
kara desu	imasu	mashita	naide kudasai	tokoro desu
mae ni	kudasai	mashō	nakutemo ii desu	deshō
jikan ga arimasen	wa ikemasen	tai desu		bakari desu
koto ga dekimasu	mo ii desu	kata o		koto ga arimasu
deshō	agemasu	shitte imasu		kamo shiremasen
toki	moraimasu	tara		ato de
tokoro desu	kuremasu			
tame ni	hoshii desu			
no desu				
sō desu				
to omoimasu				
node				

miseru	misete	mise	mise	miseta
mitsukeru	mitsukete	mitsuke	mitsuke	mitsuketa
miru	mite	mi	mi	mita
mōkeru	mōkete	mōke	mōke	mōketa
mochiageru	mochiagete	mochiage	mochiage	mochiageta
motsu	motte	mochi	mota	motta
morau	moratte	morai	morawa	moratta
yasumu	yasunde	yasumi	yasuma	yasunda
yomu	yonde	yomi	yoma	yonda
wakaru	wakatte	wakari	wakara	wakatta
wakareru	wakarete	wakare	wakare	wakareta
wasureru	wasurete	wasure	wasure	wasureta
watasu	watashite	watashi	watasa	watashita

KAITŌ

Mondai 1
1. Iie, kore wa tabako ja arimasen. (Iie, sō ja arimasen.)   2. Iie, kore wa hon demo arimasen.   3. Kore wa matchi desu.   4. Iie, kore wa enpitsu ja arimasen. (Iie, sō ja arimasen.)   5. Kore wa pen demo arimasen.   6. Kore wa haizara desu.   7. Iie, kore wa inu ja arimasen.   8. Hai, kore wa denwa desu. (Hai, sō desu.)   9. Iie, kore wa denwa ja arimasen. (Iie, sō ja arimasen.)   10. Kore wa hamaki desu.   11. Iie, kore wa pen ja arimasen. (Iie, sō ja arimasen.)   12. Kore wa hon desu.

Mondai 2
1. Iie, kore wa Tanaka-san ja arimasen.   2. Kore wa Dubaru-san desu.   3. Iie, Dubaru-san wa Doitsu-jin ja arimasen.   4. Dubaru- san wa Furansu-jin desu.   5. Shumitto-san wa Doitsu-jin desu.   6. Hai, Berutini-san wa Itaria-jin desu.   7. Iie, kore wa Berutini- san ja arimasen.   8. Kore wa Jōnzu-san desu.   9. Iie, Jōnzu-san wa Itaria-jin ja arimasen.   10. Jōnzu-san wa Igirisu- jin desu.

Mondai 3
1. Iie, denwa wa ōkiku arimasen.   2. Iie, denwa wa akaku arimasen.   3. Denwa wa kuroi desu.   4. Iie, hon wa kuroku arimasen.   5. Hon wa haiiro desu.   6. Kore wa tabako desu.   7. Iie, tabako wa ōkiku arimasen.   8. Hai, tabako wa shiroi desu.   9. Iie, enpitsu wa shiroku arimasen.   10. Hai, enpitsu wa kuroi desu.   11. Iie, inu wa kuroku arimasen.   12. Inu wa shiro to kuro desu.

Mondai 4
1. Iie, watashi wa sensei ja arimasen.   2. Hai, watashi wa seito desu.   3. Iie, watashi wa Nihon-jin ja arimasen.   4. Hai, Tanaka-san wa Nihon-jin desu.   5. Hai, Noguchi-san mo Nihon-jin desu.

Mondai 5
1. Pen wa midoriiro ja arimasen.   2. Tsukue wa chairo ja arimasen.   3. Watashi wa sensei ja arimasen.   4. Anata wa Doitsu-jin ja arimasen.   5. Kore wa enpitsu ja arimasen.

Mondai 6
1. Hon wa ōkii desu ka?   2. Denwa wa kiiro desu ka?   3. Isu to tsukue wa chairo desu ka?   4. Anata wa Chūgoku-jin desu ka?   5. Haizara wa chiisai desu ka?

Mondai 7
1. Noguchi-san wa nani-jin desu ka?   2. Kore wa dare desu ka?   3. Are wa nan desu ka?   4. Mōgan-san wa nani-jin desu ka?

Mondai 8
1. Enpitsu ga nagai desu.   2. Hai, kagi wa enpitsu yori mijikai desu.   3. Kagi ga hikōki yori chiisai desu.   4. Basu ga kagi yori ōkii desu.   5. Iie, enpitsu wa tabako yori mijikaku arimasen.

Mondai 9
1. Fujisawa wa toshi desu.   2. Tōkyō ga ōkii desu.   3. Sobieto wa ōkii kuni desu.   4. Nihon ga chiisai desu.   5. Nyūyōku ga ōkii desu.

Mondai 10   1. Kono denwa ga kuroi desu.   2. Ano denwa ga haiiro desu.   3. Chiisai (Shiroi) kuruma ga Tanaka-san no (kuruma) desu.   4. Mōgan-san no (Kuroi) kuruma ga ōkii desu.   5. Tanaka-san no kuruma ga shiroi desu.

Mondai 11   1. Kono hikōki wa ōkii desu ka?   2. Tōkyō wa Kyōto yori chiisai desu ka? 3. Kono enpitsu wa nagai desu ka?   4. Sono kagi wa mijikai desu ka? 5. Basu wa densha yori nagai desu ka?

Mondai 12   1. Hai, Noguchi-san wa genki desu.   2. Iie, Jōnzu-san wa Amerika-jin ja arimasen.   3. Jōnzu-san wa Igirisu-jin desu.   4. Hai, Jōnzu-san wa Berurittsu no seito desu.

Mondai 13   1. A   2. E   3. B   4. F   5. C

Mondai 14   1. anata no nekutai wa ao to aka ja arimasen.   2. anata no tabako wa nagaku arimasen.   3. anata wa tabako o oite imasen.   4. watashi wa haizara o totte imasen.   5. sensei wa anata o mite imasen.   6. watashi no tsukue wa ōkiku arimasen.   7. anata no pen wa chairo ja arimasen.

Mondai 15   1. Iie, kono hikōki wa shiroku arimasen.   2. Hai, kono hikōki wa kuroi desu. 3. Iie, kono hikōki wa kuroku arimasen.   4. Shiroi hikōki ga chiisai desu. 5. Chūgoku ga (Nihon yori) ōkii desu.   6. Hai, watashi wa Berurittsu no seito desu.   7. Iie, watashi no namae wa Tanaka ja arimasen. 8. Watashi no namae wa . . . desu.   9. Watashi no sensei wa . . . -san desu.   10. Watashi no kuni wa (Nihon yori) ōkii (chiisai) desu.

Mondai 16   1. nana hachi kyū no san san go ichi   2. roku zero / rē zero / rē no ni hachi nana san   3. nana nana kyū no yon yon ichi san   4. san go zero / rē no ni hachi roku nana   5. ni ni san no yon kyū yon hachi

Mondai 17   1. Tanaka-san wa Nihon-jin desu.   2. Hai, Nihon-jin wa osake ga suki desu. 3. Shumitto-san wa biiru (no hō) ga suki desu.   4. Iie, sukiyaki wa nomimono ja arimasen.   5. Hai, tenpura wa oishii desu.

Mondai 18   1. Hai, Furansu wa ōkii desu.   2. Hai, Amerika mo ōkii desu.   3. Iie, Furansu wa Amerika yori ōkiku arimasen.   4. Sobieto ga ichi-ban ōkii desu. 5. Furansu ga ichi-ban chiisai desu.   6. Nihon ga ichi-ban chiisai desu. 7. Iie, Ginza-dōri wa nagaku arimasen.   8. Iie, Ginza-dōri wa Mishishippi yori nagaku arimasen.   9. Mishishippi no hō ga nagai desu.   10. Ginza-dōri no hō ga mijikai desu.   11. Hai, basu wa ōkii desu.   12. Hai, hikōki mo ōkii desu. 13. Hikōki no hō ga ōkii desu.   14. Iie, kuruma wa basu yori ōkiku arimasen. 15. Hikōki ga ichi- ban ōkii desu.

Mondai 19   1. Iie, hon wa tsukue no ue ni arimasen.   2. Iie, denwa wa tsukue no shita ni arimasen.   3. Denwa wa tsukue no ue ni arimasu.   4. Iie, handobaggu no naka ni hon wa arimasen.   5. Handobaggu no naka ni okane ga arimasu.

Mondai 20   1. Hai, (tsukue no ue ni) nani ka arimasu.   2. Denwa to pen ga arimasu. 3. Iie, handobaggu wa tsukue no ue ni arimasen.   4. Handobaggu wa tsukue no shita ni arimasu.   5. Iie, tsukue no shita ni enpitsu wa arimasen.   6. Iie, handobaggu no hoka ni nani mo arimasen.

Mondai 21
1. Kore wa biiru desu.   2. Iie, biiru wa bin no naka ni arimasen.   3. Biiru wa gurasu no naka ni arimasu.   4. Iie, kore wa biiru ja arimasen.   5. Kōcha desu.   6. Iie, kōcha wa gurasu no naka ni arimasen.   7. Kappu no naka ni arimasu.   8. Hai, kore wa miruku desu.   9. Miruku wa shiroi desu.
10. Miruku wa gurasu no naka ni arimasu.

Mondai 22
1. Hai, Rondon wa Igirisu ni arimasu.   2. Hai, Mishishippi wa Amerika de ichi-ban nagai kawa desu.   3. Amazon wa Burajiru ni arimasu.   4. Iie, Fujisan wa sekai de ichi-ban takai yama ja arimasen.   5. Eberesuto ga sekai de ichi-ban takai yama desu.

Mondai 23
1. Tsukue wa sensei no ushiro ni arimasu.   2. Sensei wa tatte imasu.
3. Iie, sensei wa seito no yoko ni tatte imasen.   4. Sensei wa seito no mae ni tatte imasu.   5. Sensei no ushiro ni dare mo tatte imasen.   6. Iie, seito wa tatte imasen.   7. Seito wa isu ni suwatte imasu.   8. Iie, sensei to seito no aida ni dare mo imasen.   9. Hai, kono kyōshitsu ni enpitsu ga arimasu.
10. Dare mo enpitsu o totte imasen.   11. Enpitsu wa tsukue no shita ni arimasu.   12. Sensei no ushiro ni arimasu.

Mondai 24
1. kita   2. nishi   3. kita   4. higashi   5. minami

Mondai 25
1. Tanaka-san wa resutoran ni imasu.   2. Tanaka-san wa suwatte imasu.
3. Hai, uētā wa migi no te ni enpitsu o motte imasu.   4. Uētā wa hidari no te ni kami o motte imasu.   5. Tanaka-san ga menyū o mite imasu.

Mondai 26
1. Hai, kono heya ni dare ka imasu.   2. Iie, sono hito no mae ni dare mo suwatte imasen.   3. Bin wa tsukue no ue ni arimasu.   4. Bin no naka ni uisukii ga arimasu.   5. Hai, denki wa sono hito no mae ni arimasu.   6. Iie, sono hito no migi no te ni nani mo arimasen.   7. Hai, hidari no te ni nani ka arimasu.   8. Okane ga arimasu.   9. Iie, ima okane o poketto ni irete imasen.   10. Ima okane o kazoete imasu.   11. Hai, okane o takusan kazoete imasu.   12. Iie, watashi no okane ja arimasen.

Mondai 27
A) 1. Iie, tsukue no ue ni hon wa san-satsu arimasen.   2. Hon wa ni-satsu arimasu.   3. Ōkii isu no ue ni hon ga san-satsu arimasu.   4. Chiisai isu no ue ni kami ga ichi-mai arimasu.   5. (Chiisai isu no ue ni) Enpitsu wa ni-hon arimasu.

B) 1. Yuka no ue ni hon ga go-satsu arimasu.   2. Chiisai isu no ue ni enpitsu ga ni-hon arimasu.   3. Tsukue no ue ni pen ga i-ppon arimasu.   4. Ōkii isu no ue ni kami ga ni-mai arimasu.   5. Ōkii isu no ue ni tabako ga san-bon arimasu.

Mondai 28
1. Kono onna no hito wa Nihon-jin desu.   2. Kono hito wa kimono o kite imasu.   3. Iie, watashi wa ima kimono o kite imasen.   4. Iie, Nihon-jin no tabemono wa Amerika-jin ya Furansu-jin no tabemono to onaji ja arimasen.
5. Nihon-jin wa sukiyaki ya sashimi ya tenpura ga suki desu.   6. Sashimi ya tenpura wa washoku desu.   7. Hai, Nihon no ōkii toshi ni wa yōshoku no resutoran ga takusan arimasu.   8. Watashi wa tenpura (sukiyaki) (no hō) ga suki desu.   9. Watashi wa (sukiyaki) ga ichi-ban suki desu.   10. Hai, watashi wa kekkon shite imasu. (Iie, watashi wa kekkon shite imasen.)

Mondai 29 1. Iie, kono onna no hito wa kodomo ni hanashite imasen. 2. Otoko no hito ni hanashite imasu. 3. Iie, kanojo wa chizu o misete imasen. 4. Otoko no hito ga chizu o misete imasu. 5. Onna no hito ni misete imasu. 6. Iie, kare wa Yōroppa no chizu o watashite imasen. 7. Nihon no chizu o watashite imasu. 8. Onna no hito ga chizu o totte imasu.

Mondai 30 1. Kono e ni onna no hito ga hitori imasu. 2. Otoko no hito mo hitori imasu. 3. Iie, kanojo wa suwatte imasen. 4. Otoko no hito ga suwatte imasu. 5. Onna no ko ga doresu o kite imasu. 6. Hai, kare wa uwagi o kite imasu. 7. Iie, kare wa kōhii o motte imasen. 8. Onna no hito ga kōhii o motte imasu. 9. Iie, kanojo wa kōhii o isu no ue ni oite imasen. 10. Kanojo wa otoko no hito ni (kōhii o) watashite imasu. 11. Migi no te ni kōhii o motte imasu. 12. Okusan kara kōhii o totte imasu. 13. Kodomo wa san-nin imasu. 14. Iie, otoko no ko wa nani mo kaite imasen. 15. Hai, (kare wa) nani ka yonde imasu. 16. Hon o yonde imasu. 17. Iie, ōkii onna no ko wa yonde imasen. 18. Kanojo wa denwa de hanashite imasu. 19. Kanojo wa tatte imasu. 20. Iie, hidari no te ni nani mo motte imasen.

Mondai 31 A) 1. sanjū-hachi 2. rokujū-ichi 3. hyaku-jū-shi 4. kyūjū-roku 5. hyaku-nanajū-ku

B) 1. Jū-ni hiku go wa nana desu. 2. Roku tasu roku wa jū-ni desu. 3. Hachi tasu jū wa jū-hachi desu. 4. Nijū hiku go wa jū- go desu. 5. Kyū(Ku) tasu hachi wa jū-shichi desu. 6. Hachijū-go hiku jū-go wa nanajū desu. 7. Nijū tasu nijū wa yonjū desu. 8. Sanjū-ni tasu jū-ichi wa yonjū-san desu. 9. Gojū-roku hiku hachi wa yonjū-hachi desu. 10. Jū-ni hiku jū-ni wa zero desu. 11. Jū-ku hiku kyū(ku) wa jū desu. 12. Shichi tasu hachi wa jū-go desu. 13. Nijū-go tasu hachi wa sanjū-san desu. 14. Nijū-san hiku ni wa nijū-ichi desu. 15. Jū-hachi tasu ni wa nijū desu.

Mondai 32 1. Iie, kono hito wa hidari no te de kaite imasen. 2. Migi no te de kaite imasu. 3. Iie, kare wa watashi ni kaite imasen. 4. Yamada- san ni kaite imasu. 5. Iie, Yamada-san wa watashi no tomodachi ja arimasen. 6. Hai, watashi wa ima kono mondai o yonde imasu. 7. Watashi wa me de yonde imasu. 8. Iie, watashi wa musuko to mondai o yonde imasen. 9. Iie, watashi wa kimono o kite imasen. 10. Watashi wa ima waishatsu (burausu/sēta) o kite imasu. 11. Iie, watashi wa sensei ni Chūgoku-go de hanashimasen. 12. Nihon-go de hanashimasu.

Mondai 33 1. H 2. D 3. A 4. G 5. O 6. M 7. L 8. K 9. J 10. N 11. E 12. C 13. F 14. I

Mondai 34 A) 1. Jū-ji desu. 2. San-ji-jū-go-fun mae desu. 3. Yo-ji-jū- go-fun desu. 4. Go-ji-han desu. 5. Shichi-ji-ju-ppun desu.

B) 1. Hachi-ji-han ni jimusho e ikimasu. 2. Jū-ni-ji-jū-go-fun ni resutoran de tabemasu. 3. Roku-ji-jū-go-fun mae ni uchi e kaerimasu. 4. Roku-ji ni gakkō e ikimasu. 5. Jū-ji-niju-ppun ni shinbun o yomimasu.

Mondai 35 1. Ku-ji-han ni Tanaka-san wa doko ni imasu ka? 2. Ku-ji-han ni kare wa nani

Mondai 35
(tsuzuki)

o yonde imasu ka? 3. Harada-san wa nani-iro no burausu o kite imasu ka? 4. Harada-san wa nani-iro no kutsu o haite imasu ka? 5. Harada-san wa jū-ji ni Tanaka-san ni nani o watashimasu ka? 6. Jū-ji ni Harada-san wa dare no mae ni tatte imasu ka? 7. Jū-ji ni Harada-san wa tsukue no ue ni nani o oite imasu ka? 8. Tanaka-san wa jū-ji-jū-go-fun ni nani o yomimasu ka? 9. Jū-ji-jū-go-fun ni Harada-san wa nani o shite imasu ka? 10. Jū-ni-ji-han ni Tanaka-san wa dare to resutoran de tabete imasu ka?

Mondai 36

1. Iie, ima jimusho ni imasen. 2. Ima uchi ni imasu. 3. Ima shinbun o yonde imasu. 4. Hai, jimusho de tegami o yomimasu. 5. Jū-ni-ji ni resutoran de tabemasu. 6. Tomodachi to issho ni tabemasu. 7. Iie, kare wa ima hanashite imasen. 8. Uchi de Nihon-go o hanashimasu. 9. Hai, watashi wa ima nani ka yonde imasu. (Hai, watashi wa ima kono mondai o yonde imasu.) 10. Hai, watashi wa uchi de shinbun o yomimasu. (Iie, watashi wa uchi de shinbun o yomimasen.)

Mondai 37

1. Hai, kono e ni onna no hito ga imasu. 2. Iie, kanojo wa Nagoya kara kite imasen. 3. Kyōto kara kite imasu. 4. Iie, Ōsaka e ikimasen. 5. Tōkyō e ikimasu. 6. Iie, hikōki de ikimasen. 7. Kuruma de ikimasu. 8. Iie, watashi wa (Tōkyō kara Nyūyōku made) kuruma de ikimasen. 9. Hikōki de ikimasu. 10. Watashi wa (jimusho kara resutoran made) chikatetsu de ikimasu. / Watashi wa (jimusho kara resutoran made) aruite ikimasu.

Mondai 38

1. Chiisai desu. 2. Hayai desu. 3. Onna no hito desu. 4. Kore wa . . . 5. Go-shujin desu. 6. Anata wa . . . 7. . . . no ushiro ni . . . 8. . . . no shita ni . . . 9. . . . no hidari ni . . . 10. Tatte imasu. 11. Shimete imasu. 12. Dashite imasu. 13. Oite kudasai! 14. Kaerimasu. 15. Nani mo arimasen. 16. Dare mo imasen. 17. Gogo ni-ji desu. 18. Go hiku ni wa . . . 19. Sō desu. 20. Hayaku hanashite kudasai.

Mondai 39

A) 1. ka-yōbi 2. moku-yōbi 3. getsu-yōbi 4. kin-yōbi

B) 1. do-yōbi 2. nichi-yōbi 3. moku-yōbi 4. sui-yōbi 5. getsu-yōbi 6. kin-yōbi 7. kin-yōbi 8. ka-yōbi 9. nichi-yōbi

C) 1. Asatte 2. Ashita 3. Ototoi 4. Kinō

Mondai 40

1. Shichi-ji-jū-go-fun ni kao o araimashita. 2. Asa shinbun o yomimashita ka? 3. Ofisu de "Ohayō" to iimashita. 4. Shigoto wa ku-ji-han ni hajimarimashita ka? 5. Doko de hiru-gohan o tabemashita ka? 6. Takusan taipu shimashita. 7. Jimusho ni Mōgan-san to iu hito ga kimashita. 8. Roku-ji goro uchi e kaerimashita.

Mondai 41

1. Hai, asa hachi-ji goro chikatetsu wa taihen komimasu. 2. Yoru konbanwa to iimasu. 3. Hai, ikimashō. 4. Hai, watashi wa nichi-yōbi ni wa osoku made nete imasu. 5. Iie, kinō eiga o hitori de mimasen deshita. 6. Iie, book wa Nihon-go no kotoba ja arimasen. 7. Book wa Nihon-go de hon to iimasu. 8. Watashi wa Berurittsu to iu gakkō e ikimasu. 9. Iie, Honda to iu kuruma wa takaku arimasen. 10. Nihon de ichi-ban ōkii toshi wa Tōkyō to iimasu.

Mondai 42   1. Hai, hikōki mo densha mo Tōkyō kara Ōsaka e ikimasu.   2. Iie, densha wa Kyōto e ikimasu ga, hikōki wa Kyōto e ikimasen.   3. Hikōki ga Miyazaki e ikimasu.   4. Kono densha no namae wa Kodama to iimasu.   5. Tōkyō kara Ōsaka made hikōki de ichi-jikan-go-fun kakarimasu.   6. Tōkyō kara Kyōto made densha de ni-jikan-nijū-go-fun kakarimasu.   7. Densha no hō ga osoi desu.   8. Anata wa ototoi no asa Kyōto e ikimashita.   9. Iie, anata no densha wa konde imasen deshita.   10. Anata wa yūbe osoku Tōkyō e kaette kimashita.

Mondai 43   1. Hai, Yamada-san to Sasaki-san wa tomodachi desu.   2. Iie, onaji kaisha de hataraite imasen.   3. Hai, futari wa onaji gakkō o demashita.   4. I-sshūkan ni ichi-do futari de shokuji o shimasu.   5. Ongaku-kai e ikimasu.   6. Iie, hitori de ikimasen.   7. Yamada-san to ikimasu.   8. Ongaku-kai no ato de "Asutoria"-resutoran e ikimasu.   9. Hai, ima Yamada-san wa denwa shite imasu.   10. Hai, do-yōbi no yūgata resutoran wa taihen komimasu.

Mondai 44   1. Takagi-san wa Yamada-san no hisho desu.   2. Hai, asa hayaku okimasu.   3. Shichi-ji ni asa-gohan o tabemasu.   4. Tamago to tōsuto o tabemasu.   5. Chōshoku-chū ni yomimasu.   6. Iie, kanojo wa takushii de kaisha e ikimasen.   7. Taipu shimasu.   8. Go-ji-go-fun goro kaisha o dete, chikatetsu no eki e ikimasu.   9. Hai, chikatetsu no eki wa kanojo no uchi no mae ni arimasu.   10. Ban-gohan o tabete kara, terebi o mimasu.

Mondai 45   1. Hai, mō aimashita. / Iie, mada atte imasen.   2. Hai, mō tabemashita. / Iie, mada tabete imasen.   3. Hai, mō denwa shimashita. / Iie, mada denwa shite imasen.   4. Hai, mō kakimashita. / Iie, mada kaite imasen.   5. Hai, mō hajimarimashita. / Iie, mada hajimatte imasen.

Mondai 46   1. Harada-san wa ima doko ni imasu ka?   2. Jimusho de wa nani ga takusan arimasu ka?   3. Harada-san wa nani o taipu shimasu ka?   4. Harada-san wa kopii o nan-mai torimasu ka?   5. Kanojo wa itsu jimusho o dete, uchi e kaerimasu ka?   6. Kinō wa nan-yōbi deshita ka?   7. Itsu osoku made nete imashita ka?   8. Kinō no gogo uchi de nani o shimashita ka?   9. Kinō dare to eiga ni ikimashita ka?   10. Kinō itsu uchi e kaerimashita ka?

Mondai 47   1. Kare wa Shibata-san ni aimashita.   2. Gakkō e ikimasu.   3. I- sshūkan ni san-do gakkō e ikimasu.   4. Shigoto no ato de gakkō e ikimasu.   5. Iie, gakkō de ongaku o benkyō shite imasen.   6. Eigo o benkyō shite imasu.   7. Iie, kyōshitsu de wa hon o yomimasen.   8. Kyōshitsu de wa Eigo dake hanashimasu.   9. Kyōshitsu ni seito wa hitori imasu.   10. Kare no benkyō wa gogo shichi-ji-jū-go-fun ni hajimarimasu.   11. Jugyō wa ni-jikan-han kakarimasu.   12. Hai, konban futari wa issho ni Berurittsu-gakkō e ikimasu.

Mondai 48   1. Kanojo wa Ōta-san ni konnichiwa to iimashita.   2. Kare wa yūbe tomodachi to eiga ni ikimashita.   3. Kare wa Furansu no eiga o mimashita.   4. "Ashita Pari de" to iu eiga deshita.   5. Iie, kanojo wa sono eiga o mada mite imasen.   6. Ōta-san ga konsāto no kippu o motte imasu.   7. Sore wa "Bētōben no yūbe" to iu konsāto desu.   8. Konsāto wa hachi-ji ni hajimatte, jū-ji-han goro owarimasu.   9. Konsāto wa konsāto- hōru de arimasu.   10. Kare to kanojo wa shichi-ji-han ni konsāto-hōru no mae de aimasu.

Mondai 48 *(tsuzuki)*	11. Futari wa basu de ikimasu. 12. Basu wa basu-noriba kara dete imasu.
Mondai 49	1. Kotoshi wa sen-kyūhyaku-nijū-ni-nen desu. Kyonen wa sen-kyūhyaku-nijū-ichi-nen deshita. Rainen wa sen-kyūhyaku-nijū-san-nen desu. 2. Kotoshi wa sen-happyaku-yonjū-shichi-nen desu. Kyonen wa sen-happyaku-yonjū-roku-nen deshita. Rainen wa sen-happyaku-yonjū-hachi-nen desu. 3. Kotoshi wa sen-nanahyaku-nijū-ku-nen desu. Kyonen wa sen-nanahyaku-nijū-hachi-nen deshita. Rainen wa sen-nanahyaku-sanjū-nen desu. 4. Kotoshi wa sen-gohyaku-san-nen desu. Kyonen wa sen-gohyaku-ni-nen deshita. Rainen wa sen-gohyaku-yo-nen desu. 5. Kotoshi wa sen-roppyaku-gojū-ichi-nen desu. Kyonen wa sen-roppyaku-gojū-nen deshita. Rainen wa sen-roppyaku-gojū-ni-nen desu.
Mondai 50	1. Hai, Tōkyō no natsu wa atsui desu. 2. Hai, natsu wa tokidoki ame ga furimasu. 3. Hai, fuyu wa tokidoki yuki ga furimasu. 4. Iie, aki ni wa sakura no hana o mimasen. 5. Haru ni sakura no hana o mimasu. 6. Hai, ku-gatsu ni wa yoru suzushiku narimasu. 7. Iie, haru ni wa amari ame ga furimasen. 8. Aki ni wa yuki wa mettani furimasen. 9. Iie, watashi wa itsumo Nihon-go de tegami o kakimasen. 10. Iie, watashi wa natsu ni ōbā o kimasen.
Mondai 51	1. Ima, Noguchi-san wa Ōsaka kara denwa shite imasu. 2. Hai, Ōsaka de wa sengetsu ame ga mainichi furimashita. 3. Iie, yuki wa furimasen deshita. 4. Iie, sengetsu yori waruku narimasen deshita. 5. Ōsaka no kongetsu no tenki wa yoku narimashita. 6. Ōsaka no kyō no tenki wa hare desu. 7. Iie, Ōsaka de wa yuki wa mettani furimasen. 8. Tōkyō no hō ga samui desu. 9. Noguchi-san wa sengetsu kara Ōsaka ni imasu. 10. Noguchi-san wa raigetsu Tōkyō e kaette kimasu. 11. Hai, samui desu. / Iie, samuku arimasen. 12. (Natsu / Fuyu / Aki / Haru) ga ichi- ban suki desu.
Mondai 52	1. akaruku narimasu. 2. atsuku narimasu. 3. hi ga nagaku narimasu. 4. Harada-san wa Tanaka-san no hisho ni narimashita. 5. waruku narimashita.
Mondai 53	1. Anata wa dono kisetsu (itsu) ga ichi-ban suki desu ka? 2. Nan no tame ni hikōki ga demasen ka? 3. Anata wa futsū asa-gohan ni nani o tabemasu ka? 4. Itsu (Donna toki) rēnkōto o kimasu ka? 5. Kōen de nani o shimasu ka? 6. Donna toki (Itsu) Nihon-go no tēpu o kikimasu ka? 7. Anata-tachi wa itsu Hokkaidō e ikimasu ka? 8. Tōkyō de wa nani ga yoku furimasu ka?
Mondai 54	A) 1. Roku-gatsu yokka desu. 2. Go-gatsu nanoka desu. 3. San- gatsu kokonoka desu. 4. Shichi-gatsu tōka desu. 5. Jū-ni- gatsu tsuitachi desu. 6. Shi-gatsu futsuka desu. 7. Hachi-gatsu yōka desu. B) 1. Jū-ichi-gatsu yōka ni demashita. 2. Shi-gatsu mikka ni moraimashita. 3. Shichi-gatsu muika ni aimashita. 4. Ku-gatsu tōka ni kaerimashita. 5. Ni-gatsu itsuka ni kakimashita. 6. Go-gatsu jū-roku-nichi ni ikimashita.
Mondai 55	1. Asatte wa jū-gatsu jū-ni-nichi desu. 2. Iie, kinō wa moku-yōbi ja arimasen deshita. 3. Suzuki-san wa asatte Hiroshima e ikimasu. 4. Hikōki de ikimasu. 5. Ni-jikan gurai kakarimasu. 6. (Hiroshima e) shigoto de ikimasu.

Mondai 55
(tsuzuki)

7. Suzuki-san no shuttchō wa yōka-kan desu.   8. Iie, nichi-yōbi ni wa shigoto o shimasen.   9. Nichi-yōbi ni gorufu o shimasu.   10. Hiroshima Hoteru ni tomarimasu.   11. Hai, shitte imasu. (Iie, shirimasen.)   12. Hai, ikitai desu. (Iie, ikitaku arimasen.)

Mondai 56

1. (Kyūka ni) Hakone ni ikimashita.   2. Kuruma de ikimashita.   3. Hai, (Hakone made no michi wa) utsukushikatta desu.   4. (Hakone de mainichi) gorufu o shimashita.   5. Iie, amari jōzu ni narimasen deshita.   6. (Yama no tenki wa) totemo yokatta desu.   7. Hai, (Asa to yoru wa) suzushikatta desu. 8. (Yamada-san wa) hachi-gatsu nijū-roku-nichi ni kaette kimashita. 9. (Tōkyō wa) mada atsukatta desu.   10. (Tōkyō no tomodachi ni) o-miyage o motte kaerimashita.

Mondai 57

1. Nihon-go o hanasu no wa yasashii desu.   2. Hitori de ryokō suru no ga suki desu.   3. Ongaku-kai e iku no wa tanoshikatta desu.   4. Nihon-go de kazoeru no wa muzukashii desu.   5. Kono mondai o suru no wa muzukashikatta desu.

Mondai 58

1. Iie, kare wa senshū kaisha ni imasen deshita.   2. Kyūka o totte imashita. 3. Yama e ikimashita.   4. Hai, kare mo yama ga (taihen) suki desu.   5. Hai, yama no tenki wa yokatta desu.   6. Iie, kaze wa tsuyoku arimasen deshita. 7. Iie, Tanaka-san wa (kare wa) mada kyūka o totte imasen.   8. Raigetsu kyūka o torimasu.   9. Hai, kazoku to issho ni ikimasu.   10. Kare wa umi e ikimasu.   11. Iie, kare no kyūka wa san-shūkan ja arimasen.   12. Kyūka wa ni-shūkan desu.

Mondai 59

1. Kanojo wa nekutai o kai ni ikimashita.   2. Nekutai-uriba de ten-in ni hanashimashita.   3. Iie, ten-in wa Toshiko-san ni nekutai o ju-ppon misemasen deshita.   4. San-bon misemashita.   5. Hai, kanojo wa nekutai no nedan o kikimashita.   6. Hai, kanojo wa nekutai o kaimashita.   7. Aka to ao no (nekutai) o kaimashita.   8. Iie, sono nekutai wa sanzen-en ja arimasen deshita.   9. Nisen- nihyaku-en (2,200-en) deshita.   10. Iie, kanojo wa ten-in ni chōdo nisen-nihyaku-en o watashimasen deshita.   11. Ichiman-en (10,000-en) watashimashita.   12. Ten-in wa otsuri o nanasen-happyaku-en watashimashita.

Mondai 60

1. hyaku-gojū   2. sanbyaku-rokujū   3. sen-roppyaku-sanjū   4. nanasen-kyūhyaku-gojū   5. niman-hassen   6. nanaman-sanzen- gohyaku-rokujū 7. nijū-niman-yonsen-happyaku   8. sanjū-goman   9. yonjū-sanman-yonsen-nihyaku   10. rokujū-goman-hassen-nanahyaku-gojū

Mondai 61

1. Seito wa mada kyōshitsu ni imasu. Seito wa mō kyōshitsu ni imasen. 2. Kagi wa mō poketto ni arimasen. Kagi wa mada poketto ni arimasu. 3. Tanaka-san wa mō jimusho ni imasen. Tanaka-san wa mada jimusho ni imasu.

Mondai 62

1. Watashi wa eiga-kan e eiga o mi ni ikimashita.   2. Anata wa gakkō e Nihon-go o hanashi ni kimasu.   3. Satō-san wa kaisha e tegami o kaki ni kimashita.   4. Michiko-san wa yūbin-kyoku e tegami o dashi ni ikimashita. 5. Kare wa kaisha e shigoto o shi ni ikimasu.

Mondai 63 1. Iie, kare wa zasshi o kaimasen deshita. 2. Shinbun to tabako o kaimashita. 3. Iie, bōru-pen o kaimasen deshita. 4. (Chikatetsu-noriba no) Shinbun-uriba de kaimashita. 5. Hai, tabako mo arimashita. 6. Iie, Igirisu no tabako wa arimasen deshita. 7. Nihon no tabako ga arimashita. 8. Hai, kare wa nedan o kikimashita. 9. Iie, sono hoka ni wa nani mo kaimasen deshita. 10. Zenbu de hyaku-sanjū-en ni narimashita.

Mondai 64 1. Kōbe kara Tōkyō made wa 590-kiro-mētoru arimasu. 2. Nagoya kara wa Hiroshima no hō ga tōi desu. 3. Kōbe kara wa Shizuoka no hō ga chikai desu. 4. Kyōto kara Hiroshima made no hō ga tōi desu. 5. Ōsaka kara Shizuoka made no hō ga chikai desu.

Mondai 65 1. B 2. I 3. A 4. M 5. C 6. K 7. J 8. H 9. L 10. E 11. F 12. G

Mondai 66 1. Watashi wa uchi o kau okane ga arimasen. 2. Buchō wa hiru-gohan o taberu jikan ga arimasen. 3. Hirai-san wa eiga o miru jikan ga arimasen. 4. Ōkii terebi o kau okane ga arimasen.

Mondai 67 1. Tabun 12-ji ni taberu deshō. 2. Tabun terebi o miru deshō. 3. Tabun Yoshikawa-san ni au deshō. 4. Tabun depāto de kaimono o suru deshō.

Mondai 68 1. Kono tsukue wa omo-sugimasu. 2. Atarashii kuruma wa taka- sugimasu. 3. Kono mondai wa muzukashi-sugimasu. 4. Kyō wa samu-sugimasu.

Mondai 69 1. Depāto wa yoru jū-ni-ji ni shimatte imasu. 2. Iie, depāto ni hairu koto ga dekimasen. 3. Depāto wa shimatte iru kara desu. 4. Hai, watashi wa gakkō kara resutoran made aruku koto ga dekimasu. 5. Iie, Tōkyō kara Hiroshima made aruku koto wa dekimasen. 6. Hai, tō-sugimasu. 7. Tōkyō kara Hiroshima made wa tō-sugiru kara desu.

Mondai 70 1. Iie, kanojo wa depāto e uwagi o kai ni ikimasen deshita. 2. Sūtsukēsu o kai ni ikimashita. 3. Ten-in ni hanashimashita. 4. Iie, yōfuku-uriba e ikimasen deshita. 5. Kaban-uriba e ikimashita. 6. Iie, kyūsen-en no sūtsukēsu o kaimasen deshita. 7. Taka-sugita kara desu. 8. Hai, hoka no ga arimashita. 9. Hai, mō sukoshi yasui no o kaimashita. 10. Nisen-en deshita.

Mondai 71 1. Okane nashi de shinbun o kau koto ga dekimasen. / Tanaka-san wa okane o motte imasu kara, shinbun o kau koto ga dekimasu. 2. Kagi nashi de doā o akeru koto ga dekimasen. / Suzuki-san wa kagi o motte imasu kara, doā o akeru koto ga dekimasu. 3. Taipuraitā nashi de tegami o taipu suru koto ga dekimasen. / Hisho wa taipuraitā o motte imasu kara, tegami o taipu suru koto ga dekimasu. 4. Megane nashi de hon o yomu koto ga dekimasen. / Sensei wa megane o motte imasu kara, hon o yomu koto ga dekimasu. 5. Kippu nashi de eiga-kan ni hairu koto ga dekimasen. / Satō- san wa kippu o motte imasu kara, eiga-kan ni hairu koto ga dekimasu. 6. Kuruma nashi de Yokohama e iku koto ga dekimasen. / Watashi wa kuruma o motte imasu kara, Yokohama e iku koto ga dekimasu. 7. Pasupōto nashi de Nihon kara deru koto ga dekimasen. / Satō-san wa pasupōto o motte imasu kara, Nihon kara deru koto ga dekimasu.

Mondai 72

1. Iie, kyō hayaku uchi e kaette wa ikemasen. / Iie, kyō hayaku uchi e kaeranai de kudasai.   2. Iie, shigoto-chū ni eiga ni itte wa ikemasen. / Iie, shigoto-chū ni eiga ni ikanai de kudasai.   3. Iie, uwagi o nuide wa ikemasen. / Iie, uwagi o nuganai de kudasai.   4. Iie, kutsu o haite wa ikemasen. / Iie, kutsu o hakanai de kudasai.   5. Iie, fōku de sashimi o tabete wa ikemasen. / Iie, fōku de sashimi o tabenai de kudasai.   6. Iie, enpitsu de sain o shite wa ikemasen. / Iie, enpitsu de sain o shinai de kudasai.   7. Iie, mado o shimete wa ikemasen. / Iie, mado o shimenai de kudasai.   8. Iie, ima jisho o tsukatte wa ikemasen. / Iie, ima jisho o tsukawanai de kudasai.   9. Iie, raishū kyūka o totte wa ikemasen. / Iie, raishū kyūka o toranai de kudasai.   10. Iie, ashita denwa shite wa ikemasen. / Iie, ashita denwa shinai de kudasai.

Mondai 73

1. kikitai desu   2. hanashitai desu   3. sumitai desu   4. yasumitai desu   5. kitai desu   6. noritai desu

Mondai 74

1. (Harada-san no kaisha wa) Tōkyō ni arimasu.   2. (Kanojo wa maitsuki kaisha kara) gekkyū o moraimasu.   3. (Kanojo wa gekkyū no hoka ni) bōnasu o moraimasu.   4. Futsū ichi-nen ni ni-do bōnasu ga demasu.   5. Kanojo wa kyonen no shi-gatsu ni (kono kaisha ni) hairimashita.   6. Kanojo no kyonen no gekkyū wa jū-niman-en deshita.   7. Hai, Ikeda-san wa Harada-san to onaji kaisha de hataraite imasu.   8. Ikeda-san wa kono kaisha ni nagai aida tsutomete iru kara desu. / Ikeda-san wa Harada-san yori nagaku kono kaisha ni tsutomete iru kara desu.   9. Hai, Ikeda-san mo Harada-san mo kaimono ga suki desu.   10. Futari wa yoku gekkyū-bi ni (issho ni) kaimono ni ikimasu.   11. Hai, watashi mo kaimono ga suki desu. / Iie, watashi wa kaimono ga suki ja arimasen.   12. Iie, watashi wa bōnasu o moraimasen. / Hai, watashi mo bōnasu o moraimasu.

Mondai 75

1. Isogashii toki, eiga o miru koto ga dekimasen.   2. Kaisha e iku toki, nekutai o shimasu.   3. Kyōto e iku toki, Shinkansen ni norimasu.   4. Tabako o suu toki, rōka e demasu.   5. Nihon-go o benkyō suru toki, Eigo o hanasanaide kudasai.   6. Heya ga akarukunai toki, denki o tsukemasu.   7. Bifuteki ga tabetai toki, doko e ikimasu ka?   8. Hikōki ni noru toki, hikōjō e ikimasu.   9. Ame ga futte iru toki, rēnkōto o kimasu.   10. Hitori de mochiageru koto ga dekinai toki, dare ka ni tanomimasu.

Mondai 76

1. Hisho wa kuruma o kau koto ga dekimasen. Hisho wa kuruma ga kaemasen.   2. Tanaka-san wa kyō Hiroshima e iku koto ga dekimasen. Tanaka-san wa kyō Hiroshima e ikemasen.   3. Satō-san wa Chūgoku-go o hanasu koto ga dekimasen. Satō-san wa Chūgoku- go ga hanasemasen.   4. Kanji o kaku koto ga dekimasen. Kanji ga kakemasen.   5. Anata wa kongetsu kyūka o toru koto ga dekimasen. Anata wa kongetsu kyūka ga toremasen.

Mondai 77

1. Hai, moshi watashi ga o-kanemochi nara, Kyaderakku o kaitai desu.   2. Hai, sashimi ga tabetai nara, Nihon no resutoran e ikimasu.   3. Hai, moshi anata ga tenisu ga jōzu nara, issho ni tenisu o shitai desu.   4. Hai, shigoto ga isogashikereba, eiga ni iku koto ga dekimasen.   5. Atsukereba, ōbā o nugimasu.   6. Hai, Tanaka-san ni aeba, itsumo kaisha no koto o hanashimasu.   7. Hai, sono sūtsukēsu ga takakunakereba, kaimasu.   8. Hai, ashita ame ga furanakereba, gorufu o shimasu.   9. Hai, Nihon-go o

Mondai 77
(tsuzuki)

benkyō shitakereba, Berurittsu e ikimasu.   10. Iie, kōhii o takusan nomeba, yoru nemuru koto ga dekimasen.

Mondai 78

1. Iie, kanojo wa gakkō e iku tokoro ja arimasen.   2. Depāto e iku tokoro desu.   3. Iie, (kanojo wa) depāto ni sukāto o kai ni iku tokoro ja arimasen. 4. Handobaggu o kai ni ikimasu.   5. Kanojo no handobaggu wa furuku natta kara desu.   6. Kanojo wa Keiko-san to hanashite imasu.   7. Hai, kanojo mo atarashii handobaggu o kaitai desu.   8. Hai, depāto de handobaggu ga kaemasu.   9. Iie, kanojo wa ima isogashiku arimasen.   10. Kanojo wa go-ji ni eiga-kan ni ikimasu.   11. Hai, kanojo wa Michiko-san to issho ni depāto ni ikimasu.   12. Iie, watashi wa kanojo-tachi to issho ni depāto ni ikimasen.

Mondai 79

1. Okane o kaeru tame ni, ginkō e ikimasu.   2. Shinkansen ni norikaeru tame ni, Tōkyō eki de orimasu.   3. Kusuri o kau tame ni, kusuri-ya e ikimasu. 4. Te o fuku tame ni, taoru o tsukaimasu.   5. Nihon e iku tame ni, pasupōto ga irimasu.   6. Kurejitto-kādo de harau tame ni, sain o shimasu.   7. Maemotte yakusoku suru tame ni, denwa o shimasu.   8. Yoku nemuru tame ni, osake o nomimasu.

Mondai 80

1. Watashi wa kesa Tanaka-san ni atta toki, kare to hanashimashita. 2. Nihon-go o takusan benkyō shita toki, tsukaremashita.   3. Kinō waishatsu o katta toki, ten-in ni okane o watashimashita.   4. Yamada-san wa yūbe Tōkyō ni tsuita toki, watashi ni denwa shimashita.   5. Byōki ni natta toki, byōin ni ikimashita.   6. Yamashita-san wa senshū kaze o hiita toki, kusuri o nomimashita.   7. Nihon taishikan e itta toki, watashi wa biza o moraimashita.   8. Kyonen watashi wa Yōroppa ni itta toki, hikōki ni norimashita.

Mondai 81

1. Kinō ame no naka o kasa nashi de aruita kara desu.   2. Hiru-yasumi ni ikimashita.   3. Hai, kaze o hiite iru toki, atama ga itai desu.   4. Kibun wa warui desu.   5. Hai, tsukarete iru toki, byōki ni nari-yasui desu.   6. Iie, warui kaze o hiite ireba, kaisha e ikemasen.   7. Isha wa byōin de hatarakimasu. 8. Futsū wa fuyu ni kaze o hikimasu.   9. Iie, kusuri wa aji ga yoku arimasen. 10. Hai, kusuri o nomimasu.

Mondai 82

1. Anata wa nan-yōbi ni gakkō e irasshaimashita ka?   2. Anata wa ima Nihon-go o benkyō shite irasshaimasu ka?   3. Berurittsu no jūsho o gozonji desu ka?   4. Tanaka-san wa nan to osshaimashita ka?   5. Konsāto e itsu irasshaimasu ka?   6. Mō shokuji o nasaimashita ka? 7. Kore wa Tanaka-san no kuruma de gozaimasu ka?   8. Ashita Tanaka-san ni o-ai ni narimasu ka? 9. Tegami o o-yomi ni narimashita ka?   10. Itsu sukii ni irasshaimasu ka?

Mondai 83

1. Hai, Suzuki-san wa "Shitsurei desu ga" to iimashita.   2. Hai, Yamada-san wa "Dōmo shitsurei shimashita" to iimashita.   3. Yamada-san wa hoka no mise demo kaimasu.   4. Suzuki-san wa san-shūkan mae ni kekkon shita to iimashita.   5. Suzuki-san no go-shujin wa Amerika no ginkō ni tsutomete imasu.   6. Yamada-san wa kodomo ga futari aru to iimashita.   7. Iie, Yamada-san wa musume-san no namae ga Haruko da to iimasen deshita. 8. Yamada- san no musume-san no namae wa Akiko to iimasu.   9. Hai, Yamada- san to Suzuki-san wa Suzuki-san no go-shujin ni tsuite hanashimashita.   10. Hai, futari wa kaimono no ato de, ocha o nomimasu.

Mondai 84 1. Saitō-san wa ima Kyōto ni imasu. 2. Kyō Saitō-san wa hima desu.
3. Hai, Honda-san wa Saitō-san no tomodachi desu. 4. Iie, Honda-san wa
ima Kyōto de shigoto o shite imasen. 5. Hai, Kyōto ni wa takusan no o-tera
ga arimasu. 6. Honda-san wa (Kyōto e) o-tera o mi ni kimashita. 7. Iie,
Honda-san wa Kokedera e iku michi o shirimasen. 8. Futari wa o-miyage-ya
de Kyōto no chizu o mimashita. 9. Futari wa michi ni mayotta toki,
omawarisan ni kikimashita. 10. Hai, moshi watashi ga michi ni mayottara,
omawarisan ni kikimasu. 11. Hai, omawarisan wa takusan no kankō-basu
ga mieru tokoro ga Kokedera da to iimashita. 12. Hai, watashi mo
Kokedera ni ikitai desu. / Iie, watashi wa Kokedera ni ikitaku arimasen.

Mondai 85 1. Ima hon o mite iru hito wa Shumitto-san desu. 2. Hai, kare wa Hiragana o
yomu koto ga dekimasu. 3. Shumitto-san ga itsumo iku hon-ya wa Ginza ni
arimasu. 4. "Yukiguni" wa Kawabata Yasunari ga kaita hon desu.
5. Hai, kare wa Kawabata Yasunari no hon ga suki desu. 6. Hon-ya no ten-in
wa "Yukiguni" wa muzukashii to iimashita. 7. Hai, Shumitto-san wa Nihon-go
no jisho o motte iru node, yomu koto ga dekiru to iimashita. 8. Muzukashii
kotoba ga aru toki, Shumitto-san wa jisho de kotoba no imi o benkyō
shimasu. 9. Wakaranai toki, Tanaka-san ni kikimasu. 10. Tanaka-san wa
(Nihon-go de wakaranai toki), itsu demo kiite kudasai to iimashita.

Mondai 86 1. J 2. D 3. G 4. A 5. H 6. I 7. C 8. E 9. B

Mondai 87 1. Kare wa kūkō made ikitai to untenshu ni iimashita. 2. Yo-ji no hikōki ni
noru to iimashita. 3. Hai, untenshu wa san-ji-han made ni iku koto ga dekiru
to kotaemashita. 4. Hai, kare wa kūkō made ikura kakaru ka to kikimashita.
5. Hai, untenshu wa sanzen-gohyaku-en gurai da to kotaemashita.
6. Kōsoku-dōro wa konde imashita. 7. Yo-ji-ju-ppun mae ni kūkō ni
tsukimashita. 8. Iie, kare wa kūkō no kauntā de kippu o kaimasen deshita.
9. Kauntā de kaban o watashimashita. 10. Hai, kare wa hikōki ni
maniaimashita.

Mondai 88 1. Densha ga nan-ji ni deru ka to kikimashita. 2. Ginza-dōri wa doko ni
aru ka to kikimashita. 3. Ikura ka to kikimashita. 4. Ikura datta ka to
kikimashita. 5. Doko ni sunde iru ka to kikimashita. 6. Doko de katta ka
to kikimashita. 7. Itsu kaetta ka to kikimashita.   8. Dare to hanashita ka
to kikimashita. 9. Nan-jikan gurai kakaru ka to kikimashita.   10. Kazoku
wa nan-nin ka to kikimashita.

Mondai 89 1. Iie, Satō-san ga (kare ga) jimusho e kita toki, okyaku ga kite imasen
deshita. 2. Tanaka-san kara denwa ga arimashita. 3. Hai, Tanaka-san wa
nani ka dengon o shimashita. 4. Iie, kare wa ni-ji ni kuru to iimasen deshita.
5. Hai, kanojo wa yūbin ga kite iru to iimashita. 6. Hai, hisho wa sore o ima
yomu ka dōka Satō-san ni tazunemashita. 7. Kare wa Noguchi-san to
shokuji ni iku to iimashita. 8. Hai, kanojo wa nan-ji ni jimusho e kaette kuru
ka to kikimashita. 9. Kare wa ni-ji goro kaette kuru to iimashita. 10. Iie, kare
wa konban gekijō de Tanaka-san to au to iimasen deshita.

Mondai 90 1. Futari wa (Akemi-san to Mieko-san wa) tanjōbi no pātii ni tsuite hanashite
imasu. 2. Kare no pātii wa raishū desu. 3. Hai, Satō-san wa Akemi-san o
shōtai shimashita. 4. Satō-san wa Mieko-san ni (subarashii) kōsui o
agemashita. 5. Akemi-san wa Satō-san kara nani mo moraimasen deshita.

Mondai 91

1. omawarisan ni michi o oshiete moraimasu.   2. kaisha kara kyūryō o haratte moraimasu.   3. kanai ni osake o motte kite moraimashita.
4. otōsan ni (kara) omocha o katte moraimashita.   5. okusan ni ban-gohan o tsukutte moraimasu.   6. Yoshida-san ni doā o shimete moraimashita.
7. Shimizu-san (Go-shujin) ni atarashii ōbā o katte moraimasu.   8. seito ni enpitsu o watashite moraimasu.   9. hisho ni taipu shite moraimasu.
10. musuko ni kuruma o aratte moraimasu.

Mondai 92

1. Kare wa taihen isogashikatta kara desu.   2. Kondō-san ga jibun de taipu shimashita.   3. Iie, kare wa Imai-san to issho ni bā ni iku koto ga dekimasen.   4. Shigoto no ato de kare wa uchi e kaerimasu.   5. Iie, kanojo wa genki ja arimasen.   6. Kanojo wa kaze o hikimashita.   7. Nete inakereba ikenai kara desu.   8. Kondō-san no uchi de wa kare ga ryōri o tsukuranakereba ikemasen.   9. Iie, kare wa ryōri o tsukuru koto ga dekimasen.   10. Hai, watashi mo jibun de ryōri o tsukuru koto ga dekimasu. / Iie, watashi wa jibun de ryōri o tsukuru koto ga dekimasen.

Mondai 93

1. Tegami o taipu shinakereba ikemasen./ Tegami o taipu shinakute mo ii desu.   2. Shinbun o yomanakereba ikemasen./Shinbun o yomanakute mo ii desu.   3. Atarashii kuruma o kawanakereba ikemasen./Atarashii kuruma o kawanakute mo ii desu.   4. Genkin de harawanakereba ikemasen./Genkin de harawanakute mo ii desu.   5. Kanji de namae o kakanakereba ikemasen./Kanji de namae o kakanakute mo ii desu.   6. Ashita gakkō e ikanakereba ikemasen./Ashita gakkō e ikanakute mo ii desu.   7. Ima heya o denakereba ikemasen./Ima heya o denakute mo ii desu.

Mondai 94

1. Kuruma o tori ni kimashita.   2. Iie, owarimasen deshita.   3. Iie, mamorimasen deshita.   4. Ogawa-san wa shichi-ji ni daiji na yakusoku ga arimasu.   5. Iie, soko e kuruma nashi de iku koto ga dekimasen.   6. Hai, kuruma o shūri suru hito wa Ogawa-san ni kuruma o kashite agemasu.
7. Iie, okane o harawanakute mo ii desu.   8. Iie, watashi wa Ogawa-san no kuruma ga Toyota ka dōka shirimasen.   9. Hai, watashi wa ashita no gogo made ni naoru to omoimasu. / Iie, watashi wa ashita no gogo made ni naoru to omoimasen.   10. Watashi wa jibun de shūri shimasu./ Dare ka ni shūri shite moraimasu.

Mondai 95

1. Hai (Tanaka-san ni aitakereba), maemotte denwa shinakereba ikemasen.
2. Hai, hajime ni uketsuke o tōranakereba ikemasen.   3. Iie, nekutai o shite inakute mo ii desu.   4. Iie, okyaku ni osake o agenakute mo ii desu.   5. Hai, kutsu o nuganakereba ikemasen.   6. Hai, kippu o motte inakereba ikemasen.   7. Iie, pasupōto o motte inakute mo ii desu.   8. Iie, ojigi o shinakute mo ii desu.   9. Hai, narubeku hayaku kaesanakereba ikemasen.
10. Hai, terebi o kesanakereba ikemasen.   11. Iie, maemotte yoyaku shinakute mo ii desu.   12. Hai, yakusoku o torikesanakereba ikemasen.

Mondai 96

1. a) Konban no shokuji o tsukuranakereba ikemasen. b) Konban no shokuji o tsukutte wa ikemasen. c) Konban no shokuji o tsukuranakute mo ii desu.
2. a) Inoue-san o pātii ni shōtai shinakereba ikemasen. b) Inoue-san o pātii ni shōtai shite wa ikemasen. c) Inoue-san o pātii ni shōtai shinakute mo ii desu.   3. a) Tonari no neko o sagasanakereba ikemasen. b) Tonari no

Mondai 96
(tsuzuki)

neko o sagashite wa ikemasen. c) Tonari no neko o sagasanakute mo ii desu.

Mondai 97

1. Watashi-tachi wa Kyūshū no Kagoshima e iku tokoro desu. 2. Iie, arimasen. 3. Densha de ikimasu. 4. Ryokō-dairiten de kippu o yoyaku shimashita. 5. Hiroshima o tōtte imasu. 6. Hakata de densha o norikaenakereba ikemasen. 7. Jū-roku-jikan gurai kakarimasu. 8. Hai, arimasu. / Iie, arimasen. 9. Hai, arimasu. / Iie, arimasen. 10. Hai, yoku ryokō shimasu. / Iie, amari ryokō shimasen. 11. Hai, ryokō-dairiten de kippu o yoyaku shite moraimasu. / Iie, ryokō-dairiten de kippu o yoyaku shite moraimasen. 12. Hikōki (ya densha) (ya jidōsha) (ya basu) o tsukaimasu.

Mondai 98

1. Watashi wa bosu to Nihon e iku tsumori desu. 2. Hikōki de iku tsumori desu. 3. Ni-shūkan Nihon ni iru tsumori desu. 4. Tōkyō Hoteru ni tomaru tsumori desu. 5. Tanaka-san ni au tsumori desu. 6. Hai, watashi no kodomo ni o-miyage o kau tsumori desu.

Mondai 99

1. Nihon ni wa yottsu no ōkii shima ga arimasu. 2. Ichi-ban chiisai shima wa Shikoku desu. 3. Ichi-ban ōkii shima wa Honshū desu. 4. Ichi-ban minami ni aru shima wa Kyūshū desu. 5. Hokkaidō ga ichi-ban samui desu.
6. Tōkyō, Ōsaka, Yokohama, Nagoya, Kōbe (nado) 7. Kyōto ni takusan no furui o-tera ya jinja ga arimasu. 8. Sapporo wa Hokkaidō ni arimasu. 9. Hai, Honshū kara densha de Kyūshū e iku koto ga dekimasu. 10. Hiroshima wa Honshū ni arimasu.

Mondai 100

1. Hai, arimasu. (Hai, Nihon ni wa ōkii kaisha ga takusan arimasu.) 2. Hai, sō desu. (Hai, Toyota ya Nissan wa jidōsha no mēkā desu.) 3. Hai, shitte imasu. / Iie, shirimasen. 4. (Sonii ya Tōshiba wa) terebi ya bideo o tsukutte imasu. 5. Hitachi ya Matsushita ya Sanyō nado desu. 6. Hai, urimasu. (Hai, Nihon no kuruma no mēkā wa sono seihin o gaikoku ni urimasu.)
7. (Nihon-sei no kamera no namae wa) Kyanon ya Nikon ya Minoruta desu.
8. (Nihon no bōeki-shōhin wa) kamotsusen de (gaikoku e) hakobaremasu.
9. (Nihon wa sekiyu o) yunyū shite imasu. 10. (Nihon wa sekiyu o) Chūkintō kara yunyū shite imasu. 11. Sekiyu wa tankā de Nihon ni hakobaremasu.
12. Hai, (watashi no kaisha wa Nihon no kaisha to torihiki ga) arimasu. / Iie, (watashi no kaisha wa Nihon no kaisha to torihiki ga) arimasen.

Mondai 101

1. rainen tatemasu. 2. gaikoku de urimasu. 3. tankā de hakobimasu.
4. tsukaimasu. 5. Hiragana de kaite imasu. 6. Amerika e yushutsu shimasu.

Mondai 102

1. K 2. A 3. N 4. J 5. E 6. O 7. L 8. M 9. I 10. D 11. B 12. G
13. F 14. C

Mondai 103

1. (Nihon de ichi-ban ōkii toshi wa) Tōkyō desu. 2. Tōkyō wa Honshū ni arimasu. 3. Tōkyō ni wa Nihon no jinkō no ju- ppāsento no hito ga sunde imasu. 4. Hai, (asa to yūgata) Tōkyō no densha ya chikatetsu wa taihen komimasu. 5. Iie, Tōkyō de hataraite iru hito wa zenbu Tōkyō ni sunde iru hito ja arimasen. 6. Hai, Chiba-ken ya Kanagawa-ken nado kara takusan no hito ga Tōkyō ni hataraki ni kimasu. 7. Hai, watashi wa Tōkyō e itta koto ga arimasu. / Iie, watashi wa Tōkyō e itta koto ga arimasen. 8. Hai,

Mondai 103 *(tsuzuki)*	watashi wa Tōkyō ni sumitai desu. / Iie, watashi wa Tōkyō ni sumitaku arimasen.
Mondai 104	1. F 2. I 3. K 4. A 5. E 6. C 7. B 8. G 9. J 10. D

Mondai 105 1. Iie, kare wa hanbai-bu de hataraite imasen. 2. Kare wa kōkoku-bu de hataraite imasu. 3. Kare wa buchō ni naru mae nijū-nenkan hataraite imashita. 4. Terebi no kōkoku o hajimeta no wa kare ga buchō ni natta ato desu. 5. Hai, (terebi no kōkoku wa) yokatta desu. 6. Hai, kamera no namae wa yūmei ni narimashita. 7. Hai, okane o mōkeru koto ga dekimashita. 8. Kyonen kamera no nedan wa agarimashita. 9. Iie, kyonen wa kamera wa amari uremasen deshita. 10. Kare wa hanbai-buchō ya shachō to sōdan shimashita. 11. Kamera no nedan o go-pāsento yasuku suru koto o kimemashita. 12. Atarashii nedan wa kyūman-gosen- en ni narimasu.

Mondai 106 1. Tokei o shūri shimasu. / naoshimasu. 2. Shokubutsu. 3. Taihen chikai desu. 4. Sore wa takai desu ne. 5. Kusuri wa nomi-yasui desu. 6. Kare wa binbō desu. 7. Ōfuku-kippu o kudasai. 8. Kaette wa ikemasen. 9. Yushutsu shimasu. 10. Defure. 11. Shisha ni tsutomete imasu. 12. Denki o tsukete kudasai. 13. Okane o kaeshimasu./Okane o karimasu. 14. Bukka ga sagarimasu. 15. Hanbun ni narimashita. 16. Nakunarimashita. 17. Sore o wasuremashita. 18. Chotto sukuna-sugimasu. 19. Kore wa fuben desu ne! 20. Watashi wa toshiyori desu. 21. Michi o oshiemasu. 22. Yōfuku o nugimasu./Kimono o kimasu. 23. Densha o orimasu. 24. Inaka ni sunde imasu. 25. Nōgyō ga sakan desu.

Mondai 107 1. K, F 2. D, O 3. B 4. L, H 5. A 6. N 7. C, M 8. E 9. I 10. J

TĒPU DAI ICH (1)

Ichi-ban no tēpu desu.
Konnichiwa!   Konnichiwa!

Kiite kudasai!

(denwa)

denwa
Are wa denwa desu.

(doā)

doā
Are wa doā desu.

(inu)

inu
Are wa inu desu.

(neko)

neko
Are wa neko desu.

Kotaete kudasai!

(denwa)

Are wa denwa desu ka?   Hai, are wa denwa desu.

(doā)

Are wa doā desu ka?   Hai, are wa doā desu.

(denwa)

Are wa neko desu ka?   Iie, are wa neko ja arimasen.
Doā desu ka?   Iie, doā de mo arimasen.
Are wa nan desu ka?   Are wa denwa desu.

(inu)

Are mo denwa desu ka?   Iie, are wa denwa ja arimasen.
Are wa nan desu ka?   Are wa inu desu.

(neko)

Are wa nan desu ka?   Are wa neko desu.

(doā)

Are mo neko desu ka?   Iie, are wa neko ja arimasen.
Are wa nan desu ka?   Are wa doā desu.

Hai, sō desu!

(kami)

Are wa denwa desu ka?   Iie, are wa denwa ja arimasen.
Enpitsu desu ka, soretomo kami
   desu ka?   Kami desu.

(matchi)

Are mo kami desu ka? Iie, . . .   Iie, are wa kami ja arimasen.
Are wa kami desu ka, soretomo
   matchi desu ka?   Are wa matchi desu.

(inu)

Are wa matchi desu ka?   Iie, are wa matchi ja arimasen.
Neko desu ka?   Iie, neko de mo arimasen.
Are wa nan desu ka?   Are wa inu desu.

(ōkii inu)

Are wa ōkii inu desu ka, soretomo
   chiisai inu desu ka?   Are wa ōkii inu desu.

(chiisai inu)

Are mo inu desu ka?   Hai, are mo inu desu.
Are mo ōkii inu desu ka?   Iie, are wa ōkii inu ja arimasen.
Are wa donna inu desu ka?   Are wa chiisai inu desu.

Yoku dekimashita! *you spok well*

Itte kudasai! *Please say*
Inu wa ōkii desu.
Matchi wa ōkiku arimasen.
Matchi wa chiisai desu.
Inu wa chiisaku arimasen.

Kotaete kudasai!
Matchi wa ōkii desu ka, soretomo
   chiisai desu ka?   Matchi wa chiisai desu.
Doā mo chiisai desu ka?   Iie, doā wa chiisaku arimasen.
Doā wa ōkii desu ka, soretomo
   chiisai desu ka?   Doā wa ōkii desu.
Kabe mo ōkii desu ka?   Hai, kabe mo ōkii desu.
Kami mo ōkii desu ka?   Iie, kami wa ōkiku arimasen.
Kami wa ōkii desu ka, soretomo
   chiisai desu ka?   Kami wa chiisai desu.
Tōkyō mo chiisai desu ka?   Iie, Tōkyō wa chiisaku arimasen.
Tōkyō wa ōkii desu ka, soretomo
   chiisai desu ka?   Tōkyō wa ōkii desu.

Hai, sō desu!

Kiite kudasai!

(ōkii inu)

Are wa chiisai inu desu ka, soretomo
  ōkii inu desu ka?

Are wa ōkii inu desu.

Itte kudasai!
Ōkii inu wa kuroi desu.
Chiisai inu wa shiroi desu.

Kotaete kudasai!
Chiisai inu wa shiroi desu ka?
Ōkii inu mo shiroi desu ka?
Ōkii inu wa aoi desu ka?
Ōkii inu wa nani-iro desu ka?
Chiisai inu wa nani-iro desu ka?
Hamaki mo shiroi desu ka?
Akai desu ka?
Hamaki wa kiiro desu ka, soretomo
  chairo desu ka?
Tabako mo chairo desu ka?
Tabako wa nani-iro desu ka?

Hai, chiisai inu wa shiroi desu.
Iie, ōkii inu wa shiroku arimasen.
Iie, ōkii inu wa aoku arimasen.
Ōkii inu wa kuroi desu.
Chiisai inu wa shiroi desu.
Iie, hamaki wa shiroku arimasen.
Iie, akaku arimasen.

Hamaki wa chairo desu.
Iie, tabako wa chairo ja arimasen.
Tabako wa shiroi desu.

Hai, yoku dekimashita!

Itte kudasai!
shi-ro
shiro
shiroi
Tabako wa shiroi desu.

ku-ro
kuro
kuroi
Inu wa kuroi desu.

en-pi-tsu
enpitsu
Kore wa enpitsu desu.
Are wa enpitsu ja arimasen.

tsu-ku-e
tsukue
Kore wa tsukue desu.
Are wa tsukue ja arimasen.

Yoku dekimashita!

Mō ichi-do kiite kudasai! — once more

(Katō)

Are wa Katō-san desu.
Katō-san wa Nihon-jin desu.

(Michiko)

Are wa Michiko-san desu.
Michiko-san mo Nihon-jin desu.

Kotaete kudasai!

(Katō)

Are wa Michiko-san desu ka?   Iie, are wa Michiko-san ja arimasen.
Are wa Satō-san desu ka?   Iie, are wa Satō-san de mo arimasen.
Are wa Satō-san desu ka, soretomo
   Katō-san desu ka?   Are wa Katō-san desu.

(Michiko)

Are wa Katō-san desu ka?   Iie, are wa Katō-san ja arimasen.
Are wa Satō-san desu ka?   Iie, are wa Satō-san de mo arimasen.
Are wa dare desu ka?   Are wa Michiko-san desu.
Michiko-san wa Amerika-jin desu ka?   Iie, Michiko-san wa Amerika-jin ja
                                               arimasen.
Furansu-jin desu ka?   Iie, Furansu-jin de mo arimasen.
Michiko-san wa nani-jin desu ka?   Michiko-san wa Nihon-jin desu.
Katō-san wa nani-jin desu ka?   Katō-san wa Nihon-jin desu.
Watashi mo Nihon-jin desu ka?   Hai, anata mo Nihon-jin desu.
Jōnzu-san mo Nihon-jin desu ka?   Iie, Jōnzu-san wa Nihon-jin ja arimasen.
Jōnzu-san wa Nihon-jin desu ka,
   soretomo Igirisu-jin desu ka?   Jōnzu-san wa Igirisu-jin desu.

Hai, sō desu!
Kore de tēpu dai ichi o owarimasu.
Ichi-ban no tēpu wa kore de owari desu.

Sayonara!   Sayonara!

TĒPU DAI NI (2)

Ni-ban no tēpu desu.
Konnichiwa!   Konnichiwa!

Kiite kudasai!

(fune)

Are wa kuruma desu ka?   Iie, are wa kuruma ja arimasen.
Basu desu ka?   Iie, basu de mo arimasen.
Are wa nan desu ka?   Are wa fune desu.

(basu)

Are mo fune desu ka?   Iie, are wa fune ja arimasen.
Are wa nan desu ka?   Are wa basu desu.

(kuruma)

Are wa nan desu ka?   Are wa kuruma desu.

Hai, yoku dekimashita ne!

Itte kudasai!

(ōkii kuruma)

Kono kuruma wa ōkii desu.

(chiisai kuruma)

Ano kuruma wa chiisai desu.
Ōkii kuruma wa kuroi desu.
Chiisai kuruma wa akai desu.

Kotaete kudasai!
Ōkii kuruma wa kuroi desu ka?   Hai, ōkii kuruma wa kuroi desu.
Chiisai kuruma mo kuroi desu ka?   Iie, chiisai kuruma wa kuroko arimasen.
Chiisai kuruma wa nani-iro desu ka?   Chiisai kuruma wa akai desu.
Dochira no kuruma ga kuroi desu ka?   Ōkii kuruma ga kuroi desu.
Dochira no kuruma ga akai desu ka?   Chiisai kuruma ga akai desu.

Hai, totemo ii desu ne!

(hikōki)

Are wa kuruma desu ka?   Iie, are wa kuruma ja arimasen.
Are wa nan desu ka?   Are wa hikōki desu.
Hikōki wa ōkii desu ka, soretomo
   chiisai desu ka?   Hikōki wa ōkii desu.

(chiisai hikōki)

Are mo hikōki desu ka?   Hai, are mo hikōki desu.
Ano hikōki wa ōkii desu ka, soretomo
   chiisai desu ka?   Ano hikōki wa chiisai desu.

Hai, sō desu ne!

(nagai fune)

Are wa hikōki desu ka?   Iie, are wa hikōki ja arimasen.
Are wa nan desu ka?   Are wa fune desu.
Ano fune wa mijikai desu ka? Iie, . . .   Iie, ano fune wa mijikaku arimasen.
Mijikai desu ka, soretomo nagai desu ka?   Nagai desu.

(mijikai fune)

Are mo fune desu ka?   Hai, are mo fune desu.
Ano fune wa nagai desu ka, soretomo
   mijikai desu ka?   Ano fune wa mijikai desu.

Hai, sō desu!
Yoku dekimashita!

Tsugi wa kaiwa desu.
Kiite kudasai!

— *Konnichiwa, Harada-san!*
— *Ara, konnichiwa, Katō-san! Anata no kuruma desu ka?*
— *Hai, watashi no desu.*
— *Toyota desu ka?*
— *Iie, Honda desu yo.*

Kotaete kudasai!
Katō-san no kuruma wa Toyota desu
  ka? Iie, . . .
Toyota desu ka, soretomo Honda
  desu ka?
Honda wa ōkii kuruma desu ka?
Honda wa donna kuruma desu ka?
Kyaderakku mo chiisai kuruma
  desu ka?
Kyaderakku wa donna kuruma
  desu ka?

Iie, Katō-san no kuruma wa Toyota ja
  arimasen.

Honda desu.
Iie, Honda wa ōkii kuruma ja arimasen.
Honda wa chiisai kuruma desu.
Iie, Kyaderakku wa chiisai kuruma ja
  arimasen.

Kyaderakku wa ōkii kuruma desu.

Hai, sō desu.

(Tōkyō)

Kiite kudasai!
Kore wa Tōkyō desu.

Kotaete kudasai!
Tōkyō wa ōkii desu ka?
Tōkyō wa kuni desu ka, soretomo
  toshi desu ka?
Honkon mo toshi desu ka?
Nihon wa nan desu ka?
Nihon wa ōkii kuni desu ka, soretomo
  chiisai kuni desu ka?
Sobieto mo chiisai kuni desu ka?
Sobieto wa donna kuni desu ka?
Amerika mo ōkii kuni desu ka?
Sobieto wa Nihon yori ōkii desu ka?
Amerika mo Nihon yori ōkii desu ka?
Amerika to Sobieto to, dochira ga
  ōkii desu ka?
Nihon to Chūgoku to, dochira ga
  ōkii desu ka?

Hai, Tōkyō wa ōkii desu.

Tōkyō wa toshi desu.
Hai, Honkon mo toshi desu.
Nihon wa kuni desu.

Nihon wa chiisai kuni desu.
Iie, Sobieto wa chiisai kuni ja arimasen.
Sobieto wa ōkii kuni desu.
Hai, Amerika mo ōkii kuni desu.
Hai, Sobieto wa Nihon yori ōkii desu.
Hai, Amerika mo Nihon yori ōkii desu.

Sobieto ga ōkii desu.

Chūgoku ga ōkii desu.

Yoku dekimashita!

Tsugi wa itte kudasai!
Sobieto wa Nihon yori ōkii desu.
Nihon wa Sobieto yori chiisai desu.

Kyaderakku wa Toyota yori ōkii desu.
  Toyota wa . . .

Toyota wa Kyaderakku yori chiisai desu.

Kono densha wa ano densha yori
  nagai desu.
  Ano densha wa . . .
Kyoto wa Tōkyō yori chiisai desu.
  Tōkyō wa . . .

Ano densha wa kono densha yori mijikai
desu.

Tōkyō wa Kyōto yori ōkii desu.

Hai, jōzu ni dekimashita!

Tsugi wa kaiwa desu.
Kiite kudasai!

— *Tanaka-san, konnichiwa!*
— *Ā, Noguchi-san, o-genki desu ka?*
— *Ē, okagesamade genki desu. Tanaka-san, kochira wa Jōnzu-san desu.*
— *Sō desu ka! Jōnzu-san, hajimemashite!*
— *Hajimemashite! Dōzo yoroshiku!*
— *Jōnzu-san wa Amerika-jin desu ka?*
— *Iie, Amerika-jin ja arimasen. Igirisu-jin desu.*

Hai, sō desu.

Kotaete kudasai!
Jōnzu-san wa Nihon-jin desu ka?
Jōnzu-san wa nani-jin desu ka?
Dare ga Nihon-jin desu ka?

Iie, Jōnzu-san wa Nihon-jin ja arimasen.
Jōnzu-san wa Igirisu-jin desu.
Tanaka-san to Noguchi-san ga Nihon-jin
desu.

Tanaka-san wa seito desu ka?
Dare ga seito desu ka?
Jōnzu-san wa Berurittsu no seito
  desu ka?

Iie, Tanaka-san wa seito ja arimasen.
Jōnzu-san ga seito desu.
Hai, Jōnzu-san wa Berurittsu no seito
desu.

Yoku dekimashita!

Kaiwa o mō ichi-do kiite kudasai!
Soshite itte kudasai!

— *Tanaka-san, konnichiwa!*
— *Ā, Noguchi-san, o-genki desu ka?*
— *Ē, okagesamade genki desu. Tanaka-san, kochira wa Jōnzu-san desu.*
— *Sō desu ka! Jōnzu-san, hajimemashite!*
— *Hajimemashite! Dōzo yoroshiku!*
— *Jōnzu-san wa Amerika-jin desu ka?*
— *Iie, Amerika-jin ja arimasen. Igirisu-jin desu.*

Hai, sō desu. Yoku dekimashita.
Kore de tēpu dai ni o owarimasu.
Ni-ban no tēpu wa kore de owari desu.

Sayonara!

Sayonara!

TĒPU DAI SAN (3)

San-ban no tēpu desu.
Konnichiwa!   Konnichiwa!

Itte kudasai!
ichi—ni—san—shi—go
ichi, ni, san, shi, go
roku—shichi—hachi—ku—jū
roku, shichi, hachi, ku, jū

Yoku dekimashita!

Motto kazoete kudasai!
jū-ichi—jū-ni—jū-san—jū-shi—jū-go
jū-ichi, jū-ni, jū-san, jū-shi, jū-go
jū-roko—jū-shichi—jū-hachi—jū-ku—nijū
jū-roku, jū-shichi, jū-hachi, jū-ku, nijū

Itte kudasai!
Ni tasu ni wa yon desu.

Kotaete kudasai!
Ni tasu ni wa yon desu ka?   Hai, ni tasu ni wa yon desu.
Ni tasu san wa yon desu ka?   Iie, ni tasu san wa yon ja arimasen.
Ni tasu san wa roku desu ka?   Iie, ni tasu san wa roku ja arimasen.
Ni tasu san wa ikutsu desu ka?   Ni tasu san wa go desu.
Dewa, ni tasu yon wa ikutsu desu ka?   Ni tasu yon wa roku desu.
Ni tasu go wa ikutsu desu ka?   Ni tasu go wa nana desu.
Go tasu ni wa ikutsu desu ka?   Go tasu ni mo nana desu.
Go hiku ni wa ni desu ka?   Iie, go hiku ni wa ni ja arimasen.
Go hiku ni wa ikutsu desu ka?   Go hiku ni wa san desu.

Hontō ni yoku dekimashita!

Kiite kudasai!

— *Sumimasen ga, koko ni denwa ga arimasu ka?*
— *E? Nan desu ka?*
— *Denwa! Denwa ga arimasu ka?*
— *Hai, arimasu. Ano kabe ni arimasu.*

Kotaete kudasai!
Kono heya ni kuruma ga arimasu ka?
   Iie, . . .   Iie, kono heya ni kuruma wa arimasen.
Hikōki ga arimasu ka?   Iie, hikōki mo arimasen.
Heya ni nani ga arimasu ka?   Heya ni denwa ga arimasu.
Denwa wa tsukue no ue ni arimasu ka? Iie, denwa wa tsukue no ue ni arimasen.
Isu no ue ni arimasu ka?   Iie, isu no ue ni mo arimasen.
Doko ni arimasu ka?   Kabe ni arimasu.
Sumimasen ga, nani ga kabe ni
   arimasu ka?   Denwa ga arimasu.

Yoku dekimashita!

Kiite kudasai!

— *Harada-san, sore wa nan desu ka?*
— *Okane desu.*
— *Okane wa doko ni arimasu ka?*
— *Isu no ue ni arimasu.*

Kotaete kudasai!
Okane wa tsukue no ue ni arimasu
  ka? Iie, . . .
Yuka no ue ni arimasu ka?
Okane wa doko ni arimasu ka?

Iie, okane wa tsukue no ue ni arimasen.
Iie, yuka no ue ni mo arimasen.
Okane wa isu no ue ni arimasu.

Hai, sō desu!

Kiite kudasai!

— *Harada-san, okane o isu kara totte kudasai!*
— *Hai!*
— *Soshite tsukue no ue ni oite kudasai!*
— *Hai, wakarimashita!*

Kotaete kudasai!
Harada-san wa okane o yuka kara
  totte imasu ka?
Hikidashi kara totte imasu ka?
Harada-san wa okane o doko kara
  totte imasu ka?
Okane o yuka no ue ni oite imasu ka?
Doko ni oite imasu ka?

Iie, Harada-san wa okane o yuka kara
  totte imasen.
Iie, hikidashi kara totte imasen.
Harada-san wa okane o isu kara totte
  imasu.
Iie, okane o yuka no ue ni oite imasen.
Tsukue no ue ni oite imasu.

Hai, yoku dekimashita ne!

Kiite kudasai!
Tsukue no ue ni shinbun ga arimasu.
Watashi wa shinbun no ue ni hako o oite imasu.

Kotaete kudasai!
Tsukue no ue ni shinbun ga arimasu
  ka?
Hako mo arimasu ka?
Shinbun wa hako no ue ni arimasu
  ka?
Shinbun wa doko ni arimasu ka?
Hako wa doko ni arimasu ka?
Anata wa hako o shinbun no ue ni
  oite imasu ka?
Dare ga hako o shinbun no ue ni oite
  imasu ka?
Anata wa kono shinbun o mite
  imasu ka?

Hai, tsukue no ue ni shinbun ga
  arimasu.
Hai, hako mo arimasu.

Iie, shinbun wa hako no ue ni arimasen.
Shinbun wa hako no shita ni arimasu.
Hako wa shinbun no ue ni arimasu.
Iie, watashi wa hako o shinbun no ue ni
  oite imasen.
Anata ga hako o shinbun no ue ni oite
  imasu.

Iie, kono shinbun o mite imasen.

Hai, sō desu!

Kiite kudasai!

— *Konnichiwa, Harada-san! O-genki desu ka?*
— *Ē, okagesamade.*
— *Harada-san, kōhii wa ikaga desu ka?*
— *Iie, kekkō desu.*
— *Biiru wa?*
— *Arigatō! Itadakimasu!*
— *Sumimasen.*
— *Nan deshō ka?*
— *Biiru o kudasai!*
— *Hai, dōzo!*

(biiru)

Kotaete kudasai!
Kore wa osake desu ka?	Iie, kore wa osake ja arimasen.
Budōshu desu ka?	Iie, budōshu de mo arimasen.
Kore wa nan desu ka?	Kore wa biiru desu.
Biiru wa hikidashi no naka ni arimasu ka?	Iie, biiru wa hikidashi no naka ni arimasen.
Chawan no naka ni arimasu ka?	Iie, chawan no naka ni mo arimasen.
Biiru wa nani no naka ni arimasu ka?	Biiru wa gurasu no naka ni arimasu.

Yoku dekimashita!

Kotaete kudasai!
Biiru wa oishii desu ka? Hai, . . .	Hai, biiru wa oishii desu.
Osake mo oishii desu ka?	Hai, osake mo oishii desu.
Nihon-jin wa osake ga suki desu ka?	Hai, Nihon-jin wa osake ga suki desu.
Furansu-jin mo osake ga suki desu ka? Iie, . . .	Iie, Furansu-jin wa osake ga suki ja arimasen.
Furansu-jin wa miruku ga suki desu ka, soretomo budōshu ga suki desu ka?	Furansu-jin wa budōshu ga suki desu.
Roshia-jin wa uokka ga suki desu ka?	Hai, Roshia-jin wa uokka ga suki desu.

Jōzu ni dekimashita!

Tsugi wa kaiwa desu.
Itte kudasai!

(denwa)

— *Moshimoshi . . .*
— *Aoki-san desu ka?*
— *Iie, chigaimasu.*
— *Sochira wa roku roku ichi no roku ichi roku ichi ja arimasen ka?*
— *Iie, roku roku ichi no roku ichi roku ni desu.*
— *Dōmo sumimasen!*
— *Dō-itashimshite!*

Yoku dekimashita!

Kore de tēpu dai san o owarimasu.
San-ban no tēpu wa kore de owari desu.

Sayonara!   Sayonara!

TĒPU DAI YON (4)

Yon-ban no tēpu desu.
Konnichiwa!   Konnichiwa!

Kotaete kudasai!
Kore wa tēpu dai ichi desu ka?   Iie, kore wa tēpu dai ichi ja arimasen.
Nan-ban no tēpu desu ka?   Yon-ban no tēpu desu.

Kiite kudasai!
Watashi wa tsukue no ue ni enpitsu o oite imasu.
i-ppon, ni-hon, san-bon

Kotaete kudasai!
Watashi wa enpitsu o go-hon oite   Iie, anata wa enpitsu o go-hon oite
    imasu ka?   imasen.
Yon-hon oite imasu ka?   Iie, yon-hon oite imasen.
Watashi wa enpitsu o nan-bon oite
    imasu ka?   Anata wa enpitsu o san-bon oite imasu.

Hai, sō desu.

Kiite kudasai!
Kore wa kōhii desu.
Watashi wa tsukue no ue ni kōhii o oite imasu.
i-ppai, ni-hai, san-bai, yon-hai

Kotaete kudasai!
Watashi wa tsukue no ue ni hon o oite   Iie, anata wa tsukue no ue ni hon o
    imasu ka?   oite imasen.
Watashi wa nani o oite imasu ka?   Anata wa kōhii o oite imasu.
Kōhii o ju-ppai oite imasu ka?   Iie, kōhii o ju-ppai oite imasen.
Nana-hai oite imasu ka?   Iie, nana-hai oite imasen.
Kōhii o nan-bai oite imasu ka?   Kōhii o yon-hai oite imasu.

Yoku dekimashita!

Kiite kudasai!
Watashi wa tsukue no ue ni kippu o oite imasu.
ichi-mai, ni-mai

Kotaete kudasai!
Anata wa kippu o oite imasu ka?   Iie, watashi wa kippu o oite imasen.
Dare ga oite imasu ka?   Anata ga oite imasu.
Isu no ue ni oite imasu ka?   Iie, isu no ue ni oite imasen.
Doko ni oite imasu ka?   Tsukue no ue ni oite imasu.
Shinbun o oite imasu ka?   Iie, shinbun o oite imasen.
Nani o oite imasu ka?   Kippu o oite imasu.

Kippu o go-mai oite imasu ka?   Iie, kippu o go-mai oite imasen.
Nan-mai oite imasu ka?   Ni-mai oite imasu.

Hai, sō desu!

Watashi wa ima apāto ni imasu.
Watashi wa ima suwatte imasu.
Watashi no mae ni doā ga arimasu.
Watashi no ushiro ni mado ga arimasu.

Kotaete kudasai!
Watashi wa ima suwatte imasu ka,
    soretomo tatte imasu ka?   Anata wa ima suwatte imasu.
Kuruma ni imasu ka?   Iie, kuruma ni imasen.
Doko ni imasu ka?   Apāto ni imasu.
Watashi no mae ni mado ga arimasu ka?   Iie, anata no mae ni mado wa arimasen.
Watashi no mae ni nani ga arimasu ka?   Anata no mae ni doā ga arimasu.
Mado wa watashi no yoko ni arimasu ka?   Iie, mado wa anata no yoko ni arimasen.
Mado wa doko ni arimasu ka?   Mado wa anata no ushiro ni arimasu.

Yoku dekimashita!

— *Michiko-san!*
— *Hai!*
— *Mado o shimete kudasai! Arigatō!*
— *Dō-itashimashite!*

Kotaete kudasai!
Michiko-san wa mado o akete imasu ka?   Iie, Michiko-san wa mado o akete imasen.
Michiko-san wa nani o shite imasu ka?   Michiko-san wa mado o shimete imasu.

Hai, sō desu!

Kiite kudasai!

(nokku)

Kotaete kudasai!
Rōka ni dare ka imasu ka?   Hai, rōka ni dare ka imasu.
Anata ga rōka ni imasu ka?   Iie, watashi wa rōka ni imasen.
Dare ga rōka ni imasu ka?
    Wakarimasu ka?   Iie, wakarimasen.

(doā)

Ā, Katō-san!

Kotaete kudasai!
Watashi wa doā o shimete imasu ka?   Iie, anata wa doā o shimete imasen.
Watashi wa nani o shite imasu ka?   Anata wa doā o akete imasu.
Katō-san wa ima suwatte imasu ka?   Iie, Katō-san wa ima suwatte imasen.
Michi ni tatte imasu ka, soretomo rōka
    ni tatte imasu ka?   Rōka ni tatte imasu.

Yoku dekimashita!
Tsugi wa mondai desu.

Itte kudasai!
Kore wa hon desu.
Are wa hon ja arimasen.
Kono hon wa ōkii desu.
Ano hon wa ōkiku arimasen.

Kore wa enpitsu desu.
   Are wa . . .

Kono enpitsu wa nagai desu.
   Ano enpitsu wa . . .

Tōkyō wa toshi desu.
   Nihon wa . . .

Nihon wa chiisai desu.
   Chūgoku wa . . .

Miruku wa shiroi desu.
   Osake wa . . .

Hon wa tsukue no ue ni arimasu.
   Enpitsu wa . . .

Migi no te ni nani ka arimasu.
   Hidari no te ni . . .

Koko ni dare ka imasu.
   Soko ni . . .

Are wa enpitsu ja arimasen.

Ano enpitsu wa nagaku arimasen.

Nihon wa toshi ja arimasen.

Chūgoku wa chiisaku arimasen.

Osake wa shiroku arimasen.

Enpitsu wa tsukue no ue ni arimasen.

Hidari no te ni nani mo arimasen.

Soko ni dare mo imasen.

Hai, sō desu. Yoku dekimashita.
Kore de tēpu dai yon o owarimasu.
Yon-ban no tēpu wa kore de owari desu.

Sayonara!

Sayonara!

TĒPU DAI GO (5)

Go-ban no tēpu desu.
Konnichiwa!

Konnichiwa!

Kiite kudasai!
Katō-san to Harada-san desu.

— *Konnichiwa, Katō-san!*
— *Ā, Harada-san, konnichiwa!*

Kotaete kudasai!
Harada-san wa ima hanashite imasu ka?
Noguchi-san ni hanashite imasu ka?
Ōta-san ni hanashite imasu ka?
Dare ni hanashite imasu ka?
Harada-san wa Furansu-go de hanashite
   imasu ka?
Roshia-go de hanashite imasu ka?
Kanojo wa nani-go de hanashite imasu ka?

Hai, kanojo wa ima hanashite imasu.
Iie, Noguchi-san ni hanashite imasen.
Iie, Ōta-san ni mo hanashite imasen.
Katō-san ni hanashite imasu.

Iie, Furansu-go de hanashite imasen.
Iie, Roshia-go de mo hanashite imasen.
Nihon-go de hanashite imasu.

Yoku dekimashita!

Mata kiite kudasai!

(denwa)

— *Moshimoshi, Katō desu ga . . .*
— *Konbanwa, Katō-san! Koyama desu!*
— *Ā, Koyama-san, konbanwa! O-genki desu ka?*
— *Ē, okagesamade! Sumimasen ga, Miyata-san no denwa-bangō o shirimasen ka?*
— *Sā, shirimasen.*
— *Sō desu ka.*

Kotaete kudasai!

Katō-san wa denwa de hanashite imasu ka?	Hai, denwa de hanashite imasu.
Anata to hanashite imasu ka?	Iie, watashi to hanashite imasen.
Dare to hanashite imasu ka?	Koyama-san to hanashite imasu.
Ima Nihon-go o hanashite imasu ka?	Hai, ima Nihon-go o hanashite imasu.
Katō-san wa Miyata-san no denwa-bangō o shirimasen ka?	Hai, Miyata-san no denwa-bangō o shirimasen.

Hai, totemo jōzu desu!

Kiite kudasai!

(tokei)

Are wa nan desu ka?	Are wa tokei desu.

Hai, sō desu!

Are wa watashi no tokei desu.
Tokei wa ima watashi no hidari no te ni arimasu.

Kotaete kudasai!

Watashi wa ima shinbun o motte imasu ka?	Iie, anata wa ima shinbun o motte imasen.
Chawan o motte imasu ka?	Iie, chawan mo motte imasen.
Watashi wa nani o motte imasu ka?	Tokei o motte imasu.
Anata no tokei desu ka?	Iie, watashi no tokei ja arimasen.
Dare no desu ka?	Anata no desu.
Tokei wa tsukue no ue ni arimasu ka?	Iie, tokei wa tsukue no ue ni arimasen.
Yuka no ue ni arimasu ka?	Iie, yuka no ue ni mo arimasen.
Poketto no naka ni arimasu ka?	Iie, poketto no naka ni mo arimasen.
Doko ni arimasu ka?	Te ni arimasu.
Watashi wa tokei o te ni motte imasu ne?	Hai, tokei o te ni motte imasu.
Migi no te ni motte imasu ka? Iie, . . .	Iie, migi no te ni motte imasen.
Dochira no te ni motte imasu ka?	Hidari no te ni motte imasu.

Hai, yoku dekimashita ne!

Hidari no te ni tokei ga arimasu.
Migi no te ni enpitsu ga arimasu.
Watashi wa kono enpitsu de kaite imasu.

Ta . . . na . . . ka, Tanaka

Kotaete kudasai!
Watashi wa ima kaite imasu ka?
Pen de kaite imasu ka?
Nan de kaite imasu ka?
Denwa-bangō o kaite imasu ka?
Jūsho o kaite imasu ka?
Nani o kaite imasu ka?
Watashi wa anata no namae o kaite
   imasu ka?
Harada-san no namae o kaite imasu ka?

Dare no namae o kaite imasu ka?
Dare ga Tanaka-san no namae o kaite
   imasu ka?

Hai, anata wa ima kaite imasu.
Iie, pen de kaite imasen.
Enpitsu de kaite imasu.
Iie, denwa-bangō o kaite imasen.
Iie, jūsho o kaite imasen.
Namae o kaite imasu.
Iie, anata wa watashi no namae o kaite
   imasen.
Iie, Harada-san no namae o kaite
   imasen.
Tanaka-san no namae o kaite imasu.

Anata ga kaite imasu.

Hai, sō desu!

Kiite kudasai!
Watashi wa ima tegami o kaite imasu.
Tanaka-san ni tegami o kaite imasu.

Kotaete kudasai!
Watashi wa ima Tanaka-san ni hanashite
   imasu ka?
Kare ni hanashite imasu ka, soretomo
   tegami o kaite imasu ka?
Anata ga tegami o kaite imasu ka?
Dare ga tegami o kaite imasu ka?

Iie, anata wa ima kare ni hanashite
   imasen.

Kare ni tegami o kaite imasu.
Iie, watashi wa tegami o kaite imasen.
Anata ga kaite imasu.

Sō desu!
Yoku dekimashita!

Kiite kudasai!

(denwa)

— *Moshimoshi.*
— *Moshimoshi, Katō desu ga, shujin wa imasu ka?*
— *Hai! Katō-san, denwa desu.*
— *Kanai desu ka?*
— *Hai, sō desu.*
— *Arigatō! Moshimoshi . . . ā . . . a sō . . . sō . . . jā . . .*

Kotaete kudasai!
Katō-san wa ima shinbun o yonde
   imasu ka?
Tegami o kaite imasu ka?
Nani o shite imasu ka?
Onna no hito ni hanashite imasu ka?
Sensei ni hanashite imasu ka?
Dare ni hanashite imasu ka?
Sumimasen ga, dare ga okusan ni
   hanashite imasu ka?

Iie, kare wa ima shinbun o yonde
   imasen.
Iie, tegami o kaite imasen.
Denwa de hanashite imasu.
Hai, onna no hito ni hanashite imasu.
Iie, sensei ni hanashite imasen.
Okusan ni hanashite imasu.

Katō-san ga okusan ni hanashite imasu.

Hai, sō desu!
Hontō ni yoku dekimashita.
Kaiwa o mō ichi-do kiite kudasai!
Soshite itte kudasai!

(denwa)

— *Moshimoshi.*
— *Moshimoshi, Katō desu ga, shujin wa imasu ka?*
— *Hai! Katō-san, denwa desu.*
— *Kanai desu ka?*
— *Hai, sō desu.*
— *Arigatō! Moshimoshi, . . . ā . . . a sō . . . sō . . . jā . . .*

Yoku dekimashita ne!
Kore de tēpu dai go o owarimasu.
Go-ban no tēpu wa kore de owarimasu.

Sayonara!   Sayonara!

TĒPU DAI ROKU (6)

Roku-ban no tēpu desu.
Konnichiwa!   Konnichiwa!

Kiite kudasai!
Katō-san wa ima resutoran ni imasu.

— *Sumimasen!*
— *Hai, nan de gozaimasu ka?*
— *Menyū o misete kudasai!*
— *Hai, dōzo!*
— *Ēto . . . sukiyaki o onegai shimasu.*
— *Hai, sukiyaki de gozaimasu ne! . . . Dōzo, sukiyaki de gozaimasu.*
— *Dōmo arigatō!*

Sā, kotaete kudasai!

Katō-san wa ima jimusho ni imasu ka?	Iie, kare wa jimusho ni imasen.
Doko ni imasu ka?	Resutoran ni imasu.
Tenpura o tabete imasu ka?	Iie, tenpura o tabete imasen.
Jā, sashimi o tabete imasu ka?	Iie, sashimi mo tabete imasen.
Nani o tabete imasu ka?	Sukiyaki o tabete imasu.
Sumimasen ga, dare ga sukiyaki o tabete imasu ka?	Katō-san ga tabete imasu.

Sō desu!
Totemo jōzu ni dekimashita!

Mō ichi-do kiite kudasai!

— *Sumimasen ga, ocha o mō i-ppai kudasai!*
— *Hai, dōzo!*

Kotaete kudasai!
Katō-san wa ima nani ka nonde imasu ne? | Hai, kare wa ima nani ka nonde imasu.
Budōshu o nonde imasu ka? | Iie, budōshu o nonde imasen.
Osake o nonde imasu ka? | Iie, osake mo nonde imasen.
Nani o nonde imasu ka? | Ocha o nonde imasu.
Anata mo Katō-san to issho ni kono resutoran ni imasu ka? | Iie, watashi wa Katō-san to issho ni kono resutoran ni imasen.
Kare to issho ni ocha o nonde imasu ka? | Iie, kare to issho ni ocha o nonde imasen.

Anata wa ima ocha o nonde imasu ka, soretomo tēpu o kiite imasu ka? | Watashi wa ima tēpu o kiite imasu.

Hai, yoku dekimashita!

(taipuraitā)

Kiite kudasai!
Are wa Harada-san desu.

Kotaete kudasai!
Harada-san wa ima resutoran ni imasu ka? | Iie, ima resutoran ni imasen.
Doko ni imasu ka? | Jimusho ni imasu.
Harada-san wa ima tabete imasu ka? | Iie, ima tabete imasen.
Jū-ni-ji ni wa resutoran de tabemasu nē? | Ē, jū-ni-ji ni wa resutoran de tabemasu.
Anata mo resutoran de tabemasu ka? | Hai, watashi mo resutoran de tabemasu.
Ima anata wa tabete imasu ka? | Iie, ima tabete imasen.
Ima Nihon-go o hanashite imasu ka? | Hai, ima Nihon-go o hanashite imasu.
Anata wa kurasu de mo Nihon-go o hanashimasu nē? | Ē, watashi wa kurasu de mo Nihon-go o hanashimasu.
Furansu-go no sensei wa kurasu de Nihon-go o hanashimasu ka? | Iie, Furansu-go no sensei wa kurasu de Nihon-go o hanashimasen.
Furansu-go no sensei wa nani-go o hanashimasu ka? | Furansu-go no sensei wa Furansu-go o hanashimasu.

Hai, sō desu nē!

Itte kudasai!
Watashi wa ima tabete imasen.
Keredomo, jū-ni-ji ni resutoran de tabemasu.

Ima tabako o sutte imasen.
   Keredomo, rōka de . . . | Rōka de tabako o suimasu.
Ima shinbun o yonde imasen.
   Keredomo, uchi de . . . | Uchi de shinbun o yomimasu.
Ima tegami o kaite imasen.
   Keredomo, jimusho de . . . | Jimusho de tegami o kakimasu.
Ima sukiyaki o tabete imasen.
   Keredomo, resutoran de . . . | Resutoran de sukiyaki o tabemasu.

Totemo ii desu yo!
Yoku dekimashita!

Kiite kudasai!

(tokei)

Are wa nan desu ka?
Chiisai tokei desu ka?
Donna tokei desu ka?

Are wa tokei desu.
Iie, chiisai tokei ja arimasen.
Ōkii tokei desu.

Kiite kudasai!

(san-ji)

Ichi . . . ni . . . san . . .

Kotaete kudasai!
Ima go-ji desu ka?
Ima yo-ji desu ka?
Jā, ima nan-ji desu ka?

Iie, ima go-ji ja arimasen.
Iie, ima yo-ji de mo arimasen.
Ima san-ji desu.

Sō desu!
Yoku dekimashita!

Kiite kudasai!
Ima gozen hachi-ji desu.
Katō-san wa gozen hachi-ji ni jimusho e ikimasu.

Kotaete kudasai!
Katō-san wa basu de jimusho e ikimasu ka?
Chikatetsu de ikimasu ka, soretomo aruite
   ikimasu ka?
Kare wa roku-ji ni jimusho e ikimasu ka?
Shichi-ji ni ikimasu ka?
Jā, nan-ji ni jimusho e ikimasu ka?
Gozen hachi-ji ni ikimasu ka, soretomo
   gogo hachi-ji ni ikimasu ka?
Jū-ni-ji ni gakkō e ikimasu ka?
Gakkō e ikimasu ka, soretomo resutoran
   e ikimasu ka?
Sumimasen ga, dare ga resutoran e
   ikimasu ka?

Iie, basu de jimusho e ikimasen.

Aruite ikimasu.
Iie, roku-ji ni jimusho e ikimasen.
Iie, shichi-ji ni mo ikimasen.
Hachi-ji ni jimusho e ikimasu.

Gozen hachi-ji ni ikimasu.
Iie, jū-ni-ji ni gakkō e ikimasen.

Resutoran e ikimasu.

Katō-san ga ikimasu.

Hai, sō desu.
Tsugi wa kaiwa desu.
Ima jū-ni-ji desu.
Katō-san wa ima resutoran ni imasu.

Itte kudasai!

— *Sumimasen!*
— *Hai, irasshaimase! Nan de gozaimasu ka?*
— *Tēburu ga arimasu ka? Menyū o onegai shimasu!*
— *Hai, dōzo!*
— *Ēto, sashimi wa arimasu ka?*
— *Iie, kyō wa sashimi wa gozaimasen.*

— *Jā, tenpura o onegai shimasu.*
— *Sumimasen ga, tenpura mo gozaimasen.*
— *Sāte, sukiyaki wa arimasu ka?*
— *Hai, gozaimasu!*
— *Jā, sore ni shimasu!*

Hai, sō desu. Jōzu ni dekimashita.
Kore de tēpu dai roku o owarimasu.
Roku-ban no tēpu wa kore de owari desu.

Sayonara!   Sayonara!

TĒPU DAI NANA (7)

Nana-ban no tēpu desu.
Konnichiwa!   Konnichiwa!

Kiite kudasai!
Ima asa go-ji desu.

Kotaete kudasai!
Kono hito wa ima shinbun o yonde
   imasu ka?   Iie, ima shinbun o yonde imasen.
Kare wa ima okite imasu ka, soretomo
   nete imasu ka?   Ima nete imasu.
Anata mo ima nete imasu ka?   Iie, watashi wa ima nete imasen.
Anata wa nete imasu ka, soretomo okite
   imasu ka?   Watashi wa okite imasu.

Kiite kudasai!

(taipuraitā)

Kochira wa Harada-san desu.

Kotaete kudasai!
Harada-san wa ima nete imasu ka?   Iie, ima nete imasen.
Denwa shite imasu ka, soretomo taipu
   shite imasu ka?   Taipu shite imasu.
Resutoran de taipu shite imasu ka?   Iie, resutoran de taipu shite imasen.
Jimusho de taipu shite imasu ka,
   soretomo gakkō de taipu shite
   imasu ka?   Jimusho de taipu shite imasu.
Anata mo ima taipu shite imasu ka?   Iie, ima taipu shite imasen.
Anata wa ima shigoto shite imasu ka,
   soretomo benkyō shite imasu ka? Ima benkyō shite imasu.
Ima shigoto shite imasen ka?   Hai, ima shigoto shite imasen.
Jimusho de shigoto shimasu ne?   Hai, jimusho de shigoto shimasu.
Gakkō de mo shigoto shimasu ka?   Iie, gakkō de wa shigoto shimasen.
Gakkō de nani o shimasu ka?   Gakkō de benkyō shimasu.

Hai, sō desu. Hontō ni yoku dekimashita.

(asa)

Kiite kudasai!
Ima gozen go-ji desu.

Kotaete kudasai!
Ima yoru go-ji desu ka, soretomo asa
  go-ji desu ka?   Ima asa go-ji desu.
Anata wa asa go-ji ni shigoto shimasu ka?   Iie, asa go-ji ni shigoto shimasen.
Asa go-ji ni shigoto shite imasu ka,
  soretomo nete imasu ka?   Asa go-ji ni nete imasu.
Asa go-ji wa hayai desu nē?   Hai, asa go-ji wa taihen hayai desu yo.

Sō desu!
Yoku dekimashita!

(ōkesutora)

Kiite kudasai!
Ima gogo hachi-ji desu.
Konsāto ga gogo hachi-ji ni hajimarimasu.

Kotaete kudasai!
Ima asa desu ka?   Iie, ima asa ja arimasen.
Ima asa desu ka, soretomo yoru desu ka?   Ima yoru desu.
Konsāto wa hachi-ji-han ni hajimarimasu   Iie, konsāto wa hachi-ji-han ni
  ka?   hajimarimasen.
Hachi-ji-han ni hajimarimasu ka, soretomo
  hachi-ji ni hajimarimasu ka?   Hachi-ji ni hajimarimasu.
Asa hachi-ji ni hajimarimasu ka?   Iie, asa hachi-ji ni hajimarimasen.
Jā, itsu hajimarimasu ka?   Yoru hachi-ji ni hajimarimasu.

Hai, sō desu!

Kiite kudasai!

(konsāto no owari)

Ima gogo jū-ji desu.

Kotaete kudasai!
Konsāto wa jū-ji ni hajimarimasu ka,
  soretomo owarimasu ka?   Jū-ji ni owarimasu.
Yo-jikan kakarimasu ka?   Iie, yo-jikan kakarimasen.
Jā, san-jikan kakarimasu ka?   Iie, san-jikan kakarimasen.
Nan-jikan kakarimasu ka?   Ni-jikan kakarimasu.
Konsāto wa nan-ji kara nan-ji made
  desu ka?   Hachi-ji kara jū-ji made desu.

Yoku dekimashita!

Kiite kudasai!
Suzuki-san wa ima Ginza-dōri o aruite imasu.
Tomodachi no Shibata-san mo Ginza-dōri o aruite imasu.

— *Konnichiwa, Shibata-san! O-genki desu ka?*
— *Konnichiwa, okagesamade! Anata mo o-genki desu ka?*
— *Ē, arigatō gozaimasu!*
— *Suzuki-san, ima doko e ikimasu ka?*
— *Gakkō e ikimasu.*
— *Gakkō e?*
— *Hai, sō desu.*
— *Nani o benkyō shite imasu ka?*
— *Eigo desu.*

Kotaete kudasai!

Suzuki-san wa ima resutoran e ikimasu ka?	Iie, ima resutoran e ikimasen.
Doko e ikimasu ka?	Gakkō e ikimasu.
Suzuki-san wa sensei desu ka, soretomo seito desu ka?	Seito desu.
Furansu-go o benkyō shite imasu ka?	Iie, Furansu-go o benkyō shite imasen.
Nani-go o benkyō shite imasu ka?	Eigo o benkyō shite imasu.

Hai, sō desu.

Kiite kudasai!

— *Suzuki-san, nani o benkyō shite imasu ka?*
— *Eigo desu.*
— *Sō desu ka! Eigo no hon o motte imasu ka?*
— *Ē, motte imasu ga, kyōshitsu de wa hon o yomimasen.*
— *Sō, desu ka! Jā, gakkō de nani o shimasu ka?*
— *Eigo dake hanashimasu.*

Kotaete kudasai!

Suzuki-san wa hon o motte imasu ne?	Hai, hon o motte imasu.
Sono hon o kyōshitsu de yomimasu ka?	Iie, sono hon o kyōshitsu de yomimasen.
Jā, kyōshitsu de wa Eigo o kakimasu ka?	Iie, kyōshitsu de wa Eigo o kakimasen.
Gakkō de Eigo o kakimasu ka, soretomo Eigo o hanashimasu ka?	Gakkō de Eigo o hanashimasu.
Eigo dake hanashimasu ne?	Hai, Eigo dake hanashimasu.

Hai, yoku dekimashita!

Kiite kudasai!

— *Eigo dake hanashimasu.*
— *Kyōshitsu wa konde imasu ka?*
— *Iie, zenzen konde imasen. Watashi hitori ga seito desu.*
— *Kyōshitsu de Nihon-go o hanashimasu ka?*
— *Iie, zenzen hanashimasen.*
— *Hontō desu ka! Doko no gakkō desu ka?*
— *Berurittsu desu.*

Kotaete kudasai!

Kyōshitsu ni wa hito ga takusan imasu ka?	Iie, kyōshitsu ni wa hito wa takusan imasen.
Seito ga san-nin imasu ka?	Iie, seito wa san-nin imasen.
Futari imasu ka?	Iie, futari imasen.

Seito wa nan-nin imasu ka?
Sensei wa nan-nin imasu ka?
Hitori dake imasu ne?
Suzuki-san no gakkō wa nan to iimasu ka?

Seito wa hitori imasu.
Sensei mo hitori imasu.
Ē, hitori dake imasu.
Gakkō wa Berurittsu to iimasu.

Hai, yoku dekimashita!
Sō desu! Suzuki-san wa Berurittsu no seito desu.
Anata mo Berurittsu no seito desu nē!
Kore de tēpu dai nana o owarimasu.
Nana-ban no tēpu wa kore de owari desu.

Sayonara!

Sayonara!

TĒPU DAI HACHI (8)

Hachi-ban no tēpu desu.
Konnichiwa!

Konnichiwa!

Kotaete kudasai!
Anata wa kyū-ban no tēpu o kiite imasu ka?
Nan-ban no tēpu o kiite imasu ka?
Nana-ban no tēpu wa mō kikimashita ka?

Iie, kyū-ban no tēpu o kiite imasen.
Hachi-ban no tēpu o kiite imasu.
Hai, nana-ban no tēpu wa mō
  kikimashita.

Roku-ban no tēpu mo mō kikimashita ka?

Hai, roku-ban no tēpu mo mō
  kikimashita.

Tēpu dai-kyū wa mō kikimashita ka?
Tēpu dai-jū wa mō kikimashita ka?

Iie, tēpu dai-kyū wa mada kiite imasen.
Iie, tēpu dai-jū wa mada kiite imasen.

Sō desu.
Sā, tsugi wa itte kudasai!
Tēpu o mō kikimashita.
Tēpu o mada kiite imasen.

Kōhii o mō nomimashita ka?
  Hai, . . .
  Iie, ...
Hiru-gohan o mō tabemashita ka?
  Hai, . . .
  Iie, . . .
Shinbun o mō yomimashita ka?
  Hai, . . .
  Iie, . . .
Hisho wa uchi e mō kaerimashita ka?
  Hai, . . .
  Iie, . . .
Densha ni mō norimashita ka?
  Hai, . . .
  Iie, . . .

Hai, mō nomimashita.
Iie, mada nonde imasen.

Hai, mō tabemashita.
Iie, mada tabete imasen.

Hai, mō yomimashita.
Iie, mada yonde imasen.

Hai, mō kaerimashita.
Iie, mada kaette imasen.

Hai, mō norimashita.
Iie, mada notte imasen.

Hai, yoku dekimashita.
Kondo wa kiite kudasai!

(densha)

Watashi-tachi wa ima densha ni notte imasu.
Densha wa Ōsaka kara Hakata e ikimasu.

Kotaete kudasai!
Watashi-tachi wa basu ni notte imasu ka?　　　Iie, basu ni notte imasen.
Nani ni notte imasu ka?　　　Densha ni notte imasu.
Kono densha wa Kyōto e ikimasu ka?　　　Iie, Kyōto e ikimasen.
Doko e ikimasu ka?　　　Hakata e ikimasu.

Sō desu.
Densha wa Hakata e ikimasu.
Yoku dekimashita!

Mō ichi-do kiite kudasai!
Kyō wa sui-yōbi desu.
Kono densha wa mainichi Hakata e ikimasu.

Kotaete kudasai!
Kyō wa ka-yōbi desu ka?　　　Iie, ka-yōbi ja arimasen.
Kyō wa nan-yōbi desu ka?　　　Kyō wa sui-yōbi desu.
Kono densha wa kyō Hakata e
　ikimasu ka?　　　Hai, kono densha wa kyō Hakata
　　　e ikimasu.
Kinō wa ka-yōbi deshita ka?　　　Hai, kinō wa ka-yōbi deshita.
Kinō kono densha wa Hakata e
　ikimashita ka?　　　Hai, kinō Hakata e ikimashita.
Ototoi wa getsu-yōbi deshita nē?　　　Hai, ototoi wa getsu-yōbi deshita.
Getsu-yōbi ni mo densha wa Hakata e　　　Hai, getsu-yōbi ni mo Hakata e
　ikimashita ka?　　　ikimashita.
Watashi-tachi wa ima densha ni notte
　imasu ka?　　　Hai, ima densha ni notte imasu.
Kinō mo kono densha ni notte imashita ka?　　　Iie, kinō wa notte imasen deshita.
Watashi-tachi wa kinō Hakata e
　ikimashita ka?　　　Iie, kinō Hakata e ikimasen deshita.

Hai, sō desu!

Kiite kudasai!
Ima ichi-ji desu.
Watashi-tachi wa kesa jū-ji ni Ōsaka o demashita.

Kotaete kudasai!
Watashi-tachi wa mō Ōsaka o
　demashita ka?　　　Hai, mō Ōsaka o demashita.
Ōsaka o ichi-jikan mae ni demashita ka?　　　Iie, ichi-jikan mae ni wa demasen
　　　deshita.
Nan-jikan mae ni demashita ka?　　　San-jikan mae ni demashita.

Hai, sō desu.
Yoku dekimashita!

(taipuraitā)

Kiite kudasai!
Kochira wa Harada-san desu.

Kotaete kudasai!

Harada-san wa ima shinbun o yonde imasu ka?	Iie, ima shinbun o yonde imasen.
Nani o shite imasu ka?	Taipu shite imasu.
Harada-san wa hisho desu ka?	Hai, hisho desu.
Hisho wa jimusho de taipu shimasu ka?	Hai, hisho wa jimusho de taipu shimasu.

Hai, ii desu yo!

(resutoran)

Kiite kudasai!
Ima jū-ni-ji desu.
Katō-san wa ima resutoran ni imasu.

— *Menyū o onegai shimasu.*
— *Hai, dōzo!*

Kotaete kudasai!

Katō-san wa ima uchi ni imasu ka?	Iie, uchi ni imasen.
Kare wa doko ni imasu ka?	Resutoran ni imasu.
Anata mo resutoran de tabemasu ka?	Hai, watashi mo resutoran de tabemasu.
Anata wa ichi-nichi ni go-do tabemasu ka?	Iie, ichi-nichi ni go-do tabemasen.
Ichi-nichi ni nan-do tabemasu ka?	San-do tabemasu.
Watashi-tachi wa itsu asa-gohan o tabemasu ka?	Asa, asa-gohan o tabemasu.
Anata wa doko de asa-gohan o tabemasu ka?	Watashi wa uchi de asa-gohan o tabemasu.
Hiru-gohan mo uchi de tabemasu ka?	Iie, hiru-gohan wa uchi de tabemasen.
Doko de hiru-gohan o tabemasu ka?	Resutoran de tabemasu.
Itsu ban-gohan o tabemasu ka?	Yoru, ban-gohan o tabemasu.

Jōzu ni dekimashita!

Tsugi wa kaiwa desu! Kiite kudasai!
Ōta-san to Koyama-san desu. Itte kudasai!

— *Ō-ta-sā-n . . . !*
— *Ā, Koyama-san, konnichiwa!*
— *Konnichiwa, Ōta-san! Yūbe anata no uchi ni denwa o shimashita ga, anata wa imasen deshita ne!*
— *Ē, yūbe wa uchi ni imasen deshita. Tomodachi to eiga ni ikimashita.*
— *Hontō? Nan no eiga o mimashita ka?*
— *Furansu no desu. Taihen ii eiga deshita.*
— *Nan to iu eiga desu ka?*
— *"Ashita Pari de" to iu eiga desu. Anata wa mō mimashita ka?*
— *Iie, mada mite imasen.*
— *Konban nani o shimasu ka?*
— *Sā, mada nani mo . . .*

— *Konsāto no kippu ga ni-mai arimasu ga, issho ni ikimasen ka?*
— *Ā, sore wa ii desu nē! Nan-ji ni hajimarimasu ka?*
— *Hachi-ji ni hajimatte, jū-ji-han goro owarimasu.*
— *Doko de aimashō ka?*
— *Konsāto-hōru no mae de shichi-ji-han ni aimashō.*
— *Doko ni arimasu ka?*
— *Kono michi o massugu ni itte, hidari ni arimasu. Asoko ni basu-noriba ga arimasu.*
    Soko kara basu ga dete imasu.
— *Sō! Dōmo arigatō! Jā mata ato de!*
— *Jā mata!*

Hai, totemo jōzu ni dekimashita!
Kore de tēpu dai hachi o owarimasu.
Hachi-ban no tēpu wa kore de owari desu.

Sayonara!   Sayonara!

TĒPU DAI KYŪ (9)

Kyū-ban no tēpu desu.
Konnichiwa!   Konnichiwa!

Kiite kudasai!
Katō-san wa kōen ni imasu.

Sā, kondo wa kotaete kudasai!
Katō-san wa ima jimusho ni imasu ka?   Iie, ima jimusho ni imasen.
Ima shigoto o shite imasen ne?   Hai, ima shigoto o shite imasen.
Denwa shite imasu ka, soretomo sanpo
   shite imasu ka?   Sanpo shite imasu.

Hai, sō desu!
Katō-san wa kōen de sanpo shite imasu.

(ame)

Ā, kiite kudasai!
Nan deshō ka, are wa? Ima ii tenki
   desu ka, warui tenki desu ka?   Ima warui tenki desu.
Ima ame ga futte imasu ka?   Hai, ima ame ga futte imasu.

Yoku dekimashita!

(ii tenki)

Kotaete kudasai!
Ima mo warui tenki desu ka?   Iie, ima wa warui tenki ja arimasen.
Ima wa warui tenki desu ka, soretomo
   ii tenki desu ka?   Ima wa ii tenki desu.
Ima wa ame ga futte imasen ne?   Hai, ima wa ame ga futte imasen.

(kaze)

Watashi-tachi wa ima Shiberia ni imasu.

Kotaete kudasai!
Shiberia wa atsui desu ka?
Jā, Shiberia wa samui desu ka?
Kesshite atsuku arimasen ne?
Tōkyō mo itsumo samui desu ka,
   soretomo tokidoki samui desu ka?
Tōkyō no natsu wa samui desu ka?

Dono kisetsu ga samui desu ka?
Nyūyōku no fuyu mo samui desu ka?
Nyūyōku de wa tokidoki ame ga
   furimasu ka?
Rondon wa tokidoki ame ga furimasu ka,
   yoku ame ga furimasu ka?
Shiberia mo yoku ame ga furimasu ka?
Yoku ame ga furimasu ka, soretomo
   yoku yuki ga furimasu ka?
Arasuka ni mo yoku yuki ga furimasu ka?

Iie, Shiberia wa atsuku arimasen.
Hai, samui desu.
Hai, kesshite atsuku arimasen.

Tōkyō wa tokidoki samui desu.
Iie, Tōkyō no natsu wa samuku
   arimasen.
Fuyu ga samui desu.
Hai, Nyūyōku no fuyu mo samui desu.
Hai, Nyūyōku de wa tokidoki ame ga
   furimasu.

Rondon wa yoku ame ga furimasu.
Iie, Shiberia wa yoku ame ga furimasen.

Yoku yuki ga furimasu.
Hai, Arasuka ni mo yoku yuki ga
   furimasu.

Hai, sō desu!
Arasuka ni mo yuki ga takusan furimasu.
Yoku dekimashita!

Kondo wa kiite kudasai!
Katō-san to Harada-san desu.

— *Katō-san, ohayō-gozaimasu!*
— *Ohayō-gozaimasu.*
— *Mainichi yoku ame ga furimasu nē!*
— *Hontō desu nē! Roku-gatsu wa kirai desu yo!*

Kotaete kudasai!
Harada-san wa Katō-san ni hanashite
   imasu ka?
Konbanwa to iimashita ka, ohayō-gozaimasu
   to iimashita ka?
Ima yoru desu ka?
Ima hiru desu ka, soretomo asa desu ka?
Mainichi ame ga futte imasu ka?
Ima hachi-gatsu desu ka?
Shichi-gatsu desu ka?
Jā, ima nan-gatsu desu ka?
Katō-san wa roku-gatsu ga suki desu ka?
Roku-gatsu ga suki desu ka, kirai desu ka?

Hai, kare ni hanashite imasu.

Ohayō-gozaimasu to iimashita.
Iie, ima yoru ja arimasen.
Ima asa desu.
Hai, mainichi ame ga futte imasu.
Iie, ima hachi-gatsu ja arimasen.
Iie, shichi-gatsu de mo arimasen.
Ima roku-gatsu desu.
Iie, roku-gatsu ga suki ja arimasen.
Roku-gatsu ga kirai desu.

Hai, yoku dekimashita nē!
Hai, sō desu.

Kiite kudasai!
Kōen ni futari no onna no hito ga imasu.

Kotaete kudasai!
Otoko no hito ga imasu ka? Iie, otoko no hito wa imasen.
Otoko no hito ga imasu ka, onna no
  hito ga imasu ka? Onna no hito ga imasu.
Onna no hito ga yo-nin imasu ka? Iie, onna no hito wa yo-nin imasen.
San-nin imasu ka? Iie, san-nin imasen.
Jā, onna no hito wa nan-nin imasu ka? Onna no hito wa futari imasu.
Eiga-kan ni imasu ka? Iie, eiga-kan ni imasen.
Doko ni imasu ka? Kōen ni imasu.

Hai, yoku dekimashita.

Tsugi wa kiite kudasai!

— *Mā, kirei!*
— *Nani ga? Nani ga kirei?*
— *Hora! Are yo! Sakura! Sakura no hana!*
— *Hontō da! Hontō ni kirei!*

Kotaete kudasai!
Futari wa ima nani ka mite imasu ka? Hai, nani ka mite imasu.
Hikōki o mite imasu ka? Iie, hikōki o mite imasen.
Dewa, hana o mite imasu ka? Hai, hana o mite imasu.
Nan no hana o mite imasu ka? Sakura no hana o mite imasu.
Sakura no hana wa fuyu ni sakimasu ka? Iie, sakura no hana wa fuyu ni
                                           sakimasen.
Aki ni sakimasu ka? Iie, aki ni mo sakimasen.
Jā, sakura no hana wa itsu
  sakimasu ka? Sakura no hana wa haru ni sakimasu.
Haru wa atsui desu ka? Iie, haru wa atsuku arimasen.
Natsu ni wa atsuku narimasu ne? Hai, natsu ni wa atsuku narimasu.
Aki wa samui desu ka? Iie, aki wa samuku arimasen.
Fuyu ni wa samuku narimasu ka? Hai, fuyu ni wa samuku narimasu.

Hai, yoku dekimashita!
Tsugi wa mondai desu.

Itte kudasai!
Fuyu wa atsuku arimasen.
Natsu ni wa atsuku narimasu.

Yoru wa akaruku arimasen.
  Asa ni wa . . . Asa ni wa akaruku narimasu.
Hiru wa kuraku arimasen.
  Yoru ni wa . . . Yoru ni wa kuraku narimasu.
Natsu wa suzushiku arimasen.
  Aki ni wa . . . Aki ni wa suzushiku narimasu.
Natsu wa yoru ga nagaku arimasen.
  Aki ni wa . . . Aki ni wa nagaku narimasu.

Hai, sō desu. Hontō ni yoku dekimashita.
Kore de tēpu dai kyū o owarimasu.
Kyū-ban no tēpu wa kore de owari desu.

Sayonara!   Sayonara!

TĒPU DAI JŪ (10)

Jū-ban no tēpu desu.
Konnichiwa!   Konnichiwa!

Kiite kudasai!
Katō-san to Harada-san desu.

— *Konnichiwa, Katō-san! O-genki desu ka?*
— *Ē, okagesamade!*
— *Senshū kaisha e irasshaimasen deshita nē!*
— *Ē, kazoku to ryokō o shite imashita.*
— *Mā, ii desu nē!*

Kotaete kudasai!
Katō-san wa senshū kaisha ni imashita ka?   Iie, senshū kaisha ni imasen deshita.
Kare wa shutchō shite imashita ka?   Iie, shutchō shite imasen deshita.
Senshū hataraite imasen deshita nē!   Hai, senshū hataraite imasen deshita.
Kare wa ryokō shite imashita ka?   Hai, kare wa ryokō shite imashita.
Kare wa anata to ryokō shite   Iie, watashi to ryokō shite imasen
  imashita ka?   deshita.
Tomodachi to ryokō shite imashita ka,
  kazoku to ryokō shite imashita ka?   Kazoku to ryokō shite imashita.
Ryokō suru no wa tanoshii desu ka?   Hai, ryokō suru no wa tanoshii desu.

Hai, sō desu.
Ryokō suru no wa totemo tanoshii desu ne!

Itte kudasai!
Ryokō shimasu.
Tanoshii desu.
Ryokō suru no wa tanoshii desu.

Yakyū o shimasu.
Omoshiroi desu.
Yakyū o suru no wa . . .   Yakyū o suru no wa omoshiroi desu.

Hashi o tsukaimasu.
Muzukashii desu.
Hashi o . . .   Hashi o tsukau no wa muzukashii desu.

Umi e ikimasu.
Tanoshii desu.
Umi e . . .   Umi e iku no wa tanoshii desu.

Asa yo-ji ni okimasu.
Taihen desu.
Asa . . .

Asa yo-ji ni okiru no wa taihen desu.

Taipu shimasu.
Yasashii desu.
Taipu . . .

Taipu suru no wa yasashii desu.

Sanpo shimasu.
Tanoshii desu.
Sanpo . . .

Sanpo suru no wa tanoshii desu.

Nihon-go o hanashimasu.
Muzukashii desu.
Nihon-go . . .

Nihon-go o hanasu no wa muzukashii
desu.

Terebi o mimasu.
Omoshiroi desu.
Terebi . . .

Terebi o miru no wa omoshiroi desu.

Hai, yoku dekimashita!

Mata kiite kudasai!
Katō-san to Harada-san desu.

— *Kazoku to ryokō o shite imashita.*
— *Mā, ii desu nē! Doko e ikimashita ka?*
— *Umi e ikimashita.*
— *Umi desu ka! Watashi mo umi ga dai-suki desu.*

Kotaete kudasai!
Katō-san wa yama e ikimashita ka?
Kawa e ikimashita ka?
Doko e ikimashita ka?
Katō-san wa umi ga suki desu ka?
Harada-san mo umi ga suki desu ka?
Umi ga dai-suki desu nē?

Iie, kare wa yama e ikimasen deshita.
Iie, kawa e mo ikimasen deshita.
Umi e ikimashita.
Hai, umi ga suki desu.
Hai, umi ga suki desu.
Hai, umi ga dai-suki desu.

Sō desu!
Totemo yoku dekimashita yo!

Tsugi wa itte kudasai!
Harada-san wa umi e yoku ikimasu.
Umi ga suki desu.
Zenzen yama e ikimasen.
Yama ga kirai desu.

Kotaete kudasai!
Katō-san wa yoku sanpo shimasu.
  Sanpo ga . . .
Mettani taipu shimasen.
  Taipu ga . . .
Itsumo tabako o sutte imasu.
Kesshite hamaki o suimasen.

Sanpo ga suki desu.

Taipu ga kirai desu.
Tabako ga suki desu.
Hamaki ga kirai desu.

Mainichi ocha o nomimasu.
Kesshite kōhii o nomimasen.

Ocha ga suki desu.
Kōhii ga kirai desu.

Hai, yoku dekimashita.

Mata Katō-san to Harada-san desu.
Kiite kudasai!

— *Umi desu ka! Watashi mo umi ga dai-suki desu. Tenki wa dō deshita ka?*
— *Taihen yokatta desu. Ichi-nichi dake ame ga furimashita.*

Kondo wa kotaete kudasai!
Warui tenki deshita ka, soretomo ii tenki
   deshita ka?

Ii tenki deshita.

Taihen ii tenki deshita ka?
Ame ga furimashita ka?
Mainichi furimashita ka?
Ichi-nichi dake furimashita ka?

Hai, taihen ii tenki deshita.
Hai, ame ga furimashita.
Iie, mainichi wa furimasen deshita.
Hai, ichi-nichi dake ame ga furimashita.

Hai, sō desu.
Yoku dekimashita!

Mata kaiwa o kiite kudasai!

— *Nan-nichikan umi e itte imashita ka?*
— *Chōdo i-sshūkan desu. Senshū no do-yōbi ni kaette kimashita.*
— *I-sshūkan desu ka! Ii desu ne!*

Sā, kotaete kudasai!
Katō-san wa senshū no moku-yōbi ni
   kaette kimashita ka?
Senshū no kin-yōbi ni kaette
   kimashita ka?
Ja, itsu kaette kimashita ka?

Iie, senshū no moku-yōbi ni wa kaette
   kimasen deshita.
Iie, senshū no kin-yōbi ni mo kaette
   kimasen deshita.
Senshū no do-yōbi ni kaette kimashita.

Hai, sō desu!
Totemo jōzu ni kotaemashita ne!

Kondo wa kaiwa o kiite kudasai!
Mata Katō-san to Harada-san desu.

— *Harada-san, anata wa mō kyūka o torimashita ka?*
— *Iie, mada totte imasen.*
— *Itsu torimasu ka?*
— *Raigetsu desu.*
— *Ā, sō desu ka. Doko e iku-no desu ka?*
— *Watashi mo umi e ikimasu.*
— *Jā, o-genki de itte irasshai.*
— *Hai, dōmo arigatō gozaimasu.*
— *Sayonara.*
— *Sayonara, Katō-san.*

Kotaete kudasai!
Harada-san wa mō kyūka o torimashita ka?

Iie, mada kyūka o totte imasen.

Kongetsu kyūka o torimasu ka, raigetsu
 kyūka o torimasu ka?

Raigetsu kyūka o torimasu.

Doko e ikimasu ka?

Umi e ikimasu.

Yoku dekimashita!
Ima no kaiwa o mata kikimashō!

Katō-san to Harada-san desu.
Itte kudasai!

— *Konnichiwa, Katō-san! O-genki desu ka?*
— *Ē, okagesamade.*
— *Senshū kaisha ni irasshaimasen deshita ne?*
— *Hai, kazoku to ryokō o shite imashita.*
— *Mā, ii desu ne! Doko e ikimashita ka?*
— *Umi e ikimashita.*
— *Umi desu ka? Watashi mo umi ga dai-suki desu. Tenki wa dō deshita ka?*
— *Taihen yokatta desu. Ichi-nichi dake ame ga furimashita.*
— *Nan-nichikan umi e itte imashita ka?*
— *Chōdo i-sshūkan desu. Senshū no do-yōbi ni kaette kimashita.*
— *I-sshūkan desu ka! Ii desu nē!*
— *Harada-san, anata wa mō kyūka o torimashita ka?*
— *Iie, mada totte imasen.*
— *Itsu torimasu ka?*
— *Raigetsu desu.*
— *Ā, sō desu ka. Doko e iku-no desu ka?*
— *Watashi mo umi e ikimasu.*
— *Jā, o-genki de itte irasshai.*
— *Hai, arigatō gozaimasu!*
— *Sayonara.*
— *Sayonara, Katō-san.*

Yoku dekimashita!
Ii desu ne!
Kono tēpu mo kore de owarimasu.
Jū-ban no tēpu wa kore de owari desu.

Sayonara!

Sayonara!

TĒPU DAI JŪ-ICHI (11)

Jū-ichi-ban no tēpu desu.
Konnichiwa!

Konnichiwa!

Sā, kotaete kudasai!
Nan-ban no tēpu o kiite imasu ka?

Jū-ichi-ban no tēpu o kiite imasu.

Tēpu dai jū-ichi wa mō owarimashita ka?

Iie, tēpu dai jū-ichi wa mada owatte
 imasen.

Anata wa tēpu dai jū-ichi o mada kiite
 imasu ka?

Hai, tēpu dai jū-ichi o mada kiite imasu.

Jū-ban no tēpu wa mō kiite imasen ne?

Hai, jū-ban no tēpu wa mō kiite imasen.

Anata wa mada Nihon-go o benkyō shite
 imasu ka?

Hai, mada Nihon-go o benkyō shite
 imasu.

Mada ichi-pēji o benkyō shite imasu ka?

Iie, mō ichi-pēji wa benkyō shite imasen.

Anata wa yūbe nemashita ka?

Hai, yūbe nemashita.

Mada nete imasu ka?

Iie, mō nete imasen.

Made okite imasu ka?

Hai, mada okite imasu.

Ima gogo san-ji desu. Hisho wa mada
 jimusho ni imasu ka?

Hai, hisho wa mada jimusho ni imasu.

Hai, yoku dekimashita!

Kiite kudasai!
Koko wa saka-ya desu.
Watashi-tachi wa saka-ya ni imasu.

Kotaete kudasai!
Watashi-tachi wa ima tabako-ya ni
 imasu ka?

Iie, ima tabako-ya ni imasen.

Doko ni imasu ka?

Saka-ya ni imasu.

Saka-ya de tabako o kaimasu ka?

Iie, saka-ya de tabako o kaimasen.

Saka-ya de nani o kaimasu ka?

Saka-ya de osake o kaimasu.

Doko de tabako o kaimasu ka?

Tabako-ya de tabako o kaimasu.

Okyaku wa tabako o kaimasu ka?

Hai, okyaku wa tabako o kaimasu.

Ten-in wa tabako o kaimasu ka,
 soretomo urimasu ka?

Ten-in wa tabako o urimasu.

Ten-in wa sakana-ya de nani o
 urimasu ka?

Ten-in wa sakana-ya de sakana o
 urimasu.

Yoku dekimashita!
Jōzu ni kotaemashita ne!

Kiite kudasai!
Katō-san desu.
Katō-san ga saka-ya e kimashita.

— *Irasshaimase. Nan de gozaimasu ka?*
— *Ēto, budōshu o kudasai.*
— *Iroiro arimasu ga . . .*
— *Aka wa arimasu ka?*
— *Hai, gozaimasu.*

Kotaete kudasai!
Katō-san wa mō saka-ya e hairimashita ka?

Hai, mō saka-ya e hairimashita.

Mō ten-in ni hanashimashita ka?

Hai, mō ten-in ni hanashimashita.

Ten-in wa mō budōshu o misemashita ka?

Iie, mada budōshu o misete imasen.

Katō-san wa mō budōshu o kaimashita ka?

Iie, mada budōshu o katte imasen.

Hai, sō desu.

Mata kiite kudasai!

— *Ēto, budōshu o kudasai.*
— *Hai, iroiro arimasu ga . . .*

— *Aka wa arimasu ka?*
— *Hai, gozaimasu. Sō desu nē, kore wa ikaga desu ka? Furansu no budōshu desu. Nisen-en
   desu ga . . .*
— *Nisen-en! Chotto takai desu nē. Mō sukoshi yasui no wa arimasen ka?*
— *Hai, gozaimasu.*

Kotaete kudasai!
Ten-in wa mō budōshu o misemashita ka?
Sono budōshu wa sanzen-en desu ka?

Ikura desu ka?
Kono nedan wa takai desu ka, yasui
   desu ka?
Sore wa Nihon no budōshu desu ka,
   Furansu no budōshu desu ka?
Mō sukoshi yasui budōshu ga arimasu ka?

Hai, mō budōshu o misemashita.
Iie, sono budōshu wa sanzen-en ja
   arimasen.
Nisen-en desu.

Kono nedan wa takai desu.

Furansu no budōshu desu.
Hai, mō sukoshi yasui budōshu ga
   arimasu.

Yoku dekimashita ne!

Mata kaiwa o kiite kudasai!
Katō-san to ten-in desu.

— *Mō sukoshi yasui budōshu wa arimasen ka?*
— *Hai, gozaimasu! Kore wa ikaga desu ka? Nihon no desu yo!*
— *Ikura desu ka?*
— *Sen-en desu.*
— *Sen-en desu ka! Sore de kekkō desu! Nihon no o kudasai!*

Sā, kotaete kudasai!
Katō-san wa takai budōshu o kaimashita
   ka?
Donna budōshu o kaimashita ka?
Furansu no budōshu o kaimashita ka?

Doko no budōshu o kaimashita ka?
Nihon no budōshu wa gohyaku-en
   desu ka?
Jā, ikura desu ka?

Iie, takai budōshu o kaimasen deshita.
Yasui budōshu o kaimashita.
Iie, Furansu no budōshu o kaimasen
   deshita.
Nihon no budōshu o kaimashita.
Iie, Nihon no budōshu wa gohyaku-en
   ja arimasen.
Sen-en desu.

Sō desu ne!
Budōshu wa i-ppon sen-en desu.

Kotaete kudasai!
Budōshu wa ni-hon nisen-en desu ka?
Jā, san-bon ikura desu ka?

Hai, budōshu wa ni-hon nisen-en desu.
San-bon sanzen-en desu.

Hai, jōzu ni kotaemashita ne!

Itte kudasai!
Kōhii wa i-ppai sanbyaku-en desu.

Kōhii wa ni-hai ikura desu ka?
San-bai ikura desu ka?

Kōhii wa ni-hai roppyaku-en desu.
San-bai kyūhyaku-en desu.

Hai, kyūhyaku-en desu.
Jōzu ni dekimashita!

Mata kaiwa o kiite kudasai!
Katō-san to ten-in desu.

— *Kore wa ikaga desu ka? Nihon no desu yo! Sen-en desu!*
— *Sen-en desu ka! Sore de kekkō desu. Nihon no o kudasai.*
— *Hoka ni nani ka?*
— *Ēto, jā kono biiru o san-bon kudasai.*
— *Hai, wakarimashita.*

Kotaete kudasai!

Katō-san wa mō budōshu o kaimashita ka?	Hai, kare wa mō budōshu o kaimashita.
Hoka ni nani ka kaimashita ka?	Hai, hoka ni nani ka kaimashita.
Hoka ni osake o kaimashita ka, biiru o kaimashita ka?	Hoka ni biiru o kaimashita.
Biiru o go-hon kaimashita ka?	Iie, biiru o go-hon kaimasen deshita.
Biiru o nan-bon kaimashita ka?	Biiru o san-bon kaimashita.

Hai, yoku dekimashita ne!

Mō ichi-do kaiwa o kiite kudasai!
Soshite itte kudasai!

— *Irasshaimase. Nan de gozaimasu ka?*
— *Ēto, budōshu o kudasai.*
— *Iroiro arimasu ga . . .*
— *Aka wa arimasu ka?*
— *Hai, gozaimasu! Sō desu nē, kore wa ikaga desu ka? Furansu no budōshu desu.*
    Nisen-en desu ga . . .
— *Nisen-en! Chotto takai desu nē! Mō sukoshi yasui no wa arimasen ka?*
— *Hai, gozaimasu. Kore wa ikaga desu ka? Nihon no desu yo! Sen-en desu.*
— *Sen-en desu ka! Sore de kekkō desu.*
— *Hoka ni nani ka?*
— *Ēto, jā, kono biiru o san-bon kudasai.*
— *Hai, wakarimashita!*

Hai, sō desu.
Totemo jōzu ni dekimashita nē!   A, dōmo arigatō!
Kore de tēpu dai jū-ichi o owarimasu.
Jū-ichi-ban no tēpu wa kore de owari desu.

Sayonara!   Sayonara!

TĒPU DAI JŪ-NI (12)

Jū-ni-ban no tēpu desu.
Konnichiwa!   Konnichiwa!

Kiite kudasai!

(Roshia-go)

Kono hito wa Roshia-go o hanashite imasu.

Kotaete kudasai!

Furansu-jin wa Roshia-go o hanashimasu ka?	Iie, Furansu-jin wa Roshia-go o hanashimasen.
Nani-jin ga Roshia-go o hanashimasu ka?	Roshia-jin ga Roshia-go o hanashimasu.
Anata wa Roshia-jin desu ka?	Iie, watashi wa Roshia-jin ja arimasen.

Dōzo! Roshia-go o hanashite kudasai!

Ā, anata wa Roshia-go o hanasu koto ga dekimasen nē!	Hai, watashi wa Roshia-go o hanasu koto ga dekimasen.
Sukoshi Nihon-go o hanasu koto ga dekimasu ka?	Hai, sukoshi Nihon-go o hanasu koto ga dekimasu.
Sensei ni Nihon-go de kotaeru koto ga dekimasu ka?	Hai, sensei ni Nihon-go de kotaeru koto ga dekimasu.
Ima anata wa tēpu-rekōdā o miru koto ga dekimasu ka?	Hai, ima tēpu-rekōdā o miru koto ga dekimasu.
Jā, anata wa ima watashi o miru koto ga dekimasu ka?	Iie, anata o miru koto ga dekimasen.
Anata no tēpu o kiku koto ga dekimasu ka?	Hai, watashi no tēpu o kiku koto ga dekimasu.
Watashi no rajio o kiku koto ga dekimasu ka?	Iie, anata no rajio o kiku koto ga dekimasen.

Sō desu.
Yoku dekimashita!

Kotaete kudasai!

Anata wa Berurittsu no hon o motte imasu ka?	Hai, watashi wa Berurittsu no hon o motte imasu.
Sono hon wa ōkii desu ne? Hai, . . .	Hai, sono hon wa ōkii desu.
Hon o poketto ni ireru koto ga dekimasu ka?	Iie, hon o poketto ni ireru koto ga dekimasen.
Dōshite desu ka? Hon wa ōki-sugimasu ka?	Hai, hon wa ōki-sugimasu.
Poketto wa chiisa-sugimasu ka?	Hai, poketto wa chiisa-sugimasu.
Hon ga ōki-sugiru kara poketto ni ireru koto ga dekimasen ne?	Hai, hon ga ōki-sugiru kara poketto ni ireru koto ga dekimasen.

Hayaku itte kudasai!
Hon ga ōki-sugiru kara poketto ni ireru koto ga dekimasen.

Hai, yoku dekimashita!
Kiite kudasai!

(hikōki)

Are wa nan desu ka?	Are wa hikōki desu.
Hikōki wa takai desu ka?	Hai, hikōki wa takai desu.
Anata wa hikōki o kau koto ga dekimasu ka?	Iie, hikōki o kau koto ga dekimasen.
Dōshite desu ka? Hikōki wa taka-sugimasu ka?	Hai, hikōki wa taka-sugimasu.

Dōshite anata wa hikōki o kau koto ga
dekimasen ka?

Hikōki wa taka-sugimasu kara kau koto
ga dekimasen.

Mō ichi-do hayaku itte kudasai!
Hikōki wa taka-sugimasu kara kau koto ga dekimasen.

Sō desu.
Kondo wa kiite kudasai!
Ima yoru jū-ji desu.

Kotaete kudasai!
Yoru wa akarui desu ka, kurai desu ka?

Yoru wa kurai desu.

Yoru denki nashi de hon o yomu koto ga
dekimasu ka?

Iie, yoru denki nashi de hon o yomu koto
ga dekimasen.

Dōshite desu ka? Yoru wa
kura-sugimasu ka?

Hai, yoru wa kura-sugimasu.

Dōshite yoru denki nashi de hon o yomu
koto ga dekimasen ka?

Yoru wa kura-sugimasu kara denki nashi
de hon o yomu koto ga dekimasen.

Mō ichi-do!
Yoru wa kura-sugimasu kara denki nashi de hon o yomu koto ga dekimasen.
Yoku dekimashita.
Mō ichi-do kotaete kudasai!

Tōkyō kara Hiroshima made wa tōi
desu ka?

Hai, Tōkyō kara Hiroshima made wa
tōi desu.

Tōkyō kara Hiroshima e aruite iku koto
ga dekimasu ka?

Iie, Tōkyō kara Hiroshima made aruite
iku koto ga dekimasen.

Tō-sugimasu ne?

Hai, tō-sugimasu.

Dōshite anata wa aruite iku koto ga
dekimasen ka?

Tō-sugimasu kara watashi wa aruite
iku koto ga dekimasen.

Mō ichi-do!
Tō-sugimasu kara watashi wa aruite iku koto ga dekimasen.
Hai, sō desu!
Tōkyō kara Hiroshima made wa tō-sugimasu ne!

Tsugi wa kaiwa desu.
Kiite kudasai!
Katō-san desu.
Katō-san wa eki made no michi o kikimasu.

— *Sumimasen ga, densha no eki wa koko kara tōi desu ka?*
— *Iie, totemo chikai desu. Kono michi o massugu itte kudasai.*
— *Aruite dono kurai kakarimasu ka?*
— *Sō desu nē . . . Go-fun gurai kakaru deshō!*
— *Dōmo arigatō!*
— *Dō-itashimashite!*

Kotaete kudasai!
Katō-san wa michi o kikimashita ka?

Hai, kare wa michi o kikimashita.

Doko made no michi o kikimashita ka?

Eki made no michi o kikimashita.

Eki wa tōi desu ka?

Iie, eki wa tōku wa arimasen.

Eki wa chikai desu ka?

Hai, chikai desu.

Totemo chikai desu ka?
Eki made aruite ichi-jikan kakarimasu ka?

Dono gurai kakarimasu ka?

Hai, sō desu!

Eki wa chikai desu ne! Sa itte kudasai!
Aruite go-fun kakarimasu.
Aruite go-fun kakaru deshō.

Hisho wa jimusho ni imasu.
  Hisho wa jimusho ni iru . . .
Ima san-ji goro desu.
  Ima . . .
Ishikawa-san wa kyō kimasu.
  Kare wa . . .
Ashita wa ame ga furimasu.
  Ashita wa . . .
Raishū kyūka o torimasu.
Hisho wa mō kite imasu.
Ishikawa-san wa go-ji ni kaerimasu.

Hai, sō desu.
Tsugi wa kaiwa desu.

Katō-san wa michi o kiite imasu. Itte kudasai!

— Sumimasen ga, densha no eki wa koko kara tōi desu ka?
— Iie, totemo chikai desu. Kono michi o massugu itte kudasai!
— Aruite dono kurai kakarimasu ka?
— Sō desu nē . . . Go-fun gurai kakaru deshō!
— Dōmo arigatō!
— Dō-itashimashite!

Yoku dekimashita!
Anata wa taihen jōzu ni iu koto ga dekimashita ne!
Kore de tēpu dai jū-ni o owarimasu.
Jū-ni-ban no tēpu wa kore de owari desu.

Sayonara!

Hai, totemo chikai desu.
Iie, eki made aruite ichi-jikan
  kakarimasen.
Go-fun gurai kakarimasu.

Hisho wa jimusho ni iru deshō.

Ima san-ji goro deshō.

Kare wa kyō kuru deshō.

Ashita wa ame ga furu deshō.
Raishū kyūka o toru deshō.
Hisho wa mō kite iru deshō.
Ishikawa-san wa go-ji ni kaeru deshō.

Sayonara!

TĒPU DAI JŪ-SAN (13)

Jū-san-ban no tēpu desu.
Konnichiwa!

Sā, kotaete kudasai!
Anata wa gakkō de Nihon-go o benkyō
  shite imasu ka?
Nihon e ikitai desu ka?

Konnichiwa!

Hai, gakkō de Nihon-go o benkyō shite
  imasu.
Hai, Nihon e ikitai desu.

Nihon-jin ni aitai desu ka?
Nihon-jin to Nihon-go de hanashitai
  desu ka?

Hai, Nihon-jin ni aitai desu.
Hai, Nihon-jin to Nihon-go de hanashitai
  desu.

Yoku dekimashita ne!

Kondo wa kiite kudasai!
Tanaka-san to Noguchi-san desu.

— *Kono heya de tabako o sutte mo ii desu ka?*
— *Sumimasen ga, koko de suwanai de kudasai!*
— *Sō desu ka! Rōka de wa sutte mo ii desu ka?*
— *Ē, mochiron ii desu yo!*

Kotaete kudasai!
Rōka de tabako o sutte mo ii desu ka?
Michi de tabako o sutte mo ii desu ka?
Kono heya de tabako o sutte mo ii
  desu ka?
Basu de tabako o sutte mo ii desu ka?

Hai, rōka de tabako o sutte mo ii desu.
Hai, michi de tabako o sutte mo ii desu.
Iie, kono heya de tabako o sutte wa
  ikemasen.
Iie, basu de tabako o sutte wa
  ikemasen.

Nihon-go no kurasu de Nihon-go o
  hanashite mo ii desu ka?
Nihon-go no kurasu de Eigo o hanashite
  mo ii desu ka?

Hai, Nihon-go no kurasu de Nihon-go o
  hanashite mo ii desu.
Iie, Nihon-go no kurasu de Eigo o
  hanashite wa ikemasen.

Hai, sō desu!
Jōzu ni kotaemashita nē!
Tsugi wa mondai desu!

Koko de tabete mo ii desu ka?
  Hai, . . .
  Iie, . . .
Uchi e kaette mo ii desu ka?
  Hai, . . .
  Iie, . . .
Osoku kite mo ii desu ka?
  Hai, . . .
  Iie, . . .

Hai, tabete mo ii desu.
Iie, tabete wa ikemasen.

Hai, kaette mo ii desu.
Iie, kaette wa ikemasen.

Hai, osoku kite mo ii desu.
Iie, osoku kite wa ikemasen.

Hai, yoku dekimashita!

Kondo wa kotaete kudasai!
Anata wa ima eiga o mitai desu ka? Iie, . . .
Eiga o mitai toki, gakkō e ikimasu ka?
Ja, eiga o mitai toki, doko e ikimasu ka?

Iie, ima eiga o mitaku arimasen.
Iie, eiga o mitai toki, gakkō e ikimasen.
Eiga o mitai toki, eiga-kan e ikimasu.

Totemo jōzu ni dekimashita ne!
Tsugi wa kono mondai o shimashō!

Itte kudasai!
Eiga-kan de eiga o mimasu.
Eiga o mitai toki, eiga-kan e ikimasu.

Gakkō de Nihon-go o hanashimasu.
Nihon-go o hanashitai toki, . . .
Kissaten de ocha o nomimasu.
Ocha o nomitai toki, . . .
Resutoran de sukiyaki o tabemasu.
Sukiyaki o tabetai toki, . . .

Nihon-go o hanashitai toki, gakkō e
ikimasu.

Ocha o nomitai toki, kissaten e ikimasu.
Sukiyaki o tabetai toki, resutoran e
ikimasu.

Hai, sō desu.

Kotaete kudasai!
Tokidoki resutoran e ikimasu ka?
Resutoran e iku toki, basu ni norimasu
ka? Hai, . . .
Nihon e iku toki, nani ni norimasu ka?

Hai, tokidoki resutoran e ikimasu.
Hai, resutoran e iku toki, basu ni
norimasu.
Nihon e iku toki, hikōki ni norimasu.

Hai, yoku dekimashita!
Tsugi wa mondai desu.

Itte kudasai!
Watashi wa Nihon e ikimasu.
Hikōki ni norimasu.
Nihon e iku toki, hikōki ni norimasu.

Shinbun o yomimasu.
Megane o tsukaimasu.
Shinbun o . . .

Shinbun o yomu toki, megane o
tsukaimasu.

Kōhii o nomimasu.
Kissaten e ikimasu.
Kōhii o nomu toki, . . .

Kōhii o nomu toki, kissaten e ikimasu.

Uchi ni imasu.
Ongaku o kikimasu.
Uchi ni . . .

Uchi ni iru toki, ongaku o kikimasu.

Hai, totemo jōzu ni dekimashita ne!
Tsugi wa kaiwa desu!

Kiite kudasai!
Noguchi-san to Burēku-san desu.
Burēku-san wa Amerika no tomodachi desu.

— Burēku-san, konnichiwa!
— Konnichiwa, Noguchi-san!
— Burēku-san, konban issho ni shokuji o shimasen ka?
— Ē, yorokonde!
— Washoku ga tabetai desu ka?
— Hai, totemo tabetai desu ne!

Kotaete kudasai!
Burēku-san wa resutoran e ikitai desu ka?
Yōshoku no resutoran e ikitai desu ka?

Hai, resutoran e ikitai desu.
Iie, yōshoku no resutoran e ikitaku
arimasen.

Nan no resutoran e ikitai desu ka?   Washoku no resutoran e ikitai desu.

Yoku dekimashita.

Mata kaiwa o kiite kudasai!
Noguchi-san to Burēku-san desu.

— *Demo Noguchi-san, watashi wa hashi de wa taberaremasen.*
— *Sō desu ka! Demo, hashi de taberu no wa zenzen muzukashiku arimasen yo! Totemo*
   yasashii desu yo!

Kotaete kudasai!
Burēku-san wa hashi de taberaremasu ka?   Iie, hashi de taberaremasen.
Noguchi-san wa hashi de taberaremasu ka?   Hai, hashi de taberaremasu.
Kagi nashi de doā ga akeraremasu ka?   Iie, kagi nashi de doā ga akeraremasen.
Kagi nashi de doā o akeru koto ga   Hai, kagi nashi de doā o akeru koto
   dekimasen ne?   ga dekimasen.

Yoku dekimashita!
Tsugi wa mondai desu.

Itte kudasai!
Kagi nashi de doā o akeru koto ga dekimasen.
Kagi nashi de doā ga akeraremasen.

Hasami nashi de kami o kiru koto ga
   dekimasen.
   Hasami nashi de . . .   Hasami nashi de kami ga kiremasen.
Rajio nashi de ongaku o kiku koto ga
   dekimasen.
   Rajio nashi de . . .   Rajio nashi de ongaku ga kikemasen.

Kotaete kudasai!
Anata wa rajio o motte imasu ka? Hai . . .   Hai, rajio o motte imasu.
Rajio de ongaku ga kikemasu ka?   Hai, rajio de ongaku ga kikemasu.
Watashi wa rajio o motte imasen.
   Watashi wa ongaku ga kikemasu ka?   Iie, anata wa ongaku ga kikemasen.
Moshi rajio o motte ireba ongaku ga   Hai, moshi rajio o motte ireba ongaku ga
   kikemasu ka?   kikemasu.
Moshi rajio o motte inakereba ongaku ga   Hai, moshi rajio o motte inakereba
   kikemasen ka?   ongaku ga kikemasen.

Mō ichi-do hayaku!
Moshi rajio o motte inakereba ongaku ga kikemasen.

Itte kudasai!
Rajio de ongaku ga kikemasu.
Rajio o motte ireba ongaku ga kikemasu.
Rajio o motte inakereba ongaku ga kikemasen.

Kagi de doā ga akeraremasu.
Kagi o motte ireba . . .   Kagi o motte ireba doā ga akeraremasu.
Kagi o motte inakereba . . .   Kagi o motte inakereba doā ga
                                                  akeraremasen.

Enpitsu de namae ga kakemasu.
Enpitsu o motte ireba . . .
Enpitsu o motte inakereba . . .

Enpitsu o motte ireba namae ga
kakemasu.
Enpitsu o motte inakereba namae ga
kakemasen.

Sō desu.
Enpitsu ga nakereba, namae ga kakemasen ne!
Totemo jōzu ni dekimashita!
Kore de tēpu dai jū-san o owarimasu.
Jū-san-ban no tēpu wa kore de owari desu.

Sayonara!

Sayonara!

TĒPU DAI JŪ-YON (14)

Jū-yon-ban no tēpu desu.
Konnichiwa!

Konnichiwa!

Kotaete kudasai!
Anata wa jōzu ni Nihon-go o hanashitai
desu ka?
Anata wa Nihon-go o benkyō shitai
desu ka?
Nihon-go o benkyō suru tame ni, tēpu
o kikimasu ne?
Sensei to hanasu tame ni, gakkō e
ikimasu ka?
Eiga o miru tame ni, kissaten e
ikimasu ka?
Ja, eiga o miru tame ni, doko e
ikimasu ka?
Kaimono o suru tame ni mo, eiga-kan e
ikimasu ka?
Kaimono o suru tame ni, ginkō e ikimasu
ka, soretomo depāto e ikimasu ka?
Kaimono o suru tame ni, ginkō e
ikimasen ne?
Okane o dasu tame ni, ginkō e
ikimasu ka?
Hikōki ni noru tame ni mo, ginkō e
ikimasu ka?
Dewa, hikōki ni noru tame ni, doko e
ikimasu ka?
Densha ni noru tame ni, doko e
ikimasu ka?

Hai, jōzu ni Nihon-go o hanashitai desu.

Hai, Nihon-go o benkyō shitai desu.

Hai, Nihon-go o benkyō suru tame ni,
tēpu o kikimasu.
Hai, sensei to hanasu tame ni, gakkō e
ikimasu.
Iie, eiga o miru tame ni, kissaten e
ikimasen.

Eiga o miru tame ni, eiga-kan e ikimasu.
Iie, kaimono o suru tame ni wa, eiga-kan
e ikimasen.
Kaimono o suru tame ni, depāto e
ikimasu.
Hai, kaimono o suru tame ni, ginkō e
ikimasen.
Hai, okane o dasu tame ni ginkō e
ikimasu.
Iie, hikōki ni noru tame ni wa, ginkō e
ikimasen.
Hikōki ni noru tame ni, kūkō e
ikimasu.
Densha ni noru tame ni, eki e
ikimasu.

Hai, yoku dekimashita ne!

Itte kudasai!
Densha ni norimasu.
Eki e ikimasu.
Densha ni noru tame ni, eki e ikimasu.

Heya ni hairimasu.
Doā o akemasu.
Heya ni hairu tame ni, . . .

Heya ni hairu tame ni, doā o akemasu.

Doā o akemasu.
Kagi o tsukaimasu.
Doā o . . .

Doā o akeru tame ni, kagi o tsukaimasu.

Tōkyō e ikimasu.
Kippu o kaimasu.
Tōkyō e . . .

Tōkyō e iku tame ni, kippu o kaimasu.

Kippu o kaimasu.
Okane ga irimasu.
Kippu o . . .

Kippo o kau tame ni, okane ga irimasu.

Okane o kaemasu.
Ginkō e ikimasu.
Okane o . . .

Okane o kaeru tame ni, ginkō e ikimasu.

Sō desu.
Totemo yoku dekimashita yo!

Kiite kudasai!
Katō-san wa ima Tōkyō-Ginkō ni imasu.
Okane o kaeru tame ni, ginkō e ikimashita.
Ima ginkō-in to hanashite imasu.

— *Irasshaimase!*
— *Amerika no doru ga kaeraremasu ka?*
— *Hai, koko de kaeraremasu. Ikura kaetai-no desu ka?*
— *Hyaku-doru o en ni kaetai-no desu ga . . .*

Kotaete kudasai!
Katō-san wa ima doko ni imasu ka?   Ima ginkō ni imasu.
Dare to hanashite imasu ka?   Ginkō-in to hanashite imasu.
Furansu no okane o kaete imasu ka?   Iie, Furansu no okane o kaete imasen.
Doko no okane o kaete imasu ka?   Amerika no okane o kaete imasu.

Hai, sō desu. Katō-san wa doru o en ni kaete imasu.

Kiite kudasai!
Katō-san to ginkō-in desu.

— *Ikura kaetai-no desu ka?*
— *Hyaku-doru o en ni kaetai-no desu ga . . .*

Kotaete kudasai!
Katō-san wa sanbyaku-doru kaetai-no   Iie, sanbyaku-doru kaetai-no ja
  desu ka?   arimasen.
Ikura kaetai-no desu ka?   Hyaku-doru kaetai-no desu.

Hai, yoku dekimashita.

Anata wa tokidoki ginkō e ikimasu ne?   Hai, watashi wa tokidoki ginkō e ikimasu.

Anata wa ginkō de ginkō-in to
 hanashimasu ka?
Anata wa sengetsu mo ginkō e
 ikimashita ka? Hai . . .
Ginkō e itta toki, ginkō-in ni
 aimashita ka?
Ginkō e itta toki, okane o kaemashita
 ka? Hai, . . .

Hai, yoku dekimashita ne!

Itte kudasai!
Ginkō e ikimashita.
Okane o kaemashita.
Ginkō e itta toki, okane o kaemashita.

Kinō depāto e ikimashita.
Kutsu o kaimashita.
Depāto e itta toki . . .

Tōkyō e ikimashita.
Ginza o arukimashita.
Tōkyō e itta toki . . .

Basu ni norimashita.
Taihen konde imashita.
Basu ni . . .

Sanpo shimashita.
Sakura no hana o mimashita.
Sanpo . . .

Kaze o hikimashita.
Byōin e ikimashita.
Kaze o . . .

Kotaete kudasai!
Anata wa tokidoki kaze o hikimasu ka?
Fuyu ni wa kaze o yoku hikimasu ka?
Fuyu ni wa kaze o hiki-yasui desu ka?
Kono tēpu wa benkyō shi-yasui desu ka?

Berurittsu no jugyō wa wakari-yasui
 desu ka?

Hai, sō desu!
Berurittsu no jugyō wa totemo wakari-yasui desu ne!
Taihen yoku dekimashita!
Totemo jōzu ni kotaeraremashita ne!
Kore de tēpu dai jū-yon o owarimasu.
Jū-yon-ban no tēpu wa kore de owari desu.

Sayonara!

Hai, watashi wa ginkō de ginkō-in to
 hanashimasu.

Hai, sengetsu mo ginkō e ikimashita.
Hai, ginkō e itta toki, ginkō-in ni
 aimashita.
Hai, ginkō e itta toki, okane o
 kaemashita.

Depāto e itta toki, kutsu o kaimashita.

Tōkyō e itta toki, Ginza o arukimashita.

Basu ni notta toki, taihen konde
 imashita.

Sanpo shita toki, sakura no hana o
 mimashita.

Kaze o hiita toki, byōin e ikimashita.

Hai, tokidoki kaze o hikimasu.
Hai, fuyu ni wa kaze o yoku hikimasu.
Hai, fuyu ni wa kaze o hiki-yasui desu.
Hai, kono tēpu wa benkyō shi-yasui
 desu.
Hai, Berurittsu no jugyō wa wakari-yasui
 desu.

Sayonara!

TĒPU DAI JŪ-GO (15)

Jū-go-ban no tēpu desu.
Konnichiwa!   Konnichiwa!

Sā, kiite kudasai!
Harada-san to Katō-san desu.

— *Konnichiwa, Katō-san! O-genki desu ka?*
— *Ē, okagesamade!*
— *Okusan mo o-genki desu ka?*
— *Hai, kanai mo genki desu!*

Kotaete kudasai!
Harada-san wa Katō-san ni nani ka
   iimashita ka?   Hai, kare ni nani ka iimashita.
Katō-san wa o-genki desu ka?   Hai, o-genki desu.
Okusan mo o-genki desu ka?   Hai, okusan mo o-genki desu.

Totemo jōzu ni dekimashita ne!

Itte kudasai!
Anata no okusan.
Watashi no kanai.
Okusan wa o-genki desu.
Kanai wa genki desu.

Kotaete kudasai!
Okusan wa o-genki desu ka?   Hai, kanai wa genki desu.
Go-kazoku wa o-genki desu ka?   Hai, kazoku wa genki desu.
Go-shujin wa o-genki desu ka?   Hai, shujin wa genki desu.
Musuko-san wa o-genki desu ka?   Hai, musuko wa genki desu.
Okāsan wa o-genki desu ka?   Hai, haha wa genki desu.
Otōsan wa o-genki desu ka?   Hai, chichi wa genki desu.

Yoku dekimashita!

Kondo wa itte kudasai!
Watashi wa Tōkyō e ikimasu.
Anata wa Tōkyō e irasshaimasu.

Watashi wa Kyōto kara kimasu.
   Anata wa . . .   Anata wa Kyōto kara irasshaimasu.
Watashi wa Tōkyō ni sunde imasu.
   Anata wa . . .   Anata wa Tōkyō ni sunde irasshaimasu.
Watashi wa biiru o nonde imasu.
   Anata wa . . .   Anata wa biiru o nonde irasshaimasu.
Watashi wa tabako o suimasu.
   Anata wa . . .   Anata wa tabako o o-sui ni narimasu.
Watashi wa hon o yomimasu.
   Anata wa . . .   Anata wa hon o o-yomi ni narimasu.
Watashi wa tegami o kakimasu.
   Anata wa . . .   Anata wa tegami o o-kaki ni narimasu.

Watashi wa konnichiwa to iimasu.
  Anata wa . . .   Anata wa konnichiwa to osshaimasu.

Hai, totemo jōzu ni dekimashita nē!

Tsugi wa Harada-san to Katō-san no kaiwa o mō ichi-do kiite kudasai!

— *Konnichiwa, Katō-san! O-genki desu ka?*
— *Ē, okagesamade!*
— *Okusan mo o-genki desu ka?*
— *Hai, kanai mo genki desu!*

Kotaete kudasai!
Harada-san wa Katō-san ni konnichiwa
  to iimashita ka?   Hai, Katō-san ni konnichiwa to iimashita.
Katō-san ni nani ka kikimashita ka?   Hai, Katō-san ni nani ka kikimashita.
O-genki desu ka to kikimashita ka?   Hai, o-genki desu ka to kikimashita.
Katō-san wa nani ka iimashita ka?   Hai, nani ka iimashita.
Harada-san ni okagesamade to iimashita ka?   Hai, okagesamade to iimashita.

Sō desu.
Tsugi wa mondai desu.
Konnichiwa!

Kotaete kudasai!
Watashi wa konnichiwa to iimashita ka?   Hai, anata wa konnichiwa to iimashita.

Tōkyō wa ōkii desu.
  Nan to iimashita ka?   Tōkyō wa ōkii to iimashita.
Sapporo wa ōkiku arimasen.
  Nan to iimashita ka?   Sapporo wa ōkiku nai to iimashita.
Densha wa nagai desu.
  Nan to iimashita ka?   Densha wa nagai to iimashita.
Kagi wa nagaku arimasen.
  Nan to iimashita ka?   Kagi wa nagaku nai to iimashita.
Katō-san wa Nihon-jin desu.
  Nan to iimashita ka?   Katō-san wa Nihon-jin da to iimashita.
Jōnzu-san wa seito desu.
  Nan to iimashita ka?   Jōnzu-san wa seito da to iimashita.
Katō-san wa seito ja arimasen.
  Nan to iimashita ka?   Katō-san wa seito ja nai to iimashita.
Kore wa Nihon-go no tēpu desu.   Kore wa Nihon-go no tēpu da to
  Nan to iimashita ka?   iimashita.
Are wa Nihon-go no tēpu ja arimasen.   Are wa Nihon-go no tēpu ja nai to
  Nan to iimashita ka?   iimashita.
Jōnzu-san wa gakkō e ikimasu.
  Nan to iimashita ka?   Jōnzu-san wa gakkō e iku to iimashita.
Katō-san wa gakkō e ikimasen.   Katō-san wa gakkō e ikanai to
  Nan to iimashita ka?   iimashita.
Jōnzu-san wa Eigo o hanashimasu.   Jōnzu-san wa Eigo o hanasu to
  Nan to iimashita ka?   iimashita.
Katō-san wa Eigo o hanashimasen.   Katō-san wa Eigo o hanasanai to
  Nan to iimashita ka?   iimashita.

Hai, taihen yoku dekimashita ne!

Kiite kudasai!
Harada-san to Katō-san desu.

(inu)

— *Katō-san, are wa nan desu ka?*
— *Inu desu! Are wa inu desu yo!*

Kotaete kudasai!
Katō-san wa Harada-san ni nani ka
   iimashita ka?   Hai, kanojo ni nani ka iimashita.
Are wa neko da to iimashita ka?   Iie, are wa neko da to iimasen deshita.
Nan to iimashita ka?   Are wa inu da to iimashita.

Hai, sō desu ne!

Mata kiite kudasai!
Harada-san to Katō-san desu.

(inu)

— *Katō-san, are wa neko ja arimasen ka?*
— *Ē, neko ja arimasen. Are wa inu desu.*

Kotaete kudasai!
Katō-san wa mata nani ka iimashita ka?   Hai, mata nani ka iimashita.
Are wa neko da to iimashita ka?   Iie, are wa neko da to iimasen deshita.
Neko da to iimashita ka neko ja nai to
   iimashita ka?   Neko ja nai to iimashita.

Totemo yoku dekimashita ne!

Kiite kudasai!
Katō-san ga ima aruite imasu.

Kotaete kudasai!
Katō-san wa nani o shite imasu ka?   Aruite imasu.
Anata mo aruite imasu ka?   Iie, aruite imasen.
Aruite iru hito wa Katō-san desu ne?   Hai, aruite iru hito wa Katō-san desu.

Sō desu. Aruite iru hito ga Katō-san desu.
Totemo jōzu ni dekimashita ne!

Itte kudasai!
Katō-san ga aruite imasu.
Aruite iru hito wa Katō-san desu.

Katō-san ga tabako o sutte imasu.   Tabako o sutte iru hito ga Katō-san
   Tabako o sutte iru . . .   desu.
Harada-san ga taipu shite imasu.   Taipu shite iru hito ga Harada-san
   Taipu shite iru . . .   desu.
Yokoi-san ga ocha o nonde imasu.   Ocha o nonde iru hito ga Yokoi-san
   Ocha o nonde . . .   desu.

Okyaku-san ga hon o katte imasu.
  Hon o katte . . .
Katō-san ga denwa shite imasu.
  Denwa shite . . .
Sasaki-san ga michi o oshiete imasu.
  Michi o oshiete . . .
Seito ga tēpu o kiite imasu.
  Tēpu o kiite . . .

Hon o katte iru hito ga Okyaku-san
  desu.

Denwa shite iru hito ga Katō-san desu.
Michi o oshiete iru hito ga Sasaki-san
  desu.

Tēpu o kiite iru hito ga seito desu.

Sō desu!
Tēpu o kiite iru hito ga seito desu.
Anata wa seito desu ne!
Anata wa kono tēpu o kiite imasu.
Kore de kono tēpu, tēpu dai jū-go o owarimasu.
Jū-go-ban no tēpu wa kore de owari desu.

Sayonara!

Sayonara!

TĒPU DAI JŪ-ROKU (16)

Jū-roku-ban no tēpu desu.
Konnichiwa!

Konnichiwa!

Kiite kudasai!
Harada-san to Tanaka-san desu.

(san-ji)

— *Harada-san, ima nan-ji desu ka?*
— *Ima san-ji desu.*
— *Arigatō!*

Kotaete kudasai!
Tanaka-san wa nani ka kikimashita ka?
Nan-yōbi ka to kikimashita ka?
Nan to kikimashita ka?
Harada-san wa Tanaka-san ni
  kotaemashita ka?
Harada-san wa ima ichi-ji da to
  kotaemashita ka?
Ni-ji da to kotaemashita ka?
Nan to kotaemashita ka?

Hai, nani ka kikimashita.
Iie, nan-yōbi ka to kikimasen deshita.
Ima nan-ji ka to kikimashita.

Hai, Tanaka-san ni kotaemashita.

Iie, ima ichi-ji da to kotaemasen deshita.
Iie, ni-ji da to kotaemasen deshita.
San-ji da to kotaemashita.

Totemo jōzu ni kotaemashita ne!

Mata Harada-san to Tanaka-san no kaiwa o kikimashō.

— *Harada-san, kyō wa kin-yōbi desu ka?*
— *Iie, kyō wa kin-yōbi ja arimasen.*

Kotaete kudasai!
Tanaka-san wa mata nani ka
  kikimashita ka?

Hai, mata nani ka kikimashita.

Kyō wa sui-yōbi ka to kikimashita ka?

Nan to kikimashita ka?
Harada-san wa kyō wa kin-yōbi da to
   kotaemashita ka?
Ja, nan to kotaemashita ka?

Yoku dekimashita!

Mō sukoshi kikimashō!
Tanaka-san to Harada-san desu.

— *Harada-san, Mori-san wa kyō kimasu ka?*
— *Sā, wakarimasen.*

Mata kotaete kudasai!
Tanaka-san wa Mori-san ga iru ka dōka
   kikimashita ka?
Nan to kikimashita ka?

Dewa, Harada-san wa Mori-san ga kyō
   kuru to kotaemashita ka?
Mori-san ga kyō konai to kotaemashita ka?

Ja, kyō kuru ka dōka wakarimasu ka?
Mori-san ga kyō kuru ka dōka wakaranai
   to iimashita ka?

Hai, hijōni yoku dekimashita ne!

Mata kiite kudasai!
Tanaka-san to Harada-san desu.

— *Harada-san, kesa denwa ga arimashita ka?*
— *Hai, arimashita.*
— *Dare kara desu ka?*
— *Okusan kara desu.*

Dewa, kotaete kudasai!
Tanaka-san wa okyaku ga atta ka dōka
   kikimashita ka?
Nan to kikimashita ka?
Harada-san wa denwa ga nakatta to
   kotaemashita ka?
Nan to kotaemashita ka?
Tanaka-san wa nan-ji ni denwa ga atta
   ka to kikimashita ka?
Nan to kikimashita ka?

Harada-san wa dare kara denwa ga atta
   ka shitte imasu ka?

Iie, kyō wa sui-yōbi ka to kikimasen
   deshita.
Kin-yōbi ka to kikimashita.
Iie, kyō wa kin-yōbi da to kotaemasen
   deshita.
Kyō wa kin-yōbi ja nai to kotaemashita.

Iie, Mori-san ga iru ka dōka kikimasen
   deshita.
Mori-san ga kyō kuru ka dōka
   kikimashita.
Iie, Mori-san ga kyō kuru to kotaemasen
   deshita.
Iie, Mori-san ga kyō konai to mo
   kotaemasen deshita.
Iie, kyō kuru ka dōka wakarimasen.
Hai, kyō kuru ka dōka wakaranai to
   iimashita.

Iie, okyaku ga atta ka dōka kikimasen
   deshita.
Denwa ga atta ka dōka kikimashita.
Iie, denwa ga nakatta to kotaemasen
   deshita.
Denwa ga atta to kotaemashita.
Iie, nan-ji ni denwa ga atta ka to
   kikimasen deshita.
Dare kara denwa ga atta ka to
   kikimashita.
Hai, dare kara denwa ga atta ka shitte
   imasu.

Mori-san kara denwa ga atta to
  iimashita ka?
Dare kare denwa ga atta to iimashita ka?
Sumimasen ga, dare ga okusan kara
  denwa ga atta to iimashita ka?

Iie, Mori-san kara denwa ga atta to
  iimasen deshita.
Okusan kara denwa ga atta to iimashita.
Harada-san ga okusan kara denwa ga
  atta to iimashita.

Hai, sō desu.
Jōzu ni dekimashita ne!

Kiite kudasai!
Tanaka-san to Harada-san desu.

— *Harada-san, kanai kara dengon ga arimashita ka?*
— *Iie, arimasen deshita. Mata denwa suru to osshaimashita.*

Kotaete kudasai!
Dengon ga arimashita ka?
Tanaka-san wa dengon ga atta ka dōka
  kikimashita ka?
Harada-san wa dengon ga atta to
  kotaemashita ka?
Ja, nan to kotaemashita ka?
Tanaka-san no okusan wa mata denwa
  shimasu ka?
Okusan wa mata denwa suru to
  iimashita ka?
Harada-san wa okusan ga mata denwa
  suru to itta to iimashita ka?

Iie, dengon ga arimasen deshita.
Hai, dengon ga atta ka dōka
  kikimashita.
Iie, dengon ga atta to kotaemasen
  deshita.
Dengon ga nakatta to kotaemashita.
Hai, Tanaka-san no okusan wa mata
  denwa shimasu.

Hai, mata denwa suru to iimashita.
Hai, okusan ga mata denwa suru to
  itta to iimashita.

Mō ichi-do itte kudasai!
Harada-san wa okusan ga mata denwa suru to itta to iimashita.

Hai, taihen yoku dekimashita!
Muzukashiku arimasen ne!
Mō sukoshi kiite kudasai!
Tanaka-san to Harada-san desu.

— *Harada-san, Kubota-san wa mada jimusho ni imasu ka?*
— *Sā, wakarimasen. Mō kaetta to omoimasu.*

Kotaete kudasai!
Harada-san wa Kubota-san ga mada
  jimusho ni iru to iimashita ka?
Kubota-san ga mada jimusho ni iru to
  omotte imasu ka?
Ja, Kubota-san ga mō jimusho ni inai to
  omotte imasu ka?
Kubota-san ga mō kaetta to omotte
  imasu ka?
Mō kaetta to omou to iimashita ka?

Iie, Kubota-san ga mada jimusho ni
  iru to iimasen deshita.
Iie, Kubota-san ga mada jimusho ni
  iru to omotte imasen.
Hai, mō jimusho ni inai to omotte
  imasu.

Hai, mō kaetta to omotte imasu.
Hai, mō kaetta to omou to iimashita.

Sō desu!
Yoku dekimashita ne!

Kono tēpu wa yasashikatta to
  omoimasu ka?

Iie, kono tēpu wa yasashikatta to
  omoimasen.

Yasashikatta to omoimasu ka,
  muzukashikatta to omoimasu ka?

Muzukashikatta to omoimasu.

Demo omoshirokatta to omoimasu ne?

Hai, omoshirokatta to omoimasu.

Sō desu! Kono tēpu wa muzukashikatta desu ne!
Demo totemo omoshirokatta desu ne!
Ja, tēpu dai jū-roku wa kore de owari desu.
Jū-roku-ban no tēpu wa kore de owarimasu.

Sayonara!

Sayonara!

TĒPU DAI JŪ-SHICHI (17)

Jū-shichi-ban no tēpu desu.
Konnichiwa!

Konnichiwa!

Kotaete kudasai!
Are wa hikōki desu ka?

Hai, are wa hikōki desu.

Hikōki ni noru toki, kippu o kaimasu ka?

Hai, hikōki ni noru toki, kippu o kaimasu.

Hikōki ni noru toki, kippu o kawanakereba
  ikemasen ne?

Hai, hikōki ni noru toki, kippu o
  kawanakereba ikemasen.

Fune ni noru toki mo, kippu o
  kawanakereba ikemasen ka?

Hai, fune ni noru toki mo, kippu o
  kawanakereba ikemasen.

Jitensha ni noru toki, kippu o
  kawanakereba ikemasen ka?

Iie, jitensha ni noru toki, kippu o
  kawanakute mo ii desu.

Chikatetsu ni noru toki mo, kippu o
  kawanakereba ikemasen ka?

Hai, chikatetsu ni noru toki mo, kippu
  o kawanakereba ikemasen.

Anata no kuruma ni noru toki, kippu o
  kawanakereba ikemasen ka?

Iie, watashi no kuruma ni noru toki,
  kippu o kawanakute mo ii desu.

Eiga-kan e iku toki, kippu o
  kawanakereba ikemasen ne?

Hai, eiga-kan e iku toki, kippu o
  kawanakereba ikemasen.

Resutoran e iku toki mo, kippu o
  kawanakereba ikemasen ka?

Iie, resutoran e iku toki, kippu o
  kawanakute mo ii desu.

Hai, totemo yoku dekimashita ne!

Kotaete kudasai!
Nihon e iku toki, hikōki ni norimasu ka?

Hai, Nihon e iku toki, hikōki ni norimasu.

Hikōki ni noru toki, kippu o kaimasu ka?

Hai, hikōki ni noru toki, kippu o kaimasu.

Itte kudasai!
Nihon e iku toki, hikōki ni norimasu.
Nihon e iku toki, hikōki ni noranakereba ikemasen.

Hikōki ni noru toki, kippu o kaimasu.
Hikōki ni noru toki, kippu o kawanakereba ikemasen.

Itte kudasai!
Nihon e iku toki, hikōki ni norimasu.
  Nihon e iku toki, hikōki ni . . .
Hikōki ni noru toki, kippu o kaimasu.
  Hikōki no noru toki, kippu o . . .
Kippu o kau toki, okane o tsukaimasu.
  Kippu o kau toki . . .
Nihon no okane o morau toki, ginkō e
ikimasu.
  Nihon no okane o morau toki . . .
Nihon no ginkō ni iru toki, Nihon-go de
hanashimasu.
  Nihon no ginkō ni iru toki . . .
Nihon-go o hanasu tame ni, Nihon-go
o benkyō shimasu.
  Nihon-go o hanasu tame ni . . .
Nihon-go o benkyō suru tame ni,
Berurittsu ni ikimasu.
  Nihon-go o benkyō suru tame ni . . .

Totemo jōzu ni dekimashita.

Kiite kudasai!
Tanaka-san to Harada-san desu.

— *Harada-san, kōhii o kudasai!*
— *Hai, dōzo!*
— *Dōmo arigatō!*

Kotaete kudasai!
Harada-san wa Tanaka-san ni nani ka
agete imasu ka?
Nani o agete imasu ka?
Tanaka-san wa Harada-san kara kōhii o
moratte imasu ne?

Jōzu ni dekimashita ne!

Kiite kudasai!
Tanaka-san to Harada-san desu.

— *Harada-san, tegami o dōzo!*
— *Hai, dōmo arigatō gozaimasu.*

Kotaete kudasai!
Dare ga tegami o moratte imasu ka?
Harada-san wa dare kara tegami o
moratte imasu ka?
Tanaka-san wa dare ni tegami o agete
imasu ka?

Sō desu ne!

Nihon e iku toki, hikōki ni
noranakereba ikemasen.
Hikōki ni noru toki, kippu
kawanakereba ikemasen.
Kippu o kau toki, okane o
tsukawanakereba ikemasen.

Nihon no okane o morau toki, ginkō e
ikanakereba ikemasen.

Nihon no ginkō ni iru toki, Nihon-go
de hanasanakereba ikemasen.

Nihon-go o hanasu tame ni, Nihon-go
o benkyō shinakereba ikemasen.

Nihon-go o benkyō suru tame ni,
Berurittsu ni ikanakereba ikemasen.

Hai, Tanaka-san ni nani ka agete
imasu.
Kōhii o agete imasu.
Hai, Harada-san kara kōhii o moratte
imasu.

Harada-san ga tegami o moratte imasu.
Tanaka-san kara tegami o moratte
imasu.

Harada-san ni tegami o agete imasu.

Kondo wa itte kudasai!
Watashi wa anata ni agemasu.
Anata wa watashi ni kuremasu.

Kotaete kudasai!

Satō-san wa buchō ni . . .	Satō-san wa buchō ni agemasu.
Hisho wa buchō ni . . .	Hisho wa buchō ni agemasu.
Watashi wa buchō ni . . .	Watashi wa buchō ni agemasu.
Buchō wa anata ni . . .	Buchō wa anata ni agemasu.
Buchō wa watashi ni . . .	Buchō wa watashi ni kuremasu.
Anata wa watashi ni . . .	Anata wa watashi ni kuremasu.
Anata wa Satō-san ni . . .	Anata wa Satō-san ni agemasu.

Totemo yoku dekimashita ne!

Kiite kudasai!
Harada-san to Tanaka-san desu.

— *Harada-san, kono tegami o taipu shite kudasai!*
— *Hai, wakarimashita! Sugu shimasu.*

Kotaete kudasai!

Tanaka-san wa Harada-san ni nani ka iimashita ka?	Hai, Harada-san ni nani ka iimashita.
Tegami o yomu yō ni tanomimashita ka, soretomo tegami o taipu suru yō ni tanomimashita ka?	Tegami o taipu suru yō ni tanomimashita.
Harada-san wa ima taipu shite imasu ka?	Hai, ima taipu shite imasu.
Soshite, Tanaka-san wa tegami o taipu shite moraimasu ka?	Hai, Tanaka-san wa tegami o taipu shite moraimasu.

Kiite kudasai!
Harada-san to Tanaka-san desu.

— *Harada-san, tegami o fairu shite kudasai!*
— *Hai, wakarimashita!*

Kotaete kudasai!

Tanaka-san wa tegami o taipu suru yō ni tanomimashita ka?	Iie, tegami o taipu suru yō ni tanomimasen deshita.
Dewa, nani o suru yō ni tanomimashita ka?	Tegami o fairu suru yō ni tanomimashita.
Harada-san wa ima tegami o fairu shite imasu ka?	Hai, ima tegami o fairu shite imasu.
Ja, dare ga tegami o fairu shite moraimasu ka?	Tanaka-san ga tegami o fairu shite moraimasu.

Yoku dekimashita!

Itte kudasai!
Hisho wa fairu shimasu.
Buchō ni fairu shite agemasu.
Watashi ni fairu shite kuremasu.

Hisho wa taipu shimasu.
  Buchō ni . . .
  Watashi ni . . .
Sensei wa doā o akemasu.
  Seito ni . . .
  Watashi ni . . .
Omawarisan wa michi o oshiemasu.
  Tanaka-san ni . . .
  Watashi ni . . .
  Watashi no musuko ni . . .

Buchō ni taipu shite agemasu.
Watashi ni taipu shite kuremasu.

Seito ni doā o akete agemasu.
Watashi ni doā o akete kuremasu.

Tanaka-san ni michi o oshiete agemasu.
Watashi ni michi o oshiete kuremasu.
Watashi no musuko ni michi o oshiete kuremasu.

Hai, sō desu!
Totemo jōzu ni dekimashita ne!
Kore de kono tēpu, tēpu dai jū-shichi o owarimasu.
Jū-shichi-ban no tēpu wa kore de owari desu.

Sayonara!

Sayonara!

TĒPU DAI JŪ-HACHI (18)

Jū-hachi-ban no tēpu desu.
Konnichiwa!

Konnichiwa!

Kiite kudasai!
Tanaka-san wa tomodachi no Yoshida-san ni hanashite imasu.

— *Tanaka-san, shibaraku deshita nē!*
— *Ā, Yoshida-san, shibaraku desu nē! Kyonen kara atte imasen nē!*
— *Sō desu! Ima Kyōto ni sunde imasu kara.*
— *Tōkyō e wa mettani kimasen nē?*
— *Hai, shibaraku koko ni kite imasen.*

Kotaete kudasai!
Tanaka-san wa tomodachi ni hanashite
  imasu ka?
Tomodachi wa Yoshida-san to iimasu ka?

Hai, tomodachi ni hanashite imasu.
Hai, tomodachi wa Yoshida-san to iimasu.

Yoshida-san wa ima Tōkyō ni sunde
  imasu ka?
Doko ni sunde imasu ka?
Tōkyō e yoku kimasu ka, soretomo
  mettani kimasen ka?

Iie, ima Tōkyō ni sunde imasen.
Kyōto ni sunde imasu.

Tōkyō e mettani kimasen.

Yoku dekimashita!

Kiite kudasai!
Tanaka-san to Yoshida-san desu.

– *Yoshida-san, shigoto de Tōkyō e irasshaimashita ka?*
– *Iie, shigoto ja arimasen. Kazoku to issho ni kyūka o totte imasu.*
– *Ā, sō desu ka! Demo mō Tōkyō o yoku shitte imasu ne?*
– *Ē, watashi wa yoku shitte imasu. Demo, kodomo-tachi ni misetai-n desu.*

Kotaete kudasai!
Yoshida-san wa shigoto de kimashita ka,
soretomo kyūka de kimashita ka?   Kyūka de kimashita.
Hitori de kimashita ka, kazoku to
kimashita ka?   Kazoku to kimashita.
Mō Tōkyō o yoku shitte imasu ka?   Hai, mō Tōkyō o yoku shitte imasu.
Kodomo-tachi mo mō shitte imasu ka?   Iie, kodomo-tachi wa mada shirimasen.

Sō desu.

Mata kiite kudasai!
Tanaka-san to Yoshida-san desu.

– *Tanaka-san, kotoshi kyūka o torimashita ka?*
– *Iie, mada totte imasen. Raigetsu toru tsumori desu.*

Kotaete kudasai!
Tanaka-san mo mō kyūka o
torimashita ka?   Iie, mada kyūka o totte imasen.
Kongetsu kyūka o toru tsumori desu ka?   Iie, kongetsu kyūka o toru tsumori ja
arimasen.
Ja, raigetsu kyūka o toru tsumori desu ka?   Hai, raigetsu kyūka o toru tsumori desu.

Yoku dekimashita!

Motto kaiwa o kikimashō!
Tanaka-san to Yoshida-san desu.

– *Mada kyūka o totte imasen ga, raigetsu toru tsumori desu.*
– *Doko e iku tsumori desu ka?*
– *Okinawa e iku tsumori desu.*
– *Ā, Okinawa wa ii desu nē. Itta koto ga arimasu ka?*
– *Iie, mada ichi-do mo itta koto ga arimasen.*

Kotaete kudasai!
Tanaka-san wa kyūka de Sapporo e iku   Iie, kyūka de Sapporo e iku tsumori
tsumori desu ka?   ja arimasen.
Doko e iku tsumori desu ka?   Okinawa e iku tsumori desu.
Okinawa e mō itta koto ga arimasu ka?   Iie, Okinawa e mada itta koto ga
arimasen.

Hai, taihen yoku dekimashita nē!

Kiite kudasai!
Mata Tanaka-san to Yoshida-san desu.

– *Yoshida-san, anata wa mō Okinawa e irasshaimashita ka?*
– *Hai, shigoto de tokidoki ikimasu. Ima made ni go-do itta koto ga arimasu.*

Kotaete kudasai!
Yoshida-san wa Okinawa e itta koto ga
  arimasu ka?

Kyūka de ikimashita ka?
Shigoto de ikimashita ka?
Yoshida-san wa Okinawa e nan-do itta
  koto ga arimasu ka?

Hai, Okinawa e itta koto ga arimasu.

Iie, kyūka de wa ikimasen deshita.
Hai, shigoto de ikimashita.

Go-do itta koto ga arimasu.

Jōzu ni kotaeru koto ga dekimashita ne!

Mata kiite kudasai!
Tanaka-san to Yoshida-san desu.

— *Tanaka-san, Okinawa e hikōki de iku tsumori desu ka?*
— *Iie, hikōki ni noru no wa suki ja arimasen. Fune de iku tsumori desu.*
— *Sō desu ka! Watashi wa mada fune de Okinawa e itta koto ga arimasen.*

Kotaete kudasai!
Tanaka-san wa Okinawa e hikōki de iku
  tsumori desu ka?
Nan de iku tsumori desu ka?
Yoshida-san wa fune de Okinawa e
  itta koto ga arimasu ka?
Okinawa e hikōki de ikemasu ka?
Hikōki ni noru tame ni, kippu o
  kawanakereba ikemasen ka?
Takushii ni noru tame ni mo, kippu o
  kawanakereba ikemasen ka?
Resutoran e iku toki, yoyaku shinakereba
  ikemasen ka?
Yoyaku suru tame ni, resutoran e
  ikanakereba ikemasen ka?
Yoyaku suru tame ni, maemotte denwa
  shite mo ii desu ka?
Resutoran ni maemotte okane o
  harawanakereba ikemasen ka?
Shokuji no ato de, haratte mo ii
  desu ka?
Shokuji o shita ato de, haratte mo ii
  desu ka?
Ocha o nonda ato de, haratte mo ii
  desu ka?

Iie, Okinawa e hikōki de iku tsumori
  ja arimasen.
Fune de iku tsumori desu.
Iie, Yoshida-san wa fune de Okinawa e
  itta koto ga arimasen.
Hai, Okinawa e hikōki de ikemasu.
Hai, hikōki ni noru tame ni, kippu o
  kawanakereba ikemasen.
Iie, takushii ni noru tame ni wa kippu o
  kawanakute mo ii desu.
Hai, resutoran e iku toki, yoyaku
  shinakereba ikemasen.
Iie, yoyaku suru tame ni, resutoran
  e ikanakute mo ii desu.
Hai, yoyaku suru tame ni, maemotte
  denwa shite mo ii desu.
Iie, resutoran ni maemotte okane o
  harawanakute mo ii desu.
Hai, shokuji no ato de, haratte mo ii
  desu.
Hai, shokuji o shita ato de, haratte mo
  ii desu.
Hai, ocha o nonda ato de, haratte mo
  ii desu.

Hai, totemo yoku dekimashita ne!
Tsugi wa mondai desu!

Itte kudasai!
Shokuji o shimasu.
Sorekara ocha o nomimasu.
Shokuji o shita ato de, ocha o nomimasu.

Ocha o nomimasu.
Uētā ni kanjō o tanomimasu.
Ocha o nonda ato de . . .

Ocha o nonda ato de, uētā ni kanjō o
tanomimasu.

Kanjōgaki o tanomimasu.
Uētā ga motte kimasu.
Kanjōgaki o . . .

Kanjōgaki o tanonda ato de, uētā ga
motte kimasu.

Tēpu o kikimasu.
Mō ichi-do kikimasu.
Tēpu o . . .

Tēpu o kiita ato de, mō ichi-do
kikimasu.

Hai, sō desu ne!
Tēpu o kiita ato de, itsumo mō ichi-do kikimashō.
Dewa kore de kono tēpu, tēpu dai jū-hachi o owarimasu.
Jū-hachi-ban no tēpu wa kore de owari desu.

Sayonara!

Sayonara!

TĒPU DAI JŪ-KYŪ (19)

Jū-kyū-ban no tēpu desu.
Konnichiwa!

Konnichiwa!

Kotaete kudasai!

(fune)

Are wa hikōki desu ka?
Ja, are wa nan desu ka?

Iie, hikōki ja arimasen.
Are wa fune desu.

Sō desu! Are wa Nihon no fune desu.
Are wa kamotsusen desu.
Ano kamotsusen wa Nihon kara Yōroppa e ikimasu.

Kotaete kudasai!
Tankā wa kamotsusen yori ōkii desu ka?

Hai, tankā wa kamotsusen yori ōkii
desu.

Tankā wa seihin o hakobimasu ka?
Dewa, tankā wa nani o hakobimasu ka?
Kamotsusen mo sekiyu o hakobimasu ka?

Iie, tankā wa seihin o hakobimasen.
Tankā wa sekiyu o hakobimasu.
Iie, kamotsusen wa sekiyu o
hakobimasen.

Ja, kamotsusen wa nani o hakobimasu ka?

Kamotsusen wa seihin o hakobimasu.

Sō desu!
Totemo yoku dekimashita ne!

Kono kamotsusen no naka ni torakku to jidōsha ga arimasu.

Kotaete kudasai!
Nihon wa takusan no torakku to
    jidōsha o urimasu ka?

Hai, Nihon wa takusan no torakku to
jidōsha o urimasu.

Amerika wa takusan no torakku to
jidōsha o kaimasu ka?

Hai, Amerika wa takusan no torakku
to jidōsha o kaimasu.

Totemo jōzu ni dekimashita ne!

Itte kudasai!
Nihon wa Amerika ni jidōsha o urimasu.
Nihon no jidōsha ga Amerika ni uraremasu.

Nihon wa takusan no jidōsha o yushutsu
shimasu.
Nihon kara takusan no jidōsha ga . . .
Nihon wa takusan no seihin o yushutsu
shimasu.
Nihon kara . . .
Nihon wa takusan no sekiyu o yunyū
shimasu.
Nihon e takusan no sekiyu ga . . .

Nihon kara takusan no jidōsha ga
yushutsu saremasu.

Nihon kara takusan no seihin ga
yushutsu saremasu.

Nihon e takusan no sekiyu ga yunyū
saremasu.

Kotaete kudasai!
Yōroppa mo takusan no sekiyu
o yunyū shimasu ka?
Yōroppa wa Nihon kara sekiyu o
yunyū shimasu ka?
Doko kara yunyū shimasu ka?
Sekiyu wa Chūkintō kara sekai-jū e
yushutsu saremasu ka?
Seihin ga Yōroppa kara sekai-jū e
yushutsu saremasu ka?
Yōroppa kara Nihon e seihin ga
yushutsu saremasu ka?
Yōroppa to Nihon wa takusan no
bōeki o shimasu ka?
Nihon wa ōkii bōeki-koku desu ka?
Nihon wa sekai de ichi-ban ōkii
bōeki-koku desu ka?
Demo, Nihon wa sekai no ōkii
bōeki-koku no hitotsu desu ne?
Monako mo sekai no ōkii bōeki-koku
no hitotsu desu ka?
Monako wa sekai no ōkii bōeki-koku
no hitotsu desu ka, chiisai bōeki-koku
no hitotsu desu ka?

Hai, Yōroppa mo takusan no sekiyu
o yunyū shimasu.
Iie, Nihon kara sekiyu o yunyū
shimasen.
Chūkintō kara yunyū shimasu.
Hai, sekiyu wa Chūkintō kara sekai-jū
e yushutsu saremasu.
Hai, seihin ga Yōroppa kara sekai-jū e
yushutsu saremasu.
Hai, Yōroppa kara Nihon e seihin ga
yushutsu saremasu.
Hai, Yōroppa to Nihon wa takusan no
bōeki o shimasu.
Hai, Nihon wa ōkii bōeki-koku desu.
Iie, Nihon wa sekai de ichi-ban ōkii
bōeki-koku ja arimasen.
Hai, Nihon wa sekai no ōkii
bōeki-koku no hitotsu desu.
Iie, Monako wa sekai no ōkii
bōeki-koku no hitotsu ja arimasen.

Monako wa sekai no chiisai bōeki-koku
no hitotsu desu.

Jōzu ni dekimashita yo!
Tsugi wa kaiwa desu.

Kiite kudasai!
Noguchi-san to Tanaka-san desu.

— *Noguchi-san, are wa nan desu ka?*
— *Atarashii biru o tatete iru-no desu yo!*

— *Apāto ni naru-no desu ka?*
— *Iie, kōjō ni narimasu.*
— *Nan no kōjō desu ka?*
— *Yoku shirimasen ga, kamera-kōjō da to omoimasu.*

Kotaete kudasai!

Asoko de apāto o tatete imasu ka?	Iie, apāto o tatete imasen.
Nani o tatete imasu ka?	Kōjō o tatete imasu.
Noguchi-san wa kōjō o tatete iru to iimashita ka?	Hai, kōjō o tatete iru to iimashita.
Jidōsha-kōjō o tatete imasu ka?	Iie, jidōsha-kōjō o tatete imasen.
Noguchi-san wa jidōsha-kōjō o tatete iru to iimashita ka?	Iie, jidōsha-kōjō o tatete iru to imasen deshita.
Kamera-kōjō o tatete iru to omotte imasu ka?	Hai, kamera-kōjō o tatete iru to omotte imasu.

Yoku dekimashita!

Mō sukoshi kaiwa o kikimashō!
Tanaka-san to Noguchi-san desu.

— *Kōjō e nan-nin kurai no jūgyō-in ga kuru-no deshō ka?*
— *Sā, jūgyō-in no kazu wa yoku shirimasen ga, tabun gohyaku-nin kurai deshō.*

Kotaete kudasai!

Tanaka-san wa Noguchi-san ni nani ka kikimashita ka?	Hai, kare wa Noguchi-san ni nani ka kikimashita.
Kare wa kaisha no namae o shiritai-no desu ka, jūgyō-in no kazu o shiritai-no desu ka?	Jūgyō-in no kazu o shiritai-no desu.
Noguchi-san wa jūgyō-in no kazu o yoku shitte imasu ka?	Iie, jūgyō-in no kazu o yoku shirimasen.
Jūgyō-in wa sen-nin kurai da to omotte imasu ka?	Iie, sen-nin kurai da to omotte imasen.
Jūgyō-in ga nan-nin kurai da to omotte imasu ka?	Jūgyō-in ga gohyaku-nin kurai da to omotte imasu.

Hai, sō desu.

Kotaete kudasai!

Depāto ni tsutomete iru hito wa ginkō-in to iimasu ka?	Iie, depāto ni tsutomete iru hito wa ginkō-in to iimasen.
Depāto ni tsutomete iru hito wa ten-in to imasu ka, soretomo ginkō-in to iimasu ka?	Depāto ni tsutomete iru hito wa ten-in to iimasu.
Kuruma o unten suru hito wa nan to iimasu ka?	Kuruma o unten suru hito wa untenshu to iimasu.
Kaisha de hataraite iru hito wa ginkō-in to iimasu ka?	Iie, kaisha de hataraite iru hito wa ginkō-in iimasen.
Kaisha de hataraite iru hito wa nan to iimasu ka?	Kaisha de hataraite iru hito wa kaisha-in to iimasu.
Dewa, ginkō de hataraite itu hito wa nan to iimasu ka?	Ginkō de hataraite iru hito wa ginkō-in to iimasu.
Yūbin-kyoku-in mo ginkō de hataraite imasu ka?	Iie, yūbin-kyoku-in wa ginkō de hataraite imasen.

Yūbin-kyoku-in wa doko de hataraite
   imasu ka?
Sensei wa doko de hatarakimasu ka?

Yūbin-kyoku-in wa yūbin-kyoku de
   hataraite imasu.
Sensei wa gakkō de hatarakimasu.

Yoku dekimashita!
Taihen ii seito desu ne!
Nan de mo yoku kotaeraremasu ne!
Kore de kono tēpu, tēpu dai jū-kyū o owarimasu.
Jū-kyū-ban no tēpu wa kore de owari desu.

Sayonara!

Sayonara!

TĒPU DAI NIJŪ (20)

Nijū-ban no tēpu desu.
Konnichiwa!

Konnichiwa!

Kiite kudasai!
Tanaka-san to Jōnzu-san desu.

— *Jōnzu-san, Nihon-go ga o-jōzu desu nē! Doko de benkyō shimashita ka?*
— *Berurittsu desu!*
— *Shigoto de Nihon-go ga hitsuyō desu ka?*
— *Hai, hitsuyō desu. Watashi wa Tōkyō shishachō desu kara.*

Kotaete kudasai!
Jōnzu-san wa Nihon-go o uchi de benkyō
   shimashita ka?
Doko de Nihon-go o benkyō shimashita ka?
Okusan to hanasu tame ni, Nihon-go o
   benkyō shimashita ka?
Okusan to hanasu tame ni wa, Nihon-go
   ga hitsuyō ja arimasen ka?
Dōshite Nihon-go ga hitsuyō desu ka?
   Shigoto suru tame ni, hitsuyō desu ka?

Iie, Nihon-go o uchi de benkyō shimasen
   deshita.
Berurittsu de benkyō shimashita.
Iie, okusan to hanasu tame ni, Nihon-go
   o benkyō shimasen deshita.
Hai, okusan to hanasu tame ni wa,
   Nihon-go ga hitsuyō ja arimasen.

Hai, shigoto suru tame ni, hitsuyō desu.

Yoku dekimashita!

Mō-ichi-do kiite kudasai!
Tanaka-san to Jōnzu-san desu.

— *Jōnzu-san, anata wa Nihon no kaisha de hataraite iru-no desu ka?*
— *Iie, Igirisu no kaisha desu.*
— *Nihon-jin wa imasu ka?*
— *Hai, takusan imasu. Tatoeba hanbai-buchō wa Nihon-jin desu. Kare wa taihen jūyō na*
   hito no hitori desu.

Kotaete kudasai!
Jōnzu-san wa Nihon no kaisha de
   hataraite iru to iimashita ka?
Doko no kaisha de hataraite iru to
   iimashita ka?

Iie, Nihon no kaisha de hataraite iru to
   iimasen deshita.
Igirisu no kaisha de hataraite iru to
   iimashita.

Sono kaisha de hataraite iru hito wa
  zenbu Igirisu-jin desu ka?

Iie, zenbu ga Igirisu-jin ja arimasen.

Sono kaisha ni wa Nihon-jin mo imasu ka?

Hai, Nihon-jin mo imasu.

Jōnzu-san wa Nihon-jin ga takusan iru
  to iimashita ka?

Hai, Nihon-jin ga takusan iru to
  iimashita.

Hai, yoku dekimashita ne!
Mō ichi-do kikimashō!

— *Nihon-jin wa imasu ka?*
— *Hai, takusan imasu. Tatoeba hanbai-buchō wa Nihon-jin desu. Kare wa taihen
    jūyō na hito no hitori desu.*

Kotaete kudasai!

Shachō wa Nihon-jin da to iimashita ka?

Iie, shachō wa Nihon-jin da to iimasen
  deshita.

Seizō-buchō wa Nihon-jin da to
  iimashita ka?

Iie, seizō-buchō wa Nihon-jin da to mo
  iimasen deshita.

Ja, hanbai-buchō wa Nihon-jin da to
  iimashita ka?

Hai, hanbai-buchō wa Nihon-jin da to
  iimashita.

Sō desu.
Hanbai-buchō ga Nihon-jin desu.

Totemo jōzu ni dekimashita!
Mō ichi-do kaiwa o kiite kudasai!
Tanaka-san to Jōnzu-san desu.

— *Jōnzu-san, anata wa shachō desu ka?*
— *Iie, watashi wa Tōkyō no shishachō desu.*
— *Honsha wa doko ni arimasu ka?*
— *Rondon ni arimasu.*
— *Nihon e itsu kimashita ka?*
— *Go-nen mae ni kimashita.*

Kotaete kudasai!

Jōnzu-san wa shachō desu ka?

Iie, shachō ja arimasen.

Buchō desu ka, soretomo shishachō
  desu ka?

Shishachō desu.

Kaisha no honsha wa Tōkyō ni arimasu ka?

Iie, Tōkyō ni arimasen.

Doko ni arimasu ka?

Rondon ni arimasu.

Jōnzu-san wa Nihon e kyonen kimashita ka?

Iie, kyonen kimasen deshita.

Ja, itsu kimashita ka?

Go-nen mae ni kimashita.

Hai, sō desu.
Totemo jōzu ni dekimashita yo!

Mō sukoshi kaiwa o kikimashō.
Tanaka-san to Jōnzu-san desu.

— *Jōnzu-san, saikin keiki wa ikaga desu ka?*
— *Taihen ii desu nē! Kotoshi wa mō hanbai ga goju-ppāsento agarimashita.*

Kotaete kudasai!
Jōnzu-san wa keiki ga warui to iimashita
ka, keiki ga ii to iimashita ka?

Hanbai wa kotoshi sagarimashita ka,
agarimashita ka?
Hyaku-pāsento agarimashita ka?
Nan-pāsento agarimashita ka?
Infure no toki wa bukka ga sagarimasu ka?

Infure no toki wa bukka ga sagarimasu ka,
agarimasu ka?
Defure no toki mo bukka ga agarimasu ka?
Defure no toki bukka wa dō narimasu ka?
Saikin bukka wa taihen agarimashita ka?
Saikin Nihon no keizai wa hijōni hatten
shimashita ka?
Sekiyu no nedan ga agareba, futsū bukka
wa agarimasu ka?

Hai, sō desu. Yoku dekimashita.

Mata kaiwa o kiite kudasai!
Tanaka-san to Jōnzu-san desu.

— Jōnzu-san, anata no kaisha wa tekkō-gaisha ja arimasen nē!
— Hai, seishi-gaisha desu.
— Ā, sō desu ka! Seishi-kōgyō wa saikin sakan desu ne!

Kotaete kudasai!
Jōnzu-san wa tekkō-gaisha de hataraite
imasu ka?
Nan no kaisha de hataraite imasu ka?
Tanaka-san wa jidōsha-kōgyō ga sakan
da to iimashita ka?
Nan no kōgyō ga sakan da to iimashita ka?
Seishi-kōgyō wa tetsu o tsukurimasu ka?
Seishi-kōgyō wa nani o tsukurimasu ka?
Zōsen-gyō mo kami o tsukurimasu ka?
Zōsen-gyō wa nani o tsukurimasu ka?
Infure wa mō owarimashita ka, soretomo
mada tsuzuite imasu ka?

Sō desu!
Mada tsuzuite imasu.
Infure wa kesshite owarimasen.
Keredomo, kono tēpu, tēpu dai nijū wa kore de owarimasu.
Nijū-ban no tēpu wa kore de owari desu.

Sayonara!

Keiki ga ii to iimashita.

Hanbai wa kotoshi agarimashita.
Ie, hyaku-pāsento agarimasen deshita.
Goju-ppāsento agarimashita.
Iie, infure no toki wa bukka ga
sagarimasen.

Infure no toki wa bukka ga agarimasu.
Iie, defure no toki bukka wa agarimasen.
Defure no toki bukka wa sagarimasu.
Ē, saikin bukka wa taihen agarimashita.
Hai, saikin Nihon no keizai wa hijōni
hatten shimashita.
Hai, sekiyu no nedan ga agareba,
futsū bukka wa agarimasu.

Iie, tekkō-gaisha de hataraite imasen.
Seishi-gaisha de hataraite imasu.
Iie, jidōsha-kōgyō ga sakan da to
iimasen deshita.
Seishi-kōgyō ga sakan da to iimashita.
Iie, seishi-kōgyō wa tetsu o tsukurimasen.
Seishi-kōgyō wa kami o tsukurimasu.
Iie, zōsen-gyō wa kami o tsukurimasen.
Zōsen-gyō wa fune o tsukurimasu.

Infure wa mada tsuzuite imasu.

Sayonara!

KASETTO 6 — KIKITORI-RENSHŪ

Totemo jōzu ni dekimashita.
Kiite kudasai!
Tanaka-san to Harada-san desu.

— *Harada-san, kōhii o kudasai!*
— *Hai, dōzo!*
— *Dōmo arigatō!*

Kotaete kudasai!

Harada-san wa Tanaka-san ni nani ka agete imasu ka?	Hai, kanojo wa Tanaka-san ni nani ka agete imasu.
Nani o agete imasu ka?	Kōhii o agete imasu.
Tanaka-san wa Harada-san kara kōhii o moratte imasu ne?	Hai, kare wa Harada-san kara kōhii o moratte imasu.

Jōzu ni dekimashita ne!
Kiite kudasai!

Tanaka-san to Harada-san desu.

— *Harada-san, tegami o dōzo!*
— *Hai, dōmo arigatō gozaimasu.*

Kotaete kudasai!

Dare ga tegami o moratte imasu ka?	Harada-san ga tegami o moratte imasu.
Harada-san wa dare kara tegami o moratte imasu ka?	Kanojo wa Tanaka-san kara tegami o moratte imasu.
Tanaka-san wa dare ni tegami o agete imasu ka?	Kare wa Harada-san ni tegami o agete imasu.

Sō desu ne!
Totemo ii desu!
Kondo wa itte kudasai!

Watashi wa anata ni agemasu.
Anata wa watashi ni kuremasu.

Kotaete kudasai!

Satō-san wa buchō ni . . .	Satō-san wa buchō ni agemasu.
Hisho wa buchō ni . . .	Hisho wa buchō ni agemasu.
Watashi wa buchō ni . . .	Watashi wa buchō ni agemasu.
Buchō wa anata ni . . .	Buchō wa anata ni agemasu.
Buchō wa watashi ni . . .	Buchō wa watashi ni kuremasu.
Anata wa watashi ni . . .	Anata wa watashi ni kuremasu.
Anata wa Satō-san ni . . .	Anata wa Satō-san ni agemasu.

Totemo yoku dekimashita ne!
Kiite kudasai!

Harada-san to Tanaka-san desu.

— *Harada-san, kono tegami o taipu shite kudasai!*
— *Hai, wakarimashita! Sugu shimasu.*
   (taipuraitā)

Kotaete kudasai!

Tanaka-san wa Harada-san ni nani ka iimashita ka?	Hai, kare wa Harada-san ni nani ka iimashita.
Tegami o yomu yō ni tanomimashita ka, soretomo tegami o taipu suru yō ni tanomimashita ka?	Tegami o taipu suru yō ni tanomimashita.
Harada-san wa ima taipu shite imasu ka?	Hai, kanojo wa ima taipu shite imasu.
Soshite, Tanaka-san wa tegami o taipu shite moraimasu ka?	Hai, Tanaka-san wa tegami o taipu shite moraimasu.

Kiite kudasai!

Harada-san to Tanaka-san desu.

— *Harada-san, tegami o fairu shite kudasai!*
— *Hai, wakarimashita!*

Kotaete kudasai!

Tanaka-san wa tegami o taipu suru yō ni tanomimashita ka?	Iie, kare wa tegami o taipu suru yō ni tanomimasen deshita.
Dewa, nani o suru yō ni tanomimashita ka?	Tegami o fairu suru yō ni tanomimashita.
Harada-san wa ima tegami o fairu shite imasu ka?	Hai, kanojo wa ima tegami o fairu shite imasu.
Ja, dare ga tegami o fairu shite moraimasu ka?	Tanaka-san ga tegami o fairu shite moraimasu.

Yoku dekimashita!
Totemo ii desu ne!
Itte kudasai!

Hisho wa fairu shimasu.
Buchō ni fairu shite agemasu.
Watashi ni fairu shite kuremasu.

Hisho wa taipu shimasu.	
Buchō ni . . .	Buchō ni taipu shite agemasu.
Watashi ni . . .	Watashi ni taipu shite kuremasu.

Sensei wa doā o akemasu.
Seito ni . . .
Watashi ni . . .
Omawarisan wa michi o oshiemasu.
Tanaka-san ni . . .

Watashi ni . . .

Watashi no musuko ni . . .

Hai, sō desu!
Totemo jōzu ni dekimashita ne!

Kore de kono tēpu, tēpu dai
  jū-shichi o owarimasu.
Jū-shichi-ban no tēpu wa kore de
  owari desu.

Sayonara!

Seito ni doā o akete agemasu.
Watashi ni doā o akete kuremasu.

Tanaka-san ni michi o oshiete
  agemasu.
Watashi ni michi o oshiete
  kuremasu.
Watashi no musuko ni michi o
  oshiete kuremasu.

Sayonara!

TĒPU DAI JŪ-HACHI (18)

Jū-hachi-ban no tēpu desu.

Konnichiwa!   Konnichiwa!

Kiite kudasai!

Tanaka-san wa tomodachi no
  Yoshida-san ni hanashite imasu.

— *Tanaka-san, shibaraku deshita nē!*
— *Ā, Yoshida-san, shibaraku desu nē! Kyonen kara atte imasen nē!*
— *Sō desu! Ima Kyōto ni sunde imasu kara.*
— *Tōkyō e wa mettani kimasen nē?*
— *Hai, shibaraku koko ni kite imasen.*

Kotaete kudasai!

Tanaka-san wa tomodachi ni
  hanashite imasu ka?
Tomodachi wa Yoshida-san to
  iimasu ka?
Yoshida-san wa ima Tōkyō ni
  sunde imasu ka?
Doko ni sunde imasu ka?
Tōkyō e yoku kimasu ka, soretomo
  mettani kimasen ka?

Hai, kare wa tomodachi ni
  hanashite imasu.
Hai, tomodachi wa Yoshida-san to
  iimasu.
Iie, ima Tōkyō ni sunde
  imasen.
Kyōto ni sunde imasu.

Tōkyō e mettani kimasen.

Yoku dekimashita!
Totemo ii desu yo!
Kiite kudasai!

Tanaka-san to Yoshida-san desu.

— Yoshida-san, shigoto de Tōkyō e irasshaimashita ka?
— Iie, shigoto ja arimasen. Kazoku to issho ni kyūka o totte imasu.
— Ā, sō desu ka! Demo mō Tōkyō o yoku shitte imasu ne?
— Ē, watashi wa yoku shitte imasu. Demo, kodomo-tachi ni misetai-n desu.

Kotaete kudasai!

Yoshida-san wa shigoto de kimashita ka,
   soretomo kyūka de kimashita ka?   Kyūka de kimashita.
Hitori de kimashita ka,
   kazoku to kimashita ka?   Kazoku to kimashita.
Mō Tōkyō o yoku shitte imasu ka?   Hai, mō Tōkyō o yoku shitte imasu.
Kodomo-tachi mo mō shitte   Iie, kodomo-tachi wa mada
   imasu ka?   shirimasen.

Hai, ii desu ne!
Mata kiite kudasai!

Tanaka-san to Yoshida-san desu.

— Tanaka-san, kotoshi kyūka o torimashita ka?
— Iie, mada totte imasen ga, raigetsu toru tsumori desu.

Kotaete kudasai!
Tanaka-san mo mō kyūka o
   torimashita ka?   Iie, mada kyūka o totte imasen.
Kongetsu kyūka o toru tsumori   Iie, kongetsu kyūka o toru
   desu ka?   tsumori ja arimasen.
Ja, raigetsu kyūka o toru tsumori Hai, raigetsu kyūka o toru
   desu ka?   tsumori desu.

Yoku dekimashita!
Motto kaiwa o kikimashō!

Tanaka-san to Yoshida-san desu.

— Mada kyūka o totte imasen ga, raigetsu toru tsumori desu.
— Doko e iku tsumori desu ka?
— Okinawa e iku tsumori desu.
— Ā, Okinawa wa ii desu nē. Itta koto ga arimasu ka?
— Iie, mada ichi-do mo itta koto ga arimasen.

Kotaete kudasai!

Tanaka-san wa kyūka de Sapporo
  e iku tsumori desu ka?
Doko e iku tsumori desu ka?
Kare wa Okinawa e mō itta koto
  ga arimasu ka?

Iie, kyūka de Sapporo e iku
  tsumori ja arimasen.
Okinawa e iku tsumori desu.
Iie, Okinawa e mada itta koto
  ga arimasen.

Hai, taihen yoku dekimashita nē!
Kiite kudasai!

Mata Tanaka-san to Yoshida-san desu.

— *Yoshida-san, anata wa mō Okinawa e irasshaimashita ka?*
— *Hai, shigoto de tokidoki ikimasu. Ima made ni go-do itta koto ga arimasu.*

Kotaete kudasai!

Yoshida-san wa Okinawa e itta
  koto ga arimasu ka?
Kyūka de ikimashita ka?
Shigoto de ikimashita ka?
Yoshida-san wa Okinawa e nan-do
  itta koto ga arimasu ka?

Hai, Okinawa e itta koto
  ga arimasu.
Iie, kyūka de wa ikimasen deshita.
Hai, shigoto de ikimashita.

Go-do itta koto ga arimasu.

Jōzu ni kotaeru koto ga dekimashita ne!
Mata kiite kudasai!

Tanaka-san to Yoshida-san desu.

— *Tanaka-san, Okinawa e hikōki de iku tsumori desu ka?*
— *Iie, hikōki ni noru no wa suki ja arimasen. Fune de iku tsumori desu.*
— *Sō desu ka! Watashi wa mada fune de Okinawa e itta koto ga arimasen.*

Kotaete kudasai!

Tanaka-san wa Okinawa e hikōki
  de iku tsumori desu ka?

Nan de iku tsumori desu ka?
Yoshida-san wa fune de Okinawa
  e itta koto ga arimasu ka?
Okinawa e hikōki de ikemasu ka?
Hikōki ni noru tame ni, kippu
  o kawanakereba ikemasen ka?
Takushii ni noru tame ni mo, kippu
  o kawanakereba ikemasen ka?

Ii resutoran e iku toki, yoyaku
  shinakereba ikemasen ka?
Yoyaku suru tame ni, resutoran
  e ikanakereba ikemasen ka?

Iie, Okinawa e hikōki de
  iku tsumori ja arimasen.

Fune de iku tsumori desu.
Iie, Yoshida-san wa fune de Okinawa
  e itta koto ga arimasen.
Hai, Okinawa e hikōki de ikemasu.
Hai, hikōki ni noru tame ni,
  kippu o kawanakereba ikemasen.
Iie, takushii ni noru tame ni wa
  kippu o kawanakute mo ii desu.

Hai, ii resutoran e iku toki,
  yoyaku shinakereba ikemasen.
Iie, yoyaku suru tame ni, resutoran
  e ikanakute mo ii desu.

Yoyaku suru tame ni, maemotte
  denwa shite mo ii desu ka?
Resutoran ni maemotte okane
  o harawanakereba ikemasen ka?
Shokuji no ato de, haratte mo
  ii desu ka?
Shokuji o shita ato de, haratte
  mo ii desu ka?
Ocha o nonda ato de, haratte
  mo ii desu ka?

Hai, yoyaku suru tame ni, maemotte
  denwa shite mo ii desu.
Iie, resutoran ni maemotte
  okane o harawanakute mo ii desu.
Hai, shokuji no ato de, haratte mo
  ii desu.
Hai, shokuji o shita ato de,
  haratte mo ii desu.
Hai, ocha o nonda ato de, haratte
  mo ii desu.

Hai, totemo yoku dekimashita ne!
Tsugi wa mondai desu!
Itte kudasai!

Shokuji o shimasu.
Sorekara ocha o nomimasu.
Shokuji o shita ato de, ocha o nomimasu.

Ocha o nomimasu.
Uētā ni kanjō o tanomimasu.
Ocha o nonda ato de . . .

Ocha o nonda ato de, uētā ni
  kanjō o tanomimasu.

Kanjōgaki o tanomimasu.
Uētā ga motte kimasu.
Kanjōgaki o . . .

Kanjōgaki o tanonda ato de,
  uētā ga motte kimasu.

Tēpu o kikimasu.
Mō ichi-do kikimasu.
Tēpu o . . .

Tēpu o kiita ato de, mō ichi-do
  kikimasu.

Hai, sō desu ne!

Tēpu o kiita ato de, itsumo
  mō ichi-do kikimashō.

Dewa kore de kono tēpu, tēpu dai
  jū-hachi o owarimasu.
Jū-hachi-ban no tēpu wa kore de owari desu.

Sayonara!

Sayonara!

TĒPU DAI JŪ-KYŪ (19)

Jū-kyū-ban no tēpu desu.

Konnichiwa!

Konnichiwa!

Kotaete kudasai!

(fune)

Are wa hikōki desu ka?
Ja, are wa nan desu ka?

Iie, hikōki ja arimasen.
Are wa fune desu.

Sō desu! Are wa Nihon no fune desu.
Are wa kamotsusen desu.
Ano kamotsusen wa Nihon kara
   Yōroppa e ikimasu.

Kotaete kudasai!

Tankā wa kamotsusen yori ōkii
   desu ka?
Tankā wa seihin o hakobimasu ka?
Dewa, tankā wa nani o hakobimasu ka?
Kamotsusen mo sekiyu o
   hakobimasu ka?
Ja, kamotsusen wa nani o
   hakobimasu ka?

Hai, tankā wa kamotsusen yori
   ōkii desu.
Iie, tankā wa seihin o hakobimasen.
Tankā wa sekiyu o hakobimasu.
Iie, kamotsusen wa sekiyu o
   hakobimasen.
Kamotsusen wa seihin o
   hakobimasu.

Sō desu!
Totemo yoku dekimashita ne!

(fune)

Kono kamotsusen no naka ni torakku
   to jidōsha ga arimasu.

Kotaete kudasai!

Nihon wa takusan no torakku
   to jidōsha o urimasu ka?
Amerika wa takusan no torakku to
   jidōsha o kaimasu ka?

Hai, Nihon wa takusan no torakku
   to jidōsha o urimasu.
Hai, Amerika wa takusan no
   torakku to jidōsha o kaimasu.

Totemo jōzu ni dekimashita ne!
Itte kudasai!

Nihon wa Amerika ni jidōsha o urimasu.
Nihon no jidōsha ga Amerika ni uraremasu.
Nihon wa takusan no jidōsha o yushutsu
   shimasu.
Nihon kara takusan no
   jidōsha ga . . .
Nihon wa takusan no seihin o
   yushutsu shimasu. Nihon kara . . .
Nihon wa takusan no sekiyu o yunyū
   shimasu. Nihon e takusan no sekiyu ga . . .

Nihon kara takusan no jidōsha
   ga yushutsu saremasu.
Nihon kara takusan no seihin ga
   yushutsu saremasu.
Nihon e takusan no sekiyu ga
   yunyū saremasu.

Hai, ii desu ne!

Kotaete kudasai!

Yōroppa mo takusan no sekiyu
　o yunyū shimasu ka?
Yōroppa wa Nihon kara sekiyu
　o yunyū shimasu ka?
Doko kara yunyū shimasu ka?

Hai, Yōroppa mo takusan no
　sekiyu o yunyū shimasu.
Iie, Nihon kara sekiyu o yunyū
　shimasen.
Chūkintō kara yunyū shimasu.

Sekiyu wa Chūkintō kara sekai-jū
　e yushutsu saremasu ka?
Seihin ga Yōroppa kara sekai-jū
　e yushutsu saremasu ka?
Yōroppa kara Nihon e seihin ga
　yushutsu saremasu ka?
Yōroppa to Nihon wa takusan no
　bōeki o shimasu ka?
Nihon wa ōkii bōeki-koku
　desu ka?
Nihon wa sekai de ichi-ban
　ōkii bōeki-koku desu ka?
Demo, Nihon wa sekai no ōkii
　bōeki-koku no hitotsu desu ne?
Monako mo sekai no ōkii bōeki-koku
　no hitotsu desu ka?
Monako wa sekai no ōkii bōeki-koku
　no hitotsu desu ka, chiisai bōeki-
　koku no hitotsu desu ka?

Hai, sekiyu wa Chūkintō kara
　sekai-jū e yushutsu saremasu.
Hai, seihin ga Yōroppa kara
　sekai-jū e yushutsu saremasu.
Hai, Yōroppa kara Nihon e seihin
　ga yushutsu saremasu.
Hai, Yōroppa to Nihon wa takusan
　no bōeki o shimasu.
Hai, Nihon wa ōkii bōeki-koku
　desu.
Iie, Nihon wa sekai de ichi-ban
　ōkii bōeki-koku ja arimasen.
Hai, Nihon wa sekai no ōkii
　bōeki-koku no hitotsu desu.
Iie, Monako wa sekai no ōkii
　bōeki-koku no hitotsu ja arimasen.

Monako wa sekai no chiisai bōeki-
　koku no hitotsu desu.

Hai, totemo ii desu ne!
Jōzu ni dekimashita yo!
Tsugi wa kaiwa desu.

(kōji)

Kiite kudasai!

Noguchi-san to Tanaka-san desu.

— *Noguchi-san, are wa nan desu ka?*
— *Atarashii biru o tatete iru-no desu yo!*
— *Apāto ni naru-no desu ka?*
— *Iie, kōjō ni narimasu.*
— *Nan no kōjō desu ka?*
— *Yoku shirimasen ga, kamera-kōjō da to omoimasu.*

Kotaete kudasai!

Asoko de apāto o tatete imasu ka?
Nani o tatete imasu ka?
Noguchi-san wa kōjō o tatete
　iru to iimashita ka?

Iie, apāto o tatete imasen.
Kōjō o tatete imasu.
Hai, kōjō o tatete iru to
　iimashita.

Jidōsha-kōjō o tatete imasu ka?
Noguchi-san wa jidōsha-kōjō o
   tatete iru to iimashita ka?
Kamera-kōjō o tatete iru to
   omotte imasu ka?

Iie, jidōsha-kōjō o tatete imasen.
Iie, jidōsha-kōjō o tatete iru
   to iimasen deshita.
Hai, kamera-kōjō o tatete iru
   to omotte imasu.

Yoku dekimashita!
Hijōni ii desu yo!
Mō sukoshi kaiwa o kikimashō!

(kōji)

Tanaka-san to Noguchi-san desu.

— *Kōjō e nan-nin kurai no jūgyō-in ga kuru-no deshō ka?*
— *Sā, jūgyō-in no kazu wa yoku shirimasen ga, tabun gohyaku-nin kurai deshō.*

Kotaete kudasai!

Tanaka-san wa Noguchi-san ni
   nani ka kikimashita ka?
Kare wa kaisha no namae o shiritai-no
   desu ka, jūgyō-in no kazu o
   shiritai-no desu ka?
Noguchi-san wa jūgyō-in no kazu
   o yoku shitte imasu ka?
Jūgyō-in wa sen-nin kurai da to
   omotte imasu ka?
Jūgyō-in ga nan-nin kurai da to
   omotte imasu ka?

Hai, kare wa Noguchi-san ni
   nani ka kikimashita.

Jūgyō-in no kazu o
   shiritai-no desu.
Iie, jūgyō-in no kazu o
   yoku shirimasen.
Iie, sen-nin kurai da to omotte
   imasen.
Jūgyō-in ga gohyaku-nin kurai da to
   omotte imasu.

Hai, ii desu!
Kotaete kudasai!

Depāto ni tsutomete iru hito wa
   ginkō-in to iimasu ka?
Depāto ni tsutomete iru hito wa
   ten-in to iimasu ka, soretomo
   ginkō-in to iimasu ka?
Kuruma o unten suru hito wa
   nan to iimasu ka?
Kaisha de hataraite iru hito
   wa ginkō-in to iimasu ka?
Kaisha de hataraite iru hito
   wa nan to iimasu ka?
Dewa, ginkō de hataraite
   iru hito wa nan to iimasu ka?
Yūbin-kyoku-in mo ginkō de
   hataraite imasu ka?
Yūbin-kyoku-in wa doko de
   hataraite imasu ka?

Iie, depāto ni tsutomete iru hito wa
   ginkō-in to iimasen.

Depāto ni tsutomete iru
   hito wa ten-in to iimasu.
Kuruma o unten suru hito
   wa untenshu to iimasu.
Iie, kaisha de hataraite iru hito
   wa ginkō-in to iimasen.
Kaisha de hataraite iru hito wa
   kaisha-in to iimasu.
Ginkō de hataraite iru hito wa
   ginkō-in to iimasu.
Iie, yūbin-kyoku-in wa ginkō
   de hataraite imasen.
Yūbin-kyoku-in wa yūbin-kyoku
   de hataraite imasu.

Sensei wa doko de hatarakimasu ka?
Anata wa sensei desu ka seito desu ka?

Yoku dekimashita!
Taihen ii seito desu ne!
Nan de mo yoku kotaeraremasu ne!

Kore de kono tēpu, tēpu dai jū-kyū
    o owarimasu.
Jū-kyū-ban no tēpu wa kore de
    owari desu.

Sayonara!

Sensei wa gakkō de hatarakimasu.
Watashi wa seito desu.

Sayonara!

TĒPU DAI NIJŪ (20)

Nijū-ban no tēpu desu.

Konnichiwa!

Konnichiwa!

Tsugi wa kaiwa desu.
Kiite kudasai!

Tanaka-san to Jōnzu-san desu.

— *Jōnzu-san, Nihon-go ga o-jōzu desu nē! Doko de benkyō shimashita ka?*
— *Berurittsu desu!*
— *Shigoto de Nihon-go ga hitsuyō desu ka?*
— *Hai, hitsuyō desu. Watashi wa Tōkyō shishachō desu kara.*

Kotaete kudasai!

Jōnzu-san wa Nihon-go o uchi de
    benkyō shimashita ka?
Doko de Nihon-go o benkyō
    shimashita ka?
Okusan to hanasu tame ni, Nihon-go
    o benkyō shimashita ka?
Okusan to hanasu tame ni wa, Nihon-go
    ga hitsuyō ja arimasen ka?
Dōshite Nihon-go ga hitsuyō desu ka?
    Shigoto suru tame ni, hitsuyō desu ka?

Iie, Nihon-go o uchi de
    benkyō shimasen deshita.

Berurittsu de benkyō shimashita.
Iie, okusan to hanasu tame ni,
    Nihon-go o benkyō shimasen deshita.
Hai, okusan to hanasu tame ni wa,
    Nihon-go ga hitsuyō ja arimasen.
Hai, shigoto suru tame ni,
    hitsuyō desu.

Yoku dekimashita!
Mō ichi-do kiite kudasai!

Tanaka-san to Jōnzu-san desu.

— *Jōnzu-san, anata wa Nihon no kaisha de hataraite iru-no desu ka?*
— *Iie, Igirisu no kaisha desu.*
— *Nihon-jin wa imasu ka?*
— *Hai, takusan imasu. Tatoeba hanbai-buchō wa Nihon-jin desu. Kare wa taihen
jūyō na hito no hitori desu.*

Kotaete kudasai!

Jōnzu-san wa Nihon no kaisha
de hataraite iru to iimashita ka?

Iie, Nihon no kaisha de hataraite
iru to iimasen deshita.

Doko no kaisha de hataraite
iru to iimashita ka?

Igirisu no kaisha de hataraite
iru to iimashita.

Sono kaisha de hataraite iru hito
wa zenbu Igirisu-jin desu ka?

Iie, zenbu ga Igirisu-jin ja
arimasen.

Sono kaisha ni wa Nihon-jin mo
imasu ka?

Hai, Nihon-jin mo imasu.

Jōnzu-san wa Nihon-jin ga
takusan iru to iimashita ka?

Hai, Nihon-jin ga takusan
iru to iimashita.

Hai, yoku dekimashita ne!
Mō ichi-do kikimashō!

— *Nihon-jin wa imasu ka?*
— *Hai, takusan imasu. Tatoeba hanbai-buchō wa Nihon-jin desu. Kare wa taihen
jūyō na hito no hitori desu.*

Kotaete kudasai!

Shachō wa Nihon-jin da to
iimashita ka?

Iie, shachō wa Nihon-jin da to
iimasen deshita.

Seizō-buchō wa Nihon-jin
da to iimashita ka?

Iie, seizō-buchō wa Nihon-jin
da to mo iimasen deshita.

Ja, hanbai-buchō wa Nihon-jin
da to iimashita ka?

Hai, hanbai-buchō wa Nihon-jin
da to iimashita.

Sō desu.
Hanbai-buchō ga Nihon-jin desu.

Totemo jōzu ni dekimashita!
Mō ichi-do kaiwa o kiite kudasai!

Tanaka-san to Jōnzu-san desu.

— *Jōnzu-san, anata wa shachō desu ka?*
— *Iie, watashi wa Tōkyō no shishachō desu.*
— *Honsha wa doko ni arimasu ka?*
— *Rondon ni arimasu.*
— *Nihon e itsu kimashita ka?*
— *Go-nen mae ni kimashita.*

Kotaete kudasai!

Jōnzu-san wa shachō desu ka?

Buchō desu ka, soretomo shishachō desu ka?

Kare no kaisha no honsha wa Tōkyō ni
    arimasu ka?

Doko ni arimasu ka?

Jōnzu-san wa Nihon e kyonen kimashita ka?

Ja, itsu kimashita ka?

Iie, shachō ja arimasen.

Shishachō desu.

Iie, Tōkyō ni arimasen.

Rondon ni arimasu.

Iie, kyonen kimasen deshita.

Go-nen mae ni kimashita.

Hai, sō desu.

Totemo jōzu ni dekimashita yo!

Mō sukoshi kaiwa o kikimashō.

Tanaka-san to Jōnzu-san desu.

— *Jōnzu-san, saikin keiki wa ikaga desu ka?*

— *Taihen ii desu nē! Kotoshi wa mō hanbai ga goju-ppāsento agarimashita.*

Kotaete kudasai!

Jōnzu-san wa keiki ga warui to iimashita
    ka, keiki ga ii to iimashita ka?

Hanbai wa kotoshi sagarimashita
    ka, agarimashita ka?

Hyaku-pāsento agarimashita ka?

Nan-pāsento agarimashita ka?

Infure no toki wa bukka ga
    sagarimasu ka?

Infure no toki wa bukka ga
    sagarimasu ka, agarimasu ka?

Defure no toki mo bukka ga
    agarimasu ka?

Defure no toki bukka wa dō
    narimasu ka?

Saikin bukka wa taihen
    agarimashita ka?

Saikin Nihon no keizai wa hijōni
    hatten shimashita ka?

Sekiyu no nedan ga agareba, futsū
    bukka wa agarimasu ka?

Keiki ga ii to iimashita.

Hanbai wa kotoshi agarimashita.

Iie, hyaku-pāsento agarimasen deshita.

Goju-ppāsento agarimashita.

Iie, infure no toki wa bukka ga
    sagarimasen.

Infure no toki wa bukka ga
    agarimasu.

Iie, defure no toki bukka wa
    agarimasen.

Defure no toki bukka wa
    sagarimasu.

Ē, saikin bukka wa taihen
    agarimashita.

Hai, saikin Nihon no keizai wa hijōni
    hatten shimashita.

Hai, sekiyu no nedan ga
    agareba, futsū bukka wa agarimasu.

Taihen ii desu ne!

Mata kaiwa o kiite kudasai!

Tanaka-san to Jōnzu-san desu.

— *Jōnzu-san, anata no kaisha wa tekkō-gaisha ja arimasen nē!*

— *Hai, seishi-gaisha desu.*

— *Ā, sō desu ka! Seishi-kōgyō wa saikin sakan desu ne!*

Kotaete kudasai!

Jōnzu-san wa tekkō-gaisha de
   hataraite imasu ka?
Nan no kaisha de hataraite imasu ka?
Tanaka-san wa jidōsha-kōgyō
   ga sakan da to iimashita ka?
Nan no kōgyō ga sakan da to
   iimashita ka?
Seishi-kōgyō wa tetsu o
   tsukurimasu ka?
Seishi-kōgyō wa nani o
   tsukurimasu ka?
Zōsen-gyō mo kami o tsukurimasu ka?
Zōsen-gyō wa nani o tsukurimasu ka?
Infure wa mō owarimashita ka,
   soretomo mada tsuzuite imasu ka?

Sō desu!
Mada tsuzuite imasu.
Infure wa kesshite owarimasen.

Keredomo, kono tēpu, tēpu dai
   nijū wa kore de owarimasu.

Nijū-ban no tēpu wa kore de owari desu.

Sayonara!

Iie, tekkō-gaisha de hataraite
   imasen.
Seishi-gaisha de hataraite imasu.
Iie, jidōsha-kōgyō ga sakan da
   to iimasen deshita.
Seishi-kōgyō ga sakan da to
   iimashita.
Iie, seishi-kōgyō wa tetsu o
   tsukurimasen.
Seishi-kōgyō wa kami o
   tsukurimasu.
Iie, zōsen-gyō wa kami o tsukurimasen.
Zōsen-gyō wa fune o tsukurimasu.

Infure wa mada tsuzuite imasu.

Sayonara!

KASETTO 6 — KIKITORI-RENSHŪ